SEVENTH EDITION

THE COLLECTOR'S ENCYCLOPEDIA OF DEPRESSION GLASS

By Gene Florence

COLLECTOR BOOKS
P.O. Box 3009
Paducah, KY 42001

The current values in this book should be used only as a guide. They are not intended to set prices, which vary from one section of the country to another. Auction prices as well as dealer prices vary greatly and are affected by condition as well as demand. Neither the Author nor the Publisher assumes responsibility for any losses that might be incurred as a result of consulting this guide.

ACKNOWLEDGEMENTS

Many thanks to each of you who sent prayers and wishes for my good health. I have taken it easier by cutting back about a dozen shows a year. It is certainly a great feeling just to be able to get a new chance at life and be able to live each day to its fullest. (If any of you have gall bladder problems, for heavens sake, don't take them for granted; they can kill you--and quickly!) While working on this, my second book this year, I have promised myself an extended vacation in two years time when Chad graduates from high school. It may mean missing a few shows that I have never missed before, but by telling you now, it may not come as a big surprise if I am not where you expect me to be. The other book just written is the second edition of the *Elegant Glassware of Depression Era* and it is being released as I am finishing this.

A special thanks to all the clubs and show promoters who have felt that my presence has been worth the expense to have me attend their shows! I have enjoyed them, learned from them, and I hope, contributed to them! I have logged more air miles this year than usual, since driving is getting to be a 41-year-old "chore" instead of a 28-year-old "pleasure". I am also getting quite familiar with O'Hare airport lounges since my flights keep getting messed up there.

I have received numerous letters giving new listings for this book; thanks to all who have written of their discoveries! The photos sent are a great help for my records, and, yes, even a bad one is better than none at all! Many people have found out first hand how difficult it is to photograph glass!

Thanks to Cathy, my wife, who became chief editor, but almost non-typist, for this book. She has gotten more independent since the publication of her own book, *Collecting Quilts* (which has been getting rave reviews). I am a hunt and peck typist and if were not for "Wordstar", I might never have gotten through this! She did have fun with her editing pen, however, spotting non-sentences and forgotten endings on words.

Many thanks to my family! Chad and Marc, my sons, just kept pushing me by asking if I were through with that book yet! They like the stereo on, not off! They want to TALK, man, NOT BE QUIET! I've heard a sarcastic "Boy , you're certainly in a GREAT mood!" a few times as I shushed them while trying to type! Grannie Bear, my Mom, did all the packing and getting the glass ready for the marathon photography session. That's several weeks of work! My Dad, Charles, Sibyl and Marie kept everything else in line while we traveled. Honestly, I couldn't do this without their help.

Glass and information for this book were furnished by Frank and Sherry McClain, Kenn and Margaret Whitmyer, Lynn and Jerry Mantione, Byron Canine, Ralph Leslie, Robert McGinnis, Ron Stephens, Ferrell Bailey, Sam and Becky Collings, Arlene Showalter, Imogene McKinney, John and Trannie Davis, Brenda Mosher and Gladys Florence. They truly made this a better book with their contributions.

Photographs for this book were made by Dana Curtis of Curtis and Mays Studio in Paducah, Ziegfried Kurz, Frank McClain, Byron Canine, Raymond Mills and Janet Boyer of the Anchor Hocking photography lab. The knee cracking "fun" of displaying glass at the photography session was performed by Steve Quertermous and Jane Fryberger. That means days of working on your hands and knees to place each piece at just the right camera angle for the photographer. ("I still can't see the base of that glass on the right, Jane". "Steve, turn your cup handle to your left". "Sorry, guys, but this whole set-up is too square". "You've lost your center; move everything 5 inches to the right" etc., etc.)

If I have inadvertently left someone out of the acknowledgements who helped, please know that I am not unappreciative of your aid! I try to keep accurate records but finding them sometimes presents a problem when it comes down to a deadline.

As we go to press on this seventh edition, I wish to thank you, my readers, for making this the best selling glass book in America, and I wish you success in your glass collecting!

FOREWORD

Depression Glass as defined in this book is the colored glassware made primarily during the Depression years in the colors of amber, green, pink, red, blue, yellow, white and crystal. There are other colors and some glass made before, as well as after, this time frame, but primarily, the glass within this book was made from the 1920's through the 1930's. This book is mostly concerned with the inexpensively made glassware turned out by machine in quantity and sold through the five and dime stores or given away as promotional inducements to buy other products during that era known as The Depression.

There have been changes in the collecting of Depression glass since my first book was sold in '72, some 300,000 copies ago! Prices have soared; seemingly plentiful patterns have been secreted into vast collections and wiped from the market place; heretofore inconsequental Depression patterns and previously ingorned crystal colors have picked up buyers; indeed, ANYTHING that is Depression glass, be it a particular pattern or not, suddenly has added value and collectibility. Collectors have become vastly more knowledgeable and sophisticated in their collecting. Many collectors are enhancing their collections of ''A to W'' (Adam to Windsor) with patterns of better glasswares made during that same time frame. This broadening of interest on the part of collectors prompted me to research and write two more books on the field of Depression glass, one on the KITCHENWARE items to be found during that era, and one on the more ELEGANT glassware of the time. In this edition, I am including some later patterns now being sought by collectors. These patterns were made in the 1950's and one, as late as the early 1960's. This is what the collector is requesting, so I am trying to provide what he wants. I am having to adjust my ways of thinking about this later glass just as many of you already have.

Information for this book has come via research, experience, fellow dealers, collectors and over 575,000 miles of travel pursuant to glassware. Too, some of the more interesting information has come from readers who were kind enough to share their photographs and special knowledge with me. These gestures I particularly treasure.

PRICING

ALL PRICES IN THIS BOOK ARE RETAIL PRICES FOR MINT CONDITION GLASSWARE. THIS BOOK IS INTENDED TO BE ONLY A GUIDE TO PRICES AS THERE ARE SOME REGIONAL PRICE DIFFERENCES WHICH CANNOT REASONABLY BE DEALT WITH HEREIN.

You may expect dealers to pay from thirty to fifty percent less than the prices quoted. Glass that is in less than mint condition, i.e. chipped, cracked, scratched or poorly molded, will bring very small prices unless extremely rare, and then, it will bring only a small percentage of the price of glass that is in mint condition.

Prices have become pretty well nationally standardized due to national advertising carried on by dealers and due to the Depression Glass Shows which are held from coast to coast. However, **there are still some regional differences in prices due** partly **to glass being more readily available in some areas than in others.** Too, companies distributed certain pieces in some areas that they did not in others. Generally speaking, however, prices are about the same among dealers from coast to coast.

Prices tend to increase dramatically on rare items and, in general, they have increased as a whole due to more and more collectors entering the field and people becoming more aware of the worth of Depression Glass.

One of the more important aspects of this book is the attempt made to illustrate as well as realistically price those items which are in demand. The desire was to give you the most accurate guide to collectible patterns of Depression Glass available.

MEASUREMENTS

To illustrate why there are discrepancies in measurements, I offer the following sample from just two years of Hocking's catalogue references:

Year		Ounces		Ounces		Ounces
1935	Pitcher	37,58,80	Flat Tumbler	5,9,13½	Footed Tumbler	10,13
1935	Pitcher	37,60,80	Flat Tumbler	5,9,10,15	Footed Tumbler	10,13
1936	Pitcher	37,65,90	Flat Tumbler	5,9,13½	Footed Tumbler	10,15
1935	Pitcher	37,60,90	Flat Tumbler	5,9,13½	Footed Tumbler	10,15

All measurements in this book are exact as to some manufacturer's listing or to acutal measurement. You may expect variance of up to ½ inch or 1-5 ounces. This may be due to mold variation or changes made by the manufacturer.

Index

Collector's Questions

WHERE DO YOU GET THE PRICES LISTED IN YOUR BOOK?

Up front, let me state that I am only **recording** (not setting) the retail prices found in this book, but those prices are gathered in various ways.

First of all, I own an antique shop, Grannie Bear Antiques, that deals in Depression era glassware. I'm constantly at markets buying stock for resale purposes. Like all dealers, I try to buy marketable glassware, not stuff that will sit on the shelves for years, and I try to buy it with a view to making a reasonable profit without alienating my good customers by overpricing. Most people readily accept that a dealer is in business to make a little money, else he can't stay in business. I try not to go for the jugular with killing profits, however, preferring to encourage repeat business at small profits. Thus, operating the shop gives me a general feel for what glass will and won't sell and for what prices.

Next, I make it a point to STUDY glass prices in my travels as both dealer and guest author. I attend anywhere from thirty to forty Depression glass shows a year in various sections of the country. So far, by May of this year, I have been to shows in Florida, Texas, Oregon, Washington, and California (twice). This doesn't count the numerous small trips to flea markets and shops in and out of state. At shows, I WORK at observing prices that the various dealers have on their glass; at show's end, I try to get around to see what glass sold--and what is still sitting on the tables! (You learn, too, by noting what 1500-2000 potential customers WEREN'T willing to pay for glass for their collections!) I talk to dealers about what is and isn't selling; I pay attention to things they've carried to the last three shows which haven't sold. I talk to the collectors as they drop by my booth to buy a book, or get an autograph, or to tell me about their unusual finds. I make mental notes when they say, "I finally found that divided relish (or whatever) that I've been looking for two years, but the dealer wanted twice what it's worth, so I let him keep it." All this tells me a great deal! On the other hand, I also listen to dealers who say they've been getting thus and so price for certain pieces with regularity. I hear when "old Joe" made $800.00 profit on some item that I've had to nine shows and can't give away, too! There are a FEW customers who will pay ANYTHING to get a piece of glass they want. That, to me, doesn't necessarily indicate that the piece is worth that much money to anyone else in the world! So, I try to do us all a service by not immediately placing that astronomical sum on a piece as a retail price. You can kill a market more quickly by OVER pricing than by any other means! (I have observed this over and over again in other collectibles. I have no intention of contributing to that phenomenon in our Depression glass). I try to give accurate, informed, RELIABLE prices.

For THIS book, I even went so far as to sit down and go over the last year of sales with several dealers who were willing to share this knowledge with me. (The majority of Depression glass dealers I know are extremely fine people who are perfectly willing to go out of their way to help create an INFORMED buying public! The more YOU know, the better customer you'll be!)

I'VE HEARD THAT THE DEPRESSION GLASS MARKET IS A BIT SOFT RIGHT NOW. HOW TRUE IS THAT?

Actually, NOW, the market is getting stronger than it has been in the past two years. True, it WAS down a bit for a time. I think that was due more to the economic crunch than anything else. People considered feeding and clothing their families more important than spending money on glass investing which, now, should be viewed as something of a long term investment, rather than a short term, quick profit, investment. Let's face it, due to many more and WISER collectors, the days when EVERY PIECE of glass purchased would automatically increase by 25%-30% annually (or when ANYONE WITH MONEY to buy it could DO NO WRONG in purchasing any Depression glass for investment) have been replaced by a time when anyone having KNOWLEDGE OF THE MARKET can do little wrong with the right purchases! Collectors, in general, are more informed today. Dealers have to be cognizant of that fact. You can't get by with the wool-over-the-eyes deals that could be pulled in those early years.

I'VE ENCOUNTERED A RUMOR THAT YOU'RE LOWERING ALL THE PRICES IN YOUR BOOK THIS YEAR. IS THAT TRUE?

I've always operated on the principle that supply and DEMAND keep prices what they are. There are MANY price INCREASES in this book; but by the same token, there are some price decreases. There are some heretofore expensive pieces of glass that are not selling at the old levels simply because there is no demand for them from collectors. SUPPLY has met the current needs of the collectors for these items, and because of the high price, NEW collectors are shying away from these patterns at the moment, and thus, there is no new DEMAND for the items. They're sitting in their high priced glory at show after show. At this time, they're NOT going to be bought unless the price is reduced to an acceptable level to the NEW collector. I can't honestly tell the public that, now, in July 1985, at markets that have been recently slowed by the country's economic recession, these items are truly worth what they have been in the past. So, yes, I've recorded some lower prices for items that are presently selling for less because of a greater supply than demand. Some of the "supply" of glass that has found its way to the market place is due, also, to that economic crunch. Some people have had to sell their collections when their husbands lost jobs and money got to be tight. It's, thus, been pretty much a buyer's market for the last couple of years. If you have a deep enough pocket, you're probably going to be smiling all the way to the bank when the market gets in full swing again.

I OVERHEARD SOME DEALERS TALKING ABOUT SOME ADVERTISING GAMES BEING TRIED. I DIDN'T QUITE UNDERSTAND WHAT THEY WERE TALKING ABOUT. CAN YOU EXPLAIN?

If I don't teach you anything else in this whole book, remember this. The ADVERTISED price of any item is not necessarily the SELLING price. It's been told that some people purposely advertise items at huge price increases pretty much knowing that no one will buy at that price. Some time later, they, or their friend, will advertise at a somewhat reduced price from the first. Thus, they've "conditioned" the potential customer (or often, other DEALERS) to believing that the second advertised price is a "bargain" because they saw that same item before at the inflated price. Even though the item is higher than "booked", people will buy believing it, a more "reasonable" price. ANY glass is WORTH what SOMEONE is willing to pay for it. Only TWO people determine that price, the buyer and the seller.

ARE THE REPRODUCTIONS HURTING THE MARKET ANYMORE?

I don't think so, at least not with the older, more knowledgeable collectors. People have "taken them in stride" so to speak. They try to keep abreast of them as they occur by buying books and newspapers that keep up-dating the small percentage of reproductions available. Too, collectors are less gullible about reproductions. They shy away from glass that doesn't quite "look right". NEW collectors, however, are somewhat hesitant to begin a pattern they know has suffered from "repros".

WHAT NEW TRENDS ARE YOU OBSERVING IN DEPRESSION GLASS COLLECTING?

Hmmm, let me think. More glassware from the 1950's (and even early 1960's) is being gathered up by collectors. I've included some patterns from this time period in this book as well as in my new, second edition of the Elegant Glassware book---simply because it's turning up at shows and markets, and people are buying it!

More and more collectors are assembling multiple sets, either for themselves or for their children and grandchildren. People who have completed, or nearly completed their "fancier" dinnerware sets are now collecting a kitchen set or an "everyday" ware. (Much of this type glassware is from the 1950's, hence, it's increased collectability.)

Many of the newer collectors are quite young, in college, just married, starting families. Most have limited funds and they tend to start collecting lower priced patterns, expecting to collect only basic, useful pieces in those patterns--just plates and tumblers or cups and saucers, or a set of four, with only an extra serving bowl or two. Many choose 1950's ware. It's more economically priced at the moment, and it's easier to find. The ones who choose true Depression patterns tend to, again, stay away from patterns that have reproduction items, and they don't choose patterns with the rare, high priced items in them.

IS RARE GLASS STILL A GOOD INVESTMENT?

Generally, yes! It helps to buy rarer glass from patterns that are in demand, however. SOME rare glass is virtually uncollectible--because there is so little found that there is no DEMAND, or no MARKET for it. During the recent economic slowdown, rare glass sold steadily AND readily!

IS THERE A FUTURE FOR DEPRESSION GLASS?

Definitely! There are STILL exciting finds being made, and there are STILL people just "discovering" Depression glass who bless us with all that eager anticipation of their finds at the next garage sale, market or show! There are numerous dealers throughout the country who are making their modest living from buying and selling the glass! Libraries constantly order, and re-order books on the subject. (They re-order from me due to wear-out, theft, "many requests", etc.). "Deals" are still being made and sought by Depression glass devotees! All this, and more, bespeaks a very viable future for Depression era glasswares!

ADAM   JEANNETTE GLASS COMPANY, 1932-1934

Colors: Pink, green, crystal, yellow; some delphite blue. *(See Reproduction Section)*

Reproduction of the butter dish (as shown in the back) has softened the price of that particular item in Adam. Harder to find cereal bowls, iced tea tumblers, and lamps have escalated in price. Understand that cereal bowls have to be mint to command the price below. Those with inner rim roughness, as is usual, should be priced lower. I say ''should'' because **you** have to determine what to pay for less-than-mint glass. Green sugar/candy covers seem to be in much shorter supply than pink.

The rarely found Adam/Sierra combination butter dish has BOTH patterns on the top. You can clearly see the Sierra striations which occur on the INSIDE of the butter top on the pink butter in the picture. Adam pattern is found on the OUTSIDE of the same top. This top has been found on both Adam and Sierra butter bottoms, so don't forget to look at the Sierra butters also. Collectors, it is **not** Adam/Sierra unless BOTH patterns are on the top.

ROUND Adam luncheon plates and saucers in yellow and pink are not being found as they once were by early collectors. These rare shapes of Adam were almost certainly experimental pieces as they were discovered in a house belonging to a former Jeannette employee. Even so, there were probably more pieces made than the few yellow and pink items that have turned up. These are so rare that there are few collectors actively looking for them; but they are treasures if found!

The Adam lamps treasured by collectors were made from sherbets which were frosted and notched to accomodate a switch. The metal cover and bulb are difficult to locate separately, though you can occasionally find a lamp base. In fact, it is the bulb and cover that are worth more than the notched base. You can see a similar lamp pictured under Floral. Prices for lamps have made some drastic increases due to several collectors having complete sets of Adam except for the lamps; and they are paying ''big bucks'' to complete their sets.

All of crystal Adam is rare, however, it is so rare that there are virtually no collectors for it! This is the one lesson that is difficult for new collectors to learn. Price is determined mostly by DEMAND; rarity only adds to price on items in great demand.

Adam pitchers come with both rounded and squared bases. The rounded bases have concentric rings, and most are a light pink color. Only the squared base pitcher carries the Adam motif. All crystal pitchers that I have seen in Adam have had round bases.

Candy and sugar lids are interchangeable. This ought to mean that there are more out there to be found; actually, this means that there are less for the candy jar than would normally be the case. There are a lot of sugar and creamer collectors who will buy only sugars with lids. This depletes the lid supply for candy jars, especially in green.

Check the inside rims of items in this pattern as they tend to chip. Don't pay ''mint'' prices for damaged glass unless it's a terribly rare, desirable or unusual piece!

	Pink	Green		Pink	Green
Ash Tray, 4¼"	20.00	16.50	**Cup	16.50	15.00
Bowl, 4¾" Dessert	10.00	9.50	Lamp	150.00	150.00
Bowl, 5¾" Cereal	27.50	22.50	Pitcher, 8", 32 oz.	25.00	30.00
Bowl, 7¾"	13.50	14.50	Pitcher, 32 oz. Round Base	35.00	
Bowl, 9", No Cover	17.50	30.00	Plate, 6" Sherbet	3.50	3.75
Bowl, Cover, 9"	20.00	27.50	***Plate, 7¾" Square Salad	7.00	8.00
Bowl, 9" Covered	37.50	57.50	Plate, 9" Square Dinner	15.00	14.00
Bowl, 10" Oval	15.00	17.50	Plate, 9" Grill	11.50	11.00
Butter Dish Bottom	20.00	50.00	Platter, 11¾"	10.50	12.00
Butter Dish Top	47.50	167.50	Relish Dish, 8" Divided	9.50	11.00
Butter Dish & Cover	55.00	225.00	Salt & Pepper, 4" Footed	40.00	70.00
Butter Dish Combination			****Saucer, 6" Square	3.00	3.00
with Sierra Pattern	457.50		Sherbet, 3"	16.00	20.00
Cake Plate, 10" Footed	12.50	16.50	Sugar	9.00	10.00
*Candlesticks, 4" Pair	50.00	65.00	Sugar/Candy Cover	15.00	27.50
Candy Jar & Cover, 2½"	50.00	60.00	Tumbler, 4½"	15.00	13.50
Coaster, 3¼"	14.00	12.00	Tumbler, 5½" Iced Tea	40.00	30.00
Creamer	11.50	12.50	Vase, 7½"	135.00	30.00

*Delphite $100.00   ***Round Pink $45.00   Yellow $85.00
**Yellow $85.00   ****Round Pink $50.00   Yellow $65.00

Please refer to Foreword for pricing information

AMERICAN PIONEER   LIBERTY WORKS, 1931-1934

Colors: Pink, green, amber, crystal.

Green is the color most in demand by collectors. Pink is, perhaps, their second choice. Crystal runs a poor third. Amber is possibly the color most rarely found; but settings can be obtained in this color with patience and searching.

Liberty called their covered pitchers "urns". More and more, pitchers are being found with liner plates indicating they were probably intended as syrup or cream pitchers. One of these was featured in an Aug. 4, 1975, issue of Newsweek magazine which contained an article on Depression Glass. The crystal urn is a rare piece; but there are few collectors of crystal.

Note that amber is priced triple that of green except for covered urns which are priced separately below. If there were more to be found, I suspect American Pioneer would skyrocket in price. Most of this pattern has been found in the northeastern areas; but it is avidly being sought by several collectors in the Texas area who are building extensive collections.

What I first called a "rose" bowl is pictured in green in front of the candy. I am now convinced that the piece is an open mayonnaise, being footed and having a flared rim. Whatever the case, you may see it listed as a rose bowl in other publications which have not caught up to the fact I changed my mind as to what I thought it ought to be.

Luncheon items (cup, saucer, plate, creamer, sugar) are more commonly found than other pieces shown here. Neither the 8¾" or the 9¼" covered bowls are easily found; wine and water goblets are practically non-existent; and a little 2¼", 2 oz. shot glass shown in front of the crystal urns in the bottom picture is still missing from several extensive collections. Don't pass these by even if you don't personally collect this pattern. A collector will be delighted to take these off your hands (particularly in green).

There may be other items in American Pioneer that I do not have in my list; if you happen to have something not listed, be sure to let me know.

	Crystal, Pink	Green		Crystal, Pink	Green
*Bowl, 5" Handled	9.00	10.00	Lamp, 5½" Round, Ball		
Bowl, 8¾" Covered	65.00	75.00	Shape (Amber $67.50)	57.50	
Bowl, 9" Handled	12.00	15.00	Lamp, 8½" Tall	75.00	85.00
Bowl, 9¼" Covered	75.00	90.00	Mayonnaise, 4¼"	37.50	55.00
Bowl, 10⅜" Console	35.00	45.00	**Pitcher, 5" Covered Urn	100.00	135.00
Candlesticks, 6½" Pair	45.00	55.00	***Pitcher, 7" Covered Urn	125.00	165.00
Candy Jar and Cover, 1 lb.	60.00	80.00	Plate, 6"	4.00	6.00
Candy Jar and Cover, 1½ lb.	60.00	85.00	*Plate, 6" Handled	8.00	10.00
Cheese and Cracker Set (In-			*Plate, 8"	5.50	6.00
dented Platter and Comport)	30.00	40.00	*Plate, 11½" Handled	9.50	12.50
Coaster, 3½"	13.50	14.50	*Saucer	3.00	4.00
Creamer, 2¾"	14.00	16.00	Sherbet, 3½"	10.00	12.50
*Creamer, 3½"	15.00	17.50	Sherbet, 4¾"	17.50	20.00
*Cup	6.00	7.50	Sugar, 2¾"	13.00	15.00
Dresser Set (2 Cologne,			*Sugar, 3½"	14.00	16.50
Powder Jar, on Indented			Tumbler, 5 oz. Juice	13.50	17.50
7½" Tray)	125.00		Tumbler, 4", 8 oz.	15.00	20.00
Goblet, 4", 3 oz. Wine	17.50	22.50	Tumbler, 5", 12 oz.	20.00	30.00
Goblet, 6", 8 oz. Water	22.50	27.50	Vase, 7", Four Styles	50.00	70.00
Ice Bucket, 6"	35.00	40.00	Whiskey, 2¼, 2 oz.	30.00	32.50

    *Amber - Triple the price of green
   **Amber $200.00
  ***Amber $250.00

AMERICAN SWEETHEART   MACBETH-EVANS GLASS COMPANY, 1930-1936

Colors: Pink, monax, red, blue; some cremax and color rimmed monax.

American Sweetheart is one of the Depression Glass patterns that has suffered from over-supply of some pieces. You will note a decrease in price in most of the basic items such as cups, saucers and plates. Do not take this as a negative sign. American Sweetheart has always been plentiful except in the hard-to-find items. Today, more is being found than there are new collectors to absorb it. So, in order to sell this pattern and reduce inventory, many dealers have been reducing prices to stimulate collectors into purchasing a bargain.

There never will be an over-supply of pitchers, tumblers and shakers; but for now there is an adequate supply of sugar lids and shakers in monax. For new collectors, I might point out that MONAX is the name that MacBeth-Evans gave to their white color.

The beige-like color is called CREMAX and is found in berry sets and a few lamp shades. These shades have even been found in Canada. Sometimes they have orange, green, blue or brown panels in them and at least one brass-based floor lamp was found having the same grooved panels as the shade! Another MINIATURE version of the large console bowl with its large, flat rim, (you can serve more off the rim than from the bowl) turned up in the east. It' a RARE little bowl about 6½" wide x 1¾" tall.

No one has found another "vase" like the one pictured. It's thought to have been some factory worker's "pet project" or simply a tumbler that failed to get cut properly. Whatever, it's unique and residing in California at present.

Pink American Sweetheart shakers continue to be in short supply and the 10 oz. tumblers have all but disappeared from the market. While commonly found items decreased in price, you will note that is not true for the harder-to-find items. More collectors increase the demand for hard-to-find items and prices react accordingly.

Novices to collecting can tell from the photo that the 80 oz. pitcher has the more bulbous shape, but either one represents a good day's find.

I have seen both red and blue tid-bit servers. See prices on the following page. Many tid-bits have been put together in recent years using old hardware and drilling into regular plates.

That fired-on green shaker has a new home in Illinois, but the fired-on, peachy-pink that came from Pittsburgh in 1975 is lost, compliments of a household move years ago. We never did find it again!

	Pink	Monax		Pink	Monax
Bowl, 3¾" Flat Berry	24.00		Plate, 15½" Server		150.00
Bowl, 4½" Cream Soup	25.00	35.00	Platter, 13" Oval	17.50	35.00
Bowl, 6" Cereal	8.50	8.50	Pitcher, 7½", 60 oz.	367.50	
Bowl, 9" Round Berry	16.50	32.50	Pitcher, 8", 80 oz.	347.50	
Bowl, 9½" Flat Soup	27.50	35.00	Salt and Pepper, Footed	245.00	185.00
Bowl, 11" Oval Vegetable	27.50	35.00	Saucer	2.50	1.50
Bowl, 18" Console		250.00	Sherbet, 3¾" Footed	10.00	
Creamer, Footed	6.50	6.00	Sherbet, 4¼" Footed		
Cup	8.00	7.00	(Design Inside or Outside)	8.00	12.50
Lampshade		425.00	Sherbet in Metal Holder		
Plate, 6" or 6½" Bread & Butter	2.00	2.50	(Crystal Only) $3.00		
Plate, 8" Salad	6.00	6.00	Sugar, Open, Footed	6.50	5.00
Plate, 9" Luncheon		7.50	Sugar Cover (Monax Only)*		150.00
Plate, 9¾" Dinner	13.00	11.00	Tidbit, 3 Tier, 8", 12" & 15½"		150.00
Plate, 10¼" Dinner		13.50	Tumbler, 3½", 5 oz.	35.00	
Plate, 11" Chop Plate		9.00	Tumbler, 4", 9 oz.	35.00	
Plate, 12" Salver	8.50	9.00	Tumbler, 4½", 10 oz.	50.00	

*Two style knobs.

Please refer to Foreword for pricing information

AMERICAN SWEETHEART (Cont'd.)

Prices for red American Sweetheart have suffered a dramatic decline due to more of it being found recently than blue. Some of the blue has also declined in price although not as drastically. I have always said that these were over-priced for the supply and now, time is proving me right. The major problem is that both of these colors are basically luncheon sets, and most collectors want more pieces than that.

The stark white monax American Sweetheart can also be found rimmed with various colors such as gold, pink, green, or "smoke" which is a blue-gray color that reaches black at the extreme edges. Of all the "trims", the "smoke" is the most highly prized and the most often confused by new collectors because some monax has a bluish-black look to it. All "smoke" will have a BLACK edge.

The pink trimmed luncheon set pictured here was found at Washington Court House, Ohio, several years ago. Before it left for a home in Michigan, I thought you might like to see it one more time.

Generally speaking, the pieces shown here are what is usually discovered in the trimmed monax American Sweetheart, relegating these sets to an attractive luncheon or serving set. It's a shame that not more of this is being found.

Some blue and red sherbets and plates have appeared having the American Sweetheart SHAPE but not having the pattern. We can't call these anything but American Sweetheart BLANKS and while they are novel, without the pattern they can command only a fraction of the cost of patterned pieces. The same can be said for the plain pink pitcher in the shape of American Sweetheart. If it does not have the pattern on it, it can not be considered anything except "shaped" like American Sweetheart.

Gold trimmed monax is difficult to match and, therefore, there are few collectors of it. If you wish to get rid of the gold, you can use a scouring pad lightly for hours and chance scratching the glass; or you can spend a few minutes with a pencil eraser. You will be quite surprised how easily the gold disappears with the latter method.

	Red	Blue	Cremax	Smoke & Other Trims
Bowl, 6" Cereal			8.00	25.00
Bowl, 9" Round Berry			33.00	62.50
Bowl, 18" Console	625.00	700.00		
Creamer, Footed	65.00	75.00		57.50
Cup	55.00	75.00		52.50
Lampshade			400.00	
Lamp (Floor with Brass Base)			600.00	
Plate, 6" Bread and Butter				13.50
Plate, 8" Salad	45.00	65.00		25.00
Plate, 9" Luncheon				30.00
Plate, 9¾" Dinner				45.00
Plate, 12" Salver	115.00	135.00		75.00
Plate, 15½" Server	225.00	285.00		
Platter, 13" Oval				87.50
Saucer	20.00	22.50		13.50
Sherbet, 4¼" Footed (Design Inside or Outside)				27.50
Sugar, Open Footed	55.00	75.00	57.50	
Tidbit, 3 Tier, 8", 12" & 15½"	425.00	525.00		

ANNIVERSARY   JEANNETTE GLASS COMPANY, 1947-1949

Colors: Pink, recently crystal and iridescent

A lot more iridized Anniversary is showing up at flea markets. Remember, this was made as late as the 1970's and shouldn't be priced more than crystal. It is NOT Carnival glass as some will say. My first experiences with iridized sets were in boxed lots at a flea market in 1971. A local auctioneer asked the dealer how he had found so much Carnival glass in the original boxes and was told that if he went to Pennsylvania, he could buy all he could haul for practically nothing.

Some pieces of Anniversary (fruit bowl, candy dish, sandwich tray, butter dish, wine glass) are not easily found. It will help if you tell every dealer what you're looking for so they will help in the search. Most are glad to look for specific items they know they can sell immediately. This holds true for any pattern.

The bottom to the butter is harder to locate than the top, and there is almost no demand for later issued crystal Anniversary except for the butter dish and the pin up vase. The supply of vases has recently dried up; so be on the lookout for these. A lot of these were used and are water stained. There is nothing that will totally remove this no matter what you are told.

	Crystal	Pink		Crystal	Pink
Bowl, 4⅞" Berry	1.50	2.50	Pickle Dish, 9"	3.00	6.00
Bowl, 7⅜" Soup	3.50	8.00	Plate, 6¼" Sherbet	1.25	2.00
Bowl, 9" Fruit	7.00	11.00	Plate, 9" Dinner	3.50	4.50
Butter Dish Bottom	10.00	20.00	Plate, 12½" Sandwich Server	4.00	6.50
Butter Dish Top	12.50	22.00	Relish Dish, 8"	4.50	6.50
Butter Dish and Cover	22.50	45.00	Saucer	1.00	1.50
Candy Jar and Cover	17.50	30.00	Sherbet, Footed	2.50	4.50
*Comport, Open, 3 Legged	3.00	7.00	Sugar	2.00	4.50
Cake Plate, 12½"	5.50	8.50	Sugar Cover	3.00	4.50
Cake Plate and Cover	10.00	12.50	Vase, 6½"	6.00	9.00
Candlestick, 4⅞" Pair	12.50		Vase, Wall Pin-up	10.00	15.00
Creamer, Footed	3.00	6.50	Wine Glass, 2½ oz.	5.00	9.50
Cup	2.00	4.50			

*Old form; presently called compote or candy.

AUNT POLLY   U.S. GLASS COMPANY, Late 1920's

Colors: Blue, green, iridescent

One drawback to collecting Aunt Polly is the absence of cups! Not being a coffee/tea person, that doesn't bother me; but the majority of people like cups and saucers in their sets of dishes. Another problem illustrated by the photograph is the variation in color. There are three distinct shades of green and two of blue. It is difficult enough to find Aunt Polly without having to deal with color discrepancies.

Be advised that the oval vegetable bowl, covered sugar and shakers are difficult to find. Most of the pieces listed have surfaced in either green or iridescent, but not all appeared in both. Iridescent Aunt Polly holds its own in price due to scarcity. An iridescent butter, in fact, is quite rare. However, there is little demand for either green or iridescent at present except by butter dish collectors.

A butter top or bottom in blue is equally hard to find. However, in green and iridescent, only the top is difficult since the bottom is the same as found in other U.S. Glass patterns such as Strawberry, Floral and Diamond and U.S. Swirl.

Two items to note in the picture are the two handled candy whose lid fits the sugar, and the lack of a distinct spout on one creamer. Techniques of quality control weren't all that advanced in the 1930's.

	Green, Iridescent	Blue		Green, Iridescent	Blue
Bowl, 4⅜" Berry	4.50	6.00	Creamer	16.50	25.00
Bowl, 4¾", 2" High	8.50	11.00	Pitcher, 8", 48 oz.		125.00
Bowl, 5½" one handled	12.50	15.00	Plate, 6" Sherbet	3.00	4.50
Bowl, 7¼" Oval, Handled Pickle	9.00	12.50	Plate, 8" Luncheon		8.50
Bowl, 7⅞" Large Berry	11.00	17.50	Salt and Pepper		150.00
Bowl, 8⅜" Oval	25.00	40.00	Sherbet	7.50	8.50
Butter Dish and Cover	187.50	147.50	Sugar	11.50	16.50
Butter Dish Bottom	42.50	72.50	Sugar Cover	30.00	45.00
Butter Dish Top	145.00	75.00	Tumbler, 3⅝", 8 oz.		18.00
Candy, Cover, 2 Handled	35.00	47.50	Vase, 6½" Footed	17.50	22.00

Please refer to Foreword for pricing information

"AURORA"   HAZEL ATLAS GLASS COMPANY, Late 1930's

Colors: Cobalt blue, pink.

This is a nice little set to collect! It comes in the highly prized cobalt blue color that has a mystique all its own with collectors; and it still falls within budget pricing!

My wife likes this. She collected what's here to use at "small meal" times when you just need a salad, sandwich and drink! She's derived a lot of pleasure from searching, buying, owning and using this set. I will have to tell you that she blends the cobalt petalware mustard bottom with this to serve fruit or custard desserts when she uses the "Aurora". I'll also have to admit the pattern has grown on me. I totally ignored it for years!

	Cobalt/Pink		Cobalt/Pink
Bowl, 4½" Deep	10.00	Plate, 6½"	3.50
Bowl, 5⅜" Cereal	4.50	Saucer	2.50
Creamer, 4½"	8.00	Tumbler, 4¾", 10 oz.	10.00
Cup	5.00		

AVOCADO, NO. 601   INDIANA GLASS COMPANY, 1923-1933

Colors: Pink, green, crystal   *(See Reproduction Section)*

Avocado has seen some resurgence in collecting lately, but not to the point it was before the reissues started in 1974. For new collectors I repeat the following history of this beautiful pattern which has numerous devotees. It was on its way to becoming one of the oustanding patterns in Depression Glass until Indiana Glass Company started remaking it for its Tiara Exclusive Home Products line. They first issued "collectible" pitcher and water sets in colors of red, peach and frosted. Unfortunately, they made the mistake of remaking it in the older pink, too, thereby rather killing the goose that was laying their golden egg. Even though the newer pink was a more orange-pink than the original, the price of the older glass stopped dead still and hasn't fully recovered in eleven years. Since then, the company has marketed green sherbets, creamers, sugars and sherbet plates. Possibly, it's only a matter of time until they market the remaining pieces. Thus, the price rise for this glassware has slowly plodded along. Traditionally, this is what happens when a pattern is reproduced--at least until the differences between old and new become common knowledge. Unfortunately, when the original company remakes their own product, any differences are negligible! I'm not saying the glass is worthless as an investment; rather that it will take another forty or fifty years before it can recover and be considered to be antique. Had the company had the foresight to remake the pattern in heretofore unknown colors, then they could have enhanced the collectibility of BOTH the older glass and the new. As it is, they've damaged the investment possibilities of their older product, thereby souring everyone's taste for their glass. Indiana's Depression glass patterns are something of a pariah among the vast field of collectors at the moment. Agreed, there is much that IS old which is antique and which should be valuable as such. Unfortunately, the much that is new tarnishes the prospect of more immediate returns in investors' eyes.

Green pitcher and tumbler sets have dried up into collections and are some of the few pieces in Avocado to be making advancements in price. Saucers are still harder to find than cups. Milk white pieces of Avocado were probably a product of the 1950's Indiana milk glass push; and a few pieces have turned up with an apple design rather than the pear. These are considered more novel than collectible. The apple pieces were recently remade in amber for Tiara.

	Pink	Green		Pink	Green
Bowl, 5¼" Two-Handled	20.00	22.50	*Pitcher, 64 ozs.	350.00	550.00
Bowl, 6" Footed Relish	14.00	18.50	***Plate, 6¾" Sherbet	9.50	11.50
Bowl, 7" One Handle Preserve	12.50	15.00	**Plate, 8¼" Luncheon	12.50	14.50
Bowl, 7½" Salad	25.00	37.50	Plate, 10¼" 2 Handled Cake	22.50	32.50
Bowl, 8" 2 Handled Oval	14.50	18.50	Saucer	15.00	20.00
Bowl, 9½", 3¼" Deep	60.00	80.00	***Sherbet	40.00	45.00
***Creamer, Footed	22.50	2500	***Sugar, Footed	22.50	25.00
Cup, Footed	25.00	25.00	*Tumbler	75.00	125.00

*Caution on pink. The orangeish-pink is new!
**Apple Design $10.00. Amber has been newly made.
***Just remade in green.

Please refer to Foreword for pricing information

BEADED BLOCK   IMPERIAL GLASS COMPANY, 1927-1930's

Colors: Pink, green, crystal, ice blue, vaseline, iridescent, amber, red, opalescent, milk white.

There are several items to be pointed out in the picture at the right. Most noteworthy is the red lily bowl shown for the first time. Several of these have been found in the Dayton, Ohio, area in the last few years. Other items are the pink and blue vases and the white lily bowl. If you look closely, you will see that these items all have straight edges with no scallops. Only the lily bowl seems to indeed be Beaded Block; and that is marked IG (Imperial Glass) which means it was made after 1951. The vases are nice "go-with" pieces; but they are not truly Beaded Block, though they are being collected as such.

Beaded Block comes in a multitude of colors with the dubious distinction of being mistaken for "Carnival", "Vaseline" or "Pattern" glassware and unknowing or misinformed dealers will price it along those lines. YOU ultimately decide what a piece is worth to you. If you feel a piece is priced exhorbitantly, pass it by unless you can convince the dealer to moderate the price.

Imperial called the two-handled bowl a "jelly" rather than a soup; and the tall, footed pieces were "footed jellies" rather than compotes. Iridized pink items being seen at flea markets are of recent vintage.

We are still looking for a white Beaded Block pitcher!

	Crystal*, Pink, Green, Amber	Other Colors		Crystal*, Pink, Green, Amber	Other Colors
Bowl, 4½" 2 Handled Jelly	6.00	12.50	Bowl, 7½" Round, Plain Edge	7.50	14.00
**Bowl, 4½ Round Lily	8.50	15.00	Bowl, 8¼" Celery	9.50	15.00
Bowl, 5½" Square	6.00	8.50	Creamer	12.50	20.00
Bowl, 5½ One Handle	6.50	8.50	Pitcher, 5¼", Pint Jug	85.00	
Bowl, 6" Deep Round	8.50	14.50	Plate, 7¾ Square	5.00	8.00
Bowl, 6¼" Round	6.50	13.50	Plate, 8¾" Round	10.00	15.00
Bowl, 6½" Round	6.50	13.50	Stemmed Jelly, 4½"	8.00	14.50
Bowl, 6½" 2 Handled Pickle	10.00	14.50	Stemmed Jelly, 4½", Flared		
Bowl, 6¾" Round, Unflared	8.50	12.50	Top	8.50	16.00
Bowl, 7¼" Round, Flared	8.00	14.50	Sugar	12.50	17.50
Bowl, 7½" Round, Fluted			Vase, 6" Bouquet	10.00	17.50
Edges	17.50	20.00			

*All pieces 25% to 40% lower.
**Red: $65.00.

"BOWKNOT"   MANUFACTURER UNKNOWN, Probably Late 1920's

Color: Green

Does anyone out there have a cereal bowl? I must have been looking in all the wrong places as I have not yet been able to find one. I would like one for the next edition!

My wife is totally charmed with this pattern, liking the shapes and what she terms the pattern's "Depression era look". Maybe she equates its dearth of pieces to the lack of everything else during the Depression!

I get letters from people thinking they've found a creamer and sugar. Thus far, all have turned out to be Fostoria's "June" pattern which also has a knotted bow design. (However, green "June" would be a rare find!)

	Green		Green
Bowl, 4½" Berry	8.00	Sherbet, Low Footed	8.00
Bowl, 5½" Cereal	10.50	Tumbler, 5", 10 oz.	11.00
Cup	5.00	Tumbler, 5", 10 oz. Footed	11.00
Plate, 7" Salad	7.50		

Please refer to Foreword for pricing information

BLOCK OPTIC, "BLOCK"   HOCKING GLASS COMPANY, 1929-1933

Colors: Green, pink, yellow, crystal, some blue

New collectors are turning to patterns which are affordable without mortaging the homestead. This is good for Depression Glass and will make dealers rethink their concepts about buying only major patterns. I have always tried to carry a lot of patterns to shows where I set up a booth. A whole four piece setting in a minor pattern can be bought for the price of one hard-to-find piece in most highly collected patterns.

Block Optic continues to be one of the more popular patterns of Depression Glass! It never seems to attract the frenetic activity of some other patterns. Rather, it just quietly continues to attract new collectors and to steadily sell while other patterns go through "ups and downs". Were you to graph the activity generated by Block Optic, you'd just see a steady, gently rising line. This is a pattern with numerous price increases over the past two years; yet it is still affordable.

New collectors should be aware that there are five styles of sugars and creamers, short, tall, footed, and flat with each having handle variations. There are also four cup types plus one mug and two different saucers with cup rings and two without rings. The cup ring saucers are worth more than the cups which is true with most of Hocking's patterns.

After advertising a pair of green candlesticks for $30.00 in the Daze newspaper (see p.222), Grannie Bear, my Mom, got calls for several months; and I was asked if we still had them at the next three shows I attended. Candlesticks are even harder to find than I thought they were. Cone shaped sherbets, luncheon and sherbet plates are readily available. The cone-shaped mayonnaise shown in front of the tumble-up, has now been found in pink for the first time; and a pink ice tub has been reported from Texas. The jug to the tumble-up set is only worth about $10.00 by itself; it is the TUMBLER that is the hard part to find. (There is a Block-like plate found in green with a snowflake design in the center which sells for about five dollars and some collectors are buying these to supplement regular dinner plates which are becoming harder to find.)

Many Block Optic items have similar shapes to the very popular Cameo pattern (also made by Hocking). Some Block Optic pieces have black fired-on feet. These are relatively scarce; but not everyone cares for them; so the price for these has remained relatively low. Crystal Block Optic sells for about one half the price of the pink, which is scarce at any price. That blue butter dish remains one of a kind.

	Green	Yellow	Pink		Green	Yellow	Pink
Bowl, 4¼" Berry	4.50		4.00	Plate, 8" Luncheon	3.00	3.75	2.50
Bowl, 5¼" Cereal	8.00		5.00	Plate, 9" Dinner	12.50	25.00	15.00
Bowl, 7" Salad	12.00	15.00	9.00	Plate, 9" Grill	6.50	12.50	9.50
Bowl, 8½" Large Berry	12.50	25.00	10.00	Plate, 10¼" Sandwich	12.50		12.50
*Butter Dish and Cover, 3" x 5"	35.00			Salt and Pepper, Footed	22.50	55.00	45.00
Butter Dish Bottom	20.00			Salt and Pepper, Squatty	30.00		
Butter Dish Top	15.00			Sandwich Server, Center Handle	35.00		35.00
Candlesticks, 1¾" Pr.	40.00		30.00	Saucer, 5¾", With Cup Ring	7.00		5.00
Candy Jar & Cover, 2¼" Tall	30.00	40.00	30.00	Saucer, 6⅛", With Cup Ring	7.00		4.50
Candy Jar & Cover, 6¼" Tall	29.50		45.00	Sherbet, Non Stemmed (Cone)	3.00		
Comport, 4" Wide Mayonnaise	17.50		35.00	Sherbet, 3¼", 5½ oz.	4.50	7.50	4.00
Creamer, Three Styles: Cone				Sherbet, 4¾", 6 oz.	9.50	12.00	8.00
Shaped, Round, Rayed Foot				Sugar, Three Styles: As			
and Flat (5 Kinds)	9.50	9.50	8.50	Creamer	8.50	9.50	8.00
Cup, Four Styles	4.50	6.00	4.00	Tumbler, 3" & 3½, 5 oz. Flat	10.00		11.00
Goblet, 4" Cocktail	15.00		12.50	Tumbler, 4", 5 oz. Footed	11.00		11.50
Goblet, 4½" Wine	15.00		11.50	Tumbler, 9 oz. Flat	9.00		120.00
Goblet, 5¾", 9 oz.	15.00		11.50	Tumbler, 9 oz. Footed	12.50	12.50	10.00
Goblet, 7¼", 9 oz. Thin	20.00	17.50	12.50	Tumbler, 10 oz. Flat	11.50		10.00
Ice Bucket	27.50		22.50	Tumbler, 6", 10 oz Footed	12.50	15.00	14.00
Ice Tub or Butter Tub, Open	25.00		35.00	Tumbler, 14 oz. Flat	15.00		
Mug, Flat Creamer, No Spout	25.00			Tumble-up Night Set: 3"			
Pitcher, 7⅝", 68 oz., Bulbous	55.00		40.00	Tumbler Bottle and Tumbler,			
Pitcher, 8½", 54 oz.	25.00		27.50	6" High	42.50		
Pitcher, 8", 80 oz.	37.50		32.50	Vase, 5¾" Blown	150.00		
Plate, 6" Sherbet	1.50	2.00	1.00	Whiskey, 1⅝"	17.50		17.50
				Whiskey, 2½"	14.50		14.50

*Blue $350.00

"BUBBLE", "BULLSEYE", "PROVINCIAL"

ANCHOR HOCKING GLASS COMPANY, 1934-1965

Colors: Pink, light blue, dark green, red, crystal and any Hocking color.

"Bubble" is a fun pattern to collect. It is easy to identify, easy to find and easy on the purse strings in most cases. I do not believe Hocking ever made a color after 1942 in which someone at the factory did not make the 8¾" bowl using that color. It's found in pink most often, but can be found in jadite, fired-on pink over white (similar to Oyster and Pearl), and even iridized. In an earlier edition, I showed topaz; so do not be surprised at any color of Bubble.

Pink is rare except for the above mentioned 8¾" berry bowl; if you find anything else, it is exceptional.

The scarcity of creamers in blue has pulled the price of the sugar bowl up too, due to some dealers refusing to separate the two items. I have never understood why the blue creamer has been twice as hard to find as the sugar. It just is and has been from the days when the pair sold for $3.00 (if you could get that much).

Green Bubble appeared in the 1950's and early '60's during the Forest Green production. Green Bubble is presently selling well. I've asked several people their reasons for buying it and gotten answers from "I'm using it for my Christmas table," to "The price is bound to go up on this, too!"

The ruby red was issued in the 1960's under the name "Provincial". Red "Bubble" is experiencing a recent surge of interest on the part of collectors, I assume, for as myriad reasons as expressed above. The tumblers and pitcher are the predominately found pieces. So far, no one has found a creamer and sugar in red. Let me know if you do!

The flat rimmed bowl pictured in the pattern shot is rarely seen. Only two or three have turned up to date. Yet, with the number of collectors of "Bubble" increasing, surely more will be spotted. Other oddities to turn up have included an amber cup with no saucer and an opalescent "Bubble" bowl with a "Moonstone" lable affixed to it. You can see that pictured with the Moonstone pattern. These items, though rare, are more intriguing than costly.

Notice that iridized green sugar bowl between the green creamer and sugar. Frankly, I can see why very little of that has surfaced. It's just plain awful.

Crystal "Bubble" sells for about half the blue, yet crystal "Bubble" sets a very attractive table. You may go years before ever seeing a pitcher in crystal, however. I once bought over seventy pieces of crystal just to get the pitcher for my sister's collection. Everyone going by the table laughed because I was buying crystal "Bubble"! What they didn't know was that I had only paid thirty dollars for the whole set, and after giving away the pitcher, I still doubled my money within two weeks.

	Dark Green	Light Blue	Ruby Red		Dark Green	Light Blue	Ruby Red
Bowl, 4" Berry	4.00	7.50		Plate, 6¾" Bread and			
Bowl, 4½" Fruit	5.00	6.00	4.00	Butter	1.50	2.00	
Bowl, 5¼" Cereal	5.00	6.50		Plate, 9⅜" Grill		9.50	
Bowl, 7¾" Flat Soup		8.00		Plate, 9⅜" Dinner	4.50	4.00	5.50
Bowl, 8⅜" Large Berry				Platter, 12" Oval		8.50	
(Pink—$3.00)	7.50	8.50	*** Saucer	1.00	1.00	1.50
Bowl, 9" Flanged		50.00		Sugar	6.50	12.50	
Candlesticks (Crystal -				Tidbit (2 Tier)			16.50
$10.00 Pr.)	17.50			Tumbler, 6 oz. Juice			6.00
Creamer	7.00	19.50		Tumbler, 9 oz. Water			5.50
*Cup	3.00	2.50	4.00	Tumbler, 12 oz. Iced Tea			8.50
Lamp, 2 styles, Crystal Only - $25.00				Tumbler, 16 oz.			
**Pitcher, 64 oz. Ice Lip			35.00	Lemonade			14.00

*Pink—$40.00
**Crystal—$40.00
***Pink—$17.50

Please refer to Foreword for pricing information

CAMEO, "BALLERINA" or "DANCING GIRL" HOCKING GLASS

COMPANY, 1930-1934

Colors: Green, yellow pink, crystal w/platinum rim. *(See Reproduction Section)*

A special thanks to Frank McClain for his photography and to Lynn and Jerry Mantione for sharing their pink Cameo and the green sandwich server. The pitcher is the first to come to light, but it suffers from a weak pattern. Blank pitchers in yellow and pink have been found for years, but until now, the Cameo design has been missing. Pink Cameo has never been easy to find, but with patience, luck and a deep pocket, a set can be assembled as you can see!

The very rare (and costly) center handled server, which few collectors own, and the Cameo oil lamp are shown for the first time in color. ENJOY!

I used to say that Cameo was one of the top five patterns in Depression glass, but now I believe it to be in the top three! There are more unique and unusual pieces in this pattern, however, than in any other which makes owning a COMPLETE set virtually impossible as well as costly. Basic sets can still be easily put together and enjoyed, so don't let the prices of the "frill" items put you off collecting Cameo. I've had ladies tell me they've enjoyed using this glassware as no other they've ever owned!

Among saucers that can still be found (sometimes in stacks of sherbet plates), Cameo saucers with the ring indent are probably the highest priced saucers in Depression glass.

Those elusive Cameo shakers were reproduced, but the pattern proved to be so weak that they were easily distinguished from the old. So far, this mould has not been improved, and, if you will look in the reproduction section, you will see that the pattern is so weak it does not photograph well.

The odd lid pictured fits only the "rope" top juice pitcher, but should it? Some have supposedly turned up with the water pitcher, but I have yet to see one that it fits as it ought to fit.

The little 3½" wine is turning out to be quite scarce.

The small size children's sets are new. (See Reproduction Section at back).

	Green	Yellow	Pink	Crys/ Plat
Bowl, 4¼" Sauce				4.00
Bowl, 4¾" Cream Soup	40.00			
Bowl, 5½" Cereal	20.00	20.00		6.00
Bowl, 7¼" Salad	25.00			
Bowl, 8¼" Large Berry	22.00		100.00	
Bowl, 9" Rimmed Soup	25.00			
Bowl, 10" Oval Vegetable	13.50	20.00		
Bowl, 11", 3 Leg Console	40.00	52.50	19.50	
Butter Dish and Cover	130.00	625.00		
Butter Dish Bottom	80.00	300.00		
Butter Dish Top	50.00	325.00		
Cake Plate, 10", 3 Legs	14.00			
Cake Plate, 10½" Flat	65.00			
Candlesticks, 4" Pr.	67.50			
Candy Jar, 4" Low and Cover	40.00	50.00	350.00	
Candy Jar, 6½" Tall and Cover	90.00			
Cocktail Shaker (Metal Lid) Appears in Crystal Only				350.00
Comport, 5" Wide Mayonnaise	17.50		150.00	

CAMEO, "BALLERINA" or "DANCING GIRL"   (Con't.)

	Green	Yellow	Pink	Crys/ Plat
Cookie Jar and Cover	35.00			
Creamer, 3¼"	16.50	12.00		
Creamer, 4¼"	16.00		50.00	
Cup, Two Styles	9.50	6.50	50.00	5.00
Decanter, 10" With Stopper	85.00			150.00
Decanter, 10" With Stopper, Frosted (Stopper Represents ½ Value of Decanter	23.50			
Domino Tray, 7" With 3" Indentation	67.50			
Domino Tray, 7" With No Indentation			147.50	87.50
Goblet, 3½" Wine	175.00			
Goblet, 4" Wine	42.50		175.00	
Goblet, 6" Water	35.00		110.00	
Ice Bowl or Open Butter, 3" Tall x 5½" Wide	100.00		400.00	175.00
Jam Jar, 2" and Cover	90.00			97.50
Pitcher, 5¾", 20 oz. Syrup or Milk	137.50	177.50		
Pitcher, 6", 36 oz. Juice	40.00			
Pitcher, 8½", 56 oz. Water	35.00		1000.00	300.00
Plate, 6" Sherbet	2.00	2.00	45.00	1.75
Plate, 7" Salad				3.00
Plate, 8" Luncheon	7.00	2.50	23.00	3.50
Plate, 8½" Square	22.50	75.00		
Plate, 9½" Dinner	11.00	6.00	30.00	
Plate, 10" Sandwich	9.50		30.00	
Plate, 10½" Grill	7.00	6.00	32.50	
Plate, 10½" Grill With Closed Handles	47.50	5.75		
Plate, 11½" With Closed Handles	6.50	5.00		
Platter, 12", Closed Handles	13.50	13.50		
Relish, 7½" Footed, 3 Part	20.00	57.50		
*Salt and Pepper, Footed Pr.	50.00		500.00	
Sandwich Server, Center Handle	2,000.00			
Saucer With Cup Ring	75.00			
Saucer, 6" (Sherbet Plate)	2.00	2.00	45.00	
Sherbet, 3⅛" molded	9.50	15.00	25.00	
Sherbet, 3⅛" blown	11.00			
Sherbet, 4⅞"	22.50	22.50	47.50	
Sugar, 3¼"	11.50	9.50		
Sugar, 4¼"	16.50		50.00	
Tumbler, 3¾", 5 oz. Juice	20.00		60.00	
Tumbler, 4", 9 oz. Water	17.00		60.00	7.50
Tumbler, 4¾", 10 oz. Flat	20.00		72.50	
Tumbler, 5", 11 oz. Flat	18.00	25.00	72.50	
Tumbler, 5¼", 15 oz.	40.00		85.00	
Tumbler, 3 oz. Footed Juice	40.00		80.00	
Tumbler, 5", 9 oz. Footed	17.00	10.00	75.00	
Tumbler, 5¾", 11 oz. Footed	40.00			
Tumbler, 6⅜", 15 oz. Footed	250.00			
Vase, 5¾"	110.00			
Vase, 8"	15.00			
Water Bottle (Dark Green) Whitehouse Vinegar	12.50			

*Beware Reproductions

CHERRY BLOSSOM JEANNETTE GLASS COMPANY, 1930-1939

Colors: Pink, green, delphite (opaque blue), crystal, jadite (opaque green), red. *(See Reproduction Section)*

It pains me to say this, but I have always tried to be honest with my many readers. If you are going to start a pattern in Depression Glass for investment purposes, I would not choose Cherry Blossom unless you are planning on very long term investment planning.

Cherry Blossom was one of the most popular patterns in Depression glass. It was easily recognized, had a good selection of pieces, and had some intriguing, odd colors and unusual pieces to titillate the instinct of ardent collectors. Unfortunately, all this made it a prime target for the copy artists. More reproductions have occured in this pattern than any other pattern of Depression glass. Naturally, prices on this glass at present have dropped due to the reproduction blitzkreig. However, though shaken, collectors need not feel their pattern has been mortally wounded, but it is in critical condition. Old Cherry Blossom is still old and still valuable. It will help to protect everyone if you try to refrain from buying the new. If there are no buyers, there will soon be no reproductions. I will endeavor to pass along to you in the back of the book some tell-tale signs which shriek ''reproduction''. An opaque, slag-like, reddish-yellow bowl has just been found.

The rare 9″ platter (pictured in pink) measures nine inches OUTSIDE edge to OUTSIDE edge.

The letters AOP in the price listing refer to pieces having an ''all over pattern''; PAT means ''pattern at the top'' only.

You will find some few pieces of crystal Cherry Blossom, but it is not considered to be collectible.

The pattern shot shows a beautiful, old, translucent green plate.

	Pink	Green	Delphite		Pink	Green	Delphite
Bowl, 4¾″ Berry	7.50	10.00	9.00	Plate, 9″ Grill	16.00	17.00	
Bowl, 5¾″ Cereal	19.00	20.00		Plate, 10″ Grill		40.00	
Bowl, 7¾″ Flat Soup	35.00	37.50		Platter, 9″ Oval	627.50		
* Bowl, 8½″ Round Berry	12.00	15.00	35.00	Platter, 11″ Oval	16.00	20.00	30.00
Bowl, 9″ Oval Vegetable	16.00	17.50	40.00	Platter, 13″ and 13″ Divided	28.00	30.00	
** Bowl, 9″ 2 Handled	11.00	15.00	12.50	Salt and Pepper (Scalloped			
** Bowl, 10½″, 3 Leg Fruit	35.00	37.50		Bottom)	925.00	650.00	
Butter Dish and Cover	50.00	65.00		Saucer	2.50	3.00	3.00
Butter Dish Bottom	15.00	20.00		Sherbet	9.00	11.00	11.00
Butter Dish Top	35.00	45.00		Sugar	9.00	10.50	15.00
Cake Plate (3 Legs) 10¼″	12.00	14.00		Sugar Cover	10.00	11.00	
Coaster	9.00	8.50		Tray, 10½″ Sandwich	10.00	12.00	13.00
Creamer	9.00	11.00	15.00	Tumbler, 3¾″, 4 oz. Footed			
Cup	10.00	12.00	12.50	AOP, Round or Scalloped	10.00	12.00	14.00
Mug, 7 oz.	145.00	135.00		Tumbler, 4½″, 9 oz. Round			
*** Pitcher, 6¾″ AOP, 36 oz.				Foot AOP	20.00	22.50	14.00
Scalloped or Round Bottom	25.00	35.00		Tumbler, 4½″, 8 oz. Scalloped			
Pitcher, 8″ PAT, 42 oz. Flat	30.00	37.50		Foot AOP	20.00	27.50	
Pitcher, 8″ PAT, 36 oz. Footed	35.00	42.50	65.00	Tumbler, 3½″, 4 oz. Flat PAT	11.00	18.00	
Plate, 6″ Sherbet	4.00	4.00	8.50	Tumbler, 4¼″, 9 oz. Flat PAT	12.00	15.00	
Plate, 7″ Salad	12.00	14.00		Tumbler, 5″, 12 oz. Flat PAT	35.00	45.00	
**** Plate, 9″ Dinner	10.00	12.00	11.00				

* Yellow—$350.00
** Jadite—$275.00
*** Jadite—$300.00
**** Translucent Green—$175.00   Jadite—$40.00

CHERRY BLOSSOM - CHILD'S JUNIOR DINNER SET

	Pink	Delphite
Creamer	25.00	27.50
Sugar	25.00	27.50
Plate, 6″	6.50	8.25(design on bottom)
Cup	20.00	25.00
Saucer	3.00	4.00
14 Piece Set	175.00	185.00

Original box sells for $15.00 extra with these sets.

Original box sells for $15.00 extra with these sets.

Please refer to Foreword for pricing information

CHINEX CLASSIC   MACBETH-EVANS DIVISION OF CORNING GLASS WORKS, Late '30's-Early '40's.

Colors: Ivory, ivory w/decal decoration.

Chinex has an embossed, scroll-like design on the dishes which will distinguish them from the Cremax pattern with which it is often confused. The scrolling is found on the lid only of the butter dish. The base has only the pie crust type edging which leads people to believe they've discovered a Cremax butter bottom. The decaled butter has the same decal on the top and bottom.

I have seen very little of this in my travels, but what I have seen has been virtually ignored by collectors unless you find castle-decorated Chinex Classic. If I had known how scarce this particular pattern was twelve years ago when I first put it in the book, I probably would not have included it. I assumed that over the years more of it would surface. Some has, but not enough to make this collectible.

	Browntone or Plain Ivory	Decal Decorated*		Browntone or Plain Ivory	Decal Decorated*
Bowl, 5¾" Cereal	4.00	5.00	Cup	3.50	4.50
Bowl, 7" Vegetable	12.50	15.00	Plate, 6¼" Sherbet	1.50	2.00
Bowl, 7¾" Soup	10.00	12.00	Plate, 9¾" Dinner	3.00	5.00
Bowl, 9" Vegetable	9.50	12.50	Plate, 11½" Sandwich		
Bowl, 11"	15.00	22.50	or Cake	6.50	8.00
Butter Dish	40.00	50.00	Saucer	1.50	2.50
Butter Dish Bottom	10.00	15.00	Sherbet, Low Footed	5.00	8.00
Butter Dish Top	30.00	35.00	Sugar, Open	4.00	7.00
Creamer	4.50	7.00			

*Castle decal about 30% higher in most areas.

CIRCLE   HOCKING GLASS COMPANY, 1930's

Colors: Green, pink

Circle is a pretty pattern and there, seemingly, is more of it available than was first believed. Granted, it will probably take a while to gather a collection, but I now believe it could be done, something I was skeptical about for a time. It's still very reasonably priced for a Depression ware pattern.

Circle is not abundant in pink, and many pieces of green are very elusive. I have been told by collectors that the dinner plates are impossible to find at any price. One of the problems with the pattern is that dealers do not carry Circle to shows since there are few collectors. It always pays to ask each dealer if they have your pattern. Maybe they have some back in their shop. Many responsible dealers carry a book of people's wants and actively search for glass to fill these needs.

The rounded cup takes a saucer WITH a cup ring whereas the flat bottomed cup takes one WITHOUT. The bi-colored stemmed ware has been found from coast to coast. I suspect there are more pieces to be found in this pattern than are listed here. Please let me know of any others you find!

	Green/Pink		Green/Pink
Bowl, 4½"	3.00	Plate, 8¼" Luncheon	3.50
Bowl, 5½" Flared	4.50	Plate, 9½" Dinner	6.00
Bowl, 8"	7.00	Saucer	1.00
Creamer	4.50	Sherbet, 3⅛"	3.50
Cup (2 Styles)	2.50	Sherbet, 4¾"	4.50
Decanter, Handled	27.50	Sugar	4.50
Goblet, 4½" Wine	4.50	Tumbler, 4 oz. Juice	3.50
Goblet, 8 oz. Water	7.50	Tumbler, 8 oz. Water	4.50
Pitcher, 80 oz.	16.50	Vase, Hat Shape	30.00
Plate, 6" Sherbet	2.00		

Please refer to Foreword for pricing information

CLOVERLEAF   HAZEL ATLAS GLASS COMPANY, 1930-1936

Colors: Pink, green, yellow, crystal, black.

We had enough Cloverleaf to set out all the known pieces of pink and crystal for the picture, but the photographer cried, "Enough! Have a heart!"

Cloverleaf sells even better than I anticipated. It only took a couple of years to sell the large, seven year accumulation of all colors that I purchased. This collection was very revealing! The 8″ bowls are harder to find than the 7″. (There appears to be no 8″ yellow Cloverleaf bowl). The green cereal bowl is harder to find than the yellow one, and the flat, 9 oz. tumbler is even more difficult to locate than I had previously thought!

Black Cloverleaf sherbet plates carry the design in the center, the saucer does not (see lower right hand corner of picture for sherbet plate). Not everybody knows Depression glass, so remember to check all black glass displays for Cloverleaf ash trays and sherbet plates.

	Pink	Green	Yellow	Black
Ash Tray, 4″, Match Holder in Center				57.50
Ash Tray, 5¾″, Match Holder in Center				70.00
Bowl, 4″ Dessert	8.00	12.50	15.00	
Bowl, 5″ Cereal		15.00	20.00	
Bowl, 7″ Deep Salad		25.00	35.00	
Bowl, 8″		45.00		
Candy Dish and Cover		37.50	95.00	
Creamer, 3⅝″ Footed		7.50	12.50	12.50
Cup	5.00	5.50	11.50	9.50
Plate, 6″ Sherbet		3.50	5.00	22.50
Plate, 8″ Luncheon	5.00	5.00	10.00	10.50
Plate, 10¼″ Grill		15.00	17.50	
Salt and Pepper, Pair		22.50	82.50	52.50
Saucer	2.00	2.50	3.00	3.00
Sherbet, 3″ Footed	4.50	4.00	8.50	12.50
Sugar, 3⅝″ Footed		7.50	12.50	12.50
Tumbler, 4″, 9 oz. Flat		30.00		
Tumbler, 3¾″, 10 oz. Flat Flared	13.50	22.50		
Tumbler, 5¾″, 10 oz. Footed		15.00	20.00	

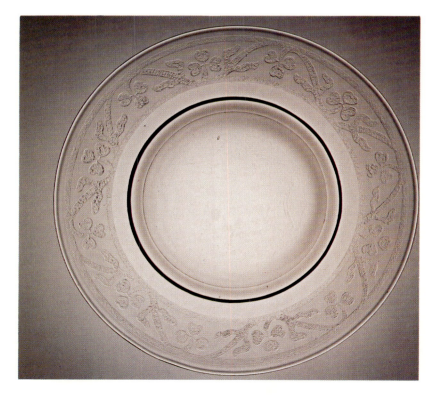

COLONIAL, "KNIFE AND FORK"   HOCKING GLASS COMPANY, 1934-1936

Colors: Pink, green, opaque white, crystal.

Colonial continues to gain the attention of new collectors, but even all these have not been able to absorb the large accumulation of green cups and saucers found in Colorado a few years ago. An abundance of shot glasses has been noted of late. Unfortunately, demand seems to be exceeding supply on some basic items in Colonial and prices are rising! Green dinner plates, 15 oz. flat tumblers, 5½″ cereal bowls, 7″ soup bowls, pink 3¾″ berry bowls and 3″ sherbets are commanding premium prices. In fact, much of Colonial has already been swallowed up into collections and more is leaving the market place daily! Spooners, (one pictured in green), are 5½″ tall whereas a sugar bowl without its lid will measure only 4¼″ tall. Often these are confused. Also, the lid of the butter will fit the wooden cheese dish. However, the cheese dish lid is ½″ shorter than the butter lid. Crystal Colonial, as listed by Hocking, is priced here. I have yet to see all these items in my travels. There are few collectors for crystal at present, but a table setting would be spectacular! A pair of shakers and a plate have turned up to match the white Colonial-like cup and saucer. From all indications, this may have been made by Corning, possibly in their Canadian plant. (By the way, from the letters I receive, there seems to be quite a bit of Depression glass being discovered in Canada.)

	Pink	Green	Crystal		Pink	Green	Crystal
Bowl, 3¾″ Berry	23.50			Plate, 6″ Sherbet	3.00	3.00	1.50
Bowl, 4½″ Berry	6.50	8.50	3.50	Plate, 8½″ Luncheon	5.50	6.00	3.00
Bowl, 5½″ Cereal	23.50	37.50	9.50	Plate, 10″ Dinner	22.50	45.00	12.00
Bowl, 4½″ Cream Soup	28.50	35.00		Plate, 10″ Grill	15.00	17.50	7.50
Bowl, 7″ Low Soup	25.00	35.00	9.00	Platter, 12″ Oval	13.50	14.50	10.00
Bowl, 9″ Large Berry	12.50	17.50	8.50	Salt and Pepper, Pair	100.00	107.50	45.00
Bowl, 10″ Oval Vegetable	13.50	18.50	9.50	Saucer (White 3.00)			
Butter Dish and Cover	400.00	42.50	30.00	(Same as Sherbet Plate)	3.50	3.50	2.00
Butter Dish Bottom	275.00	25.00	20.00	Sherbet, 3″	10.00		
Butter Dish Top	125.00	17.50	10.00	Sherbet, 3⅜″	5.50	10.00	4.00
Cheese Dish		77.50		Spoon Holder or Celery	77.50	85.00	35.00
Creamer, 5″, 8 oz. (Milk				Sugar, 5″	10.00	11.00	6.00
Pitcher)	13.50	15.00	6.50	Sugar Cover	20.00	13.50	6.50
Cup (White 7.00)	6.00	8.00	5.00	Tumbler, 3″, 5 oz. Juice	9.00	14.00	6.00
Goblet, 3¾″, 1 oz. Cordial		23.00	10.00	**Tumbler, 4″, 9 oz. Water	8.50	15.00	6.50
Goblet, 4″, 3 oz. Cocktail		16.00		Tumbler, 10 oz.	13.50	17.50	7.50
Goblet, 4½″, 2½″ oz. Wine		18.50		Tumbler, 12 oz. Iced Tea	19.50	30.00	8.50
Goblet, 5¼″, 4 oz. Claret		16.00		Tumbler, 15 oz. Lemonade	27.50	60.00	15.00
Goblet, 5¾″, 8½″ oz. Water	20.00	19.00	11.00	Tumbler, 3¼″, 8 oz. Ftd	10.00	14.00	7.00
Mug, 4½″, 12 oz.	200.00	650.00		Tumbler, 4″, 5 oz. Footed	12.50	18.50	8.00
Pitcher, 7″, 54 oz. Ice Lip				Tumbler, 5¼″, 10 oz. Ftd	15.00	20.00	10.00
or None	32.50	35.00	20.00	Whiskey, 2½″, 1½″ oz.	5.00	6.00	3.00
*Pitcher, 7¾″, 68 oz. Ice Lip							
or None	35.00	47.50	22.50				

*Beaded top in pink $750.00
**Royal Ruby $35.00

COLONIAL BLOCK   HAZEL ATLAS GLASS COMPANY, Early 1930's

Colors: Green and pink; white in '50's.

Colonial Block has always caused me to get a lot of mail. Until I included it in my book, I received many letters about the round "Block Optic" butter dish someone had just found (even though it is clearly marked with HA in the bottom which stands for Hazel Atlas and not Anchor Hocking). This time I got numerous letters wondering why I didn't include the butter tub shown in the Kitchenware book. Frankly, I forgot it last time, but here it is now, right down front.

There is still some confusion over the pitcher and goblet shown here. It could well be that Hazel Atlas did indeed manufacture these as Colonial Block pitchers. It was previously thought they were the product of U.S. Glass. So, people who bought them to "go-with" Colonial Block did the right thing! New collectors are more willing to accept pieces that "go-with" their patterns than purist collectors who started years ago and had an abundance of glass from which to choose. Several reasons come to mind, economics being foremost. Years ago, five dollars was a lot to pay for this old glassware. Today, five hundred is common place for rare items.

Notice the goblet. Often you see these labeled "Block" and so priced. They are NOT "Block Optic" and should only command a $7.00 or $8.00 price at best.

I have only seen the creamer and the sugar with lid in white. Let me know if you have or know of other pieces.

	Pink, Green	White		Pink, Green	White
Bowl, 4"	5.00		Candy Jar w/Cover	27.50	
Bowl, 7"	11.50		Creamer	7.50	5.50
Butter Dish	27.50		Goblet	8.50	
Butter Dish Bottom	7.50		Pitcher	25.00	
Butter Dish Top	20.00		Sugar	7.50	4.50
Butter Tub	27.50		Sugar Lid	5.50	3.00

COLONIAL FLUTED, "ROPE"   FEDERAL GLASS COMPANY, 1928-1933

Colors: Green, crystal

Colonial Fluted makes a great luncheon set to use for bridge parties. It is also a good way to introduce Depression glass to friends. Who knows, maybe a friend has a garage full of this old "junque" just waiting for you to expound its virtues. Don't laugh. I get letters monthly telling of such discoveries. There are STILL many people who don't know Depression glass is worth anything more than the money they paid for it years ago—which could be as little as $2.98 a set!

That's a vegetable bowl (to the right) in the background lest you think at long last we had discovered a dinner plate to go with a "luncheon" plate. Most of the depth of the piece was lost by the camera. There are some dinner plates out there bearing the Federal mark. One has the panels but no roping, the other has the roping but no panels. Thus, neither quite fit this pattern although some people are blending them into their sets quite successfully.

This pattern is often badly scratched, indicating it was widely used.

Looking closely, you should be able to see the "F" within a shield that was Federal's symbol.

	Green		Green
Bowl, 4" Berry	4.00	Plate, 6" Sherbet	1.50
Bowl, 6" Cereal	5.00	Plate, 8" Luncheon	3.00
Bowl, 6½", Deep (2½") Salad	9.00	Saucer	1.00
Bowl, 7½" Large Berry	9.00	Sherbet	4.50
Creamer	4.50	Sugar	3.00
Cup	3.50	Sugar Cover	7.50

Please refer to Foreword for pricing information

COLUMBIA   FEDERAL GLASS COMPANY, 1938-1942

Colors: Crystal, some pink

Pictured in the center is a tumbler having a plain, bulbous top seated on an inch high beaded bottom. These have turned up in boxed sets of Columbia; so, it will have to be assumed they were meant to be Columbia tumblers though they weren't catalogued as such.

This is an extremely attractive pattern that for some unknown reason has attracted few collectors to date, perhaps because it's crystal. Columbia is dressy, inexpensive and fairly easy to locate except in cereal and soup bowls and the tray for the snack set which was pictured in the 6th Edition.

Butter dishes can come with various flashed-on colors (blue, iridescent, red, purple, amethyst, green) and with decal decorated tops.

Those pink luncheon items are extremely hard to find!

	Crystal	Pink		Crystal	Pink
Bowl, 5″ Cereal	7.50		Butter Dish Top	7.00	
Bowl, 8″ Low Soup	8.50		Cup	3.50	9.50
Bowl, 8½″ Salad	8.50		Plate, 6″ Bread & Butter	1.50	3.50
Bowl, 10½″ Ruffled Edge	12.50		Plate, 9½″ Luncheon	3.50	15.00
Butter Dish and Cover	15.00		Plate, 11¾″ Chop	5.50	
Ruby Flashed (17.50)			Saucer	1.00	5.50
Other Flashed (16.00)			Snack Plate	25.00	
Butter Dish Bottom	8.00		Tumbler	8.00	

CREMAX   MACBETH-EVANS DIVISION OF CORNING GLASS WORKS, Late 1930's-Early 1940's

Colors: Cremax, Cremax with fired-on color trim

Note the demi-tasse cup and saucers shown. Only one cup was found on a saucer of the same color. All the others were found on plain cremax saucers.

If you like challenges, this is the pattern to choose! Actually, this is very rare glass, but because it's so hard to find, few people make the attempt.

There are various floral decals to be found other than those pictured here which further compounds the issue of collecting a set. As I reported last time, one lady uses hers everyday and says she enjoys it a "thousand times more than melamine"! The castle decal is the most prized decoration.

There is no butter dish in Cremax, although the base to the Chinex butter is similar to the Cremax pattern.

This PATTERN is called Cremax. MacBeth-Evans also used cremax to describe the beige-like COLOR used in some of its patterns such as American Sweetheart, Dogwood, and Petalware. Be aware of this overlapping of meaning.

	Cremax	Decal Decorated		Cremax	Decal Decorated
Bowl, 5¾″ Cereal	2.50	4.00	Plate, 9¾″ Dinner	3.00	4.00
Bowl, 9″ Vegetable	5.50	7.50	Plate, 11½″ Sandwich	3.50	5.00
Creamer	3.00	5.50	Saucer	1.00	1.00
Cup	3.00	3.50	Sugar, Open	3.00	5.50
Plate, 6¼″ Bread and Butter	1.00	2.00			

Please refer to Foreword for pricing information

CORONATION, "BANDED RIB", "SAXON"   HOCKING GLASS COMPANY,

1936-1949

Colors: Pink, green, crystal, Royal Ruby.

Repeating what I said in the 6th Edition about a trip to Hocking's plant, "Imagine my surprise. I was being shown through Hocking's morgue in 1981 and when another section was rolled out for my viewing pleasure, there sat a color of Coronation I'd never seen before--green! I could hardly believe my eyes. Since then, I've found three luncheon plates at a flea market in Indiana and that green bowl (without handles!) in northern Kentucky. The four pieces I saw in green at Hocking are shown in the smaller photograph at the bottom and were graciously photographed for all our pleasure by Anchor Hocking Glass for use in this book! I have no idea how plentiful the green actually is since I've been able to find four more pieces just this year! It's stumbling across "finds" like this that make collecting Depression glass so exciting. Keep your eyes open for other pieces in green and let me know what you find!"

In the two years since I wrote the above, I have not heard from a single reader about new finds in green. That is surprising since a new color exposed usually brings many newer discoveries shortly thereafter. Such has not been the case this time.

Notice that the handles on the pink bowls in Coronation are closed, whereas red bowls all have open handles. Why? All we know is they were made at different times. Hocking promoted a whole line of Royal Ruby products in the early '40's. Perhaps it was felt the open handles made the red bowls more attractive, less of a great red blob. It was interesting to learn that as recently as 1975 over 600 of the Coronation Royal Ruby berry sets were discovered in a warehouse still in the original Hocking packages!

You who are just learning about Depression glass should pay careful attention to the tumbler shown here in Coronation because it's often confused with the more costly Lace Edge tumbler (one pictured with Lace Edge). You will notice that the rays are well up the sides of the Coronation tumbler but only up about a third of the glass in the Lace Edge tumbler.

Perhaps there is no ruby saucer to match the Royal Ruby Coronation cup that you occasionally find simply because this cup was sold with a crystal saucer. (One thing I have learned in fifteen years of writing, is never say never.)

	Pink	Royal Ruby	Green		Pink	Royal Ruby	Green
Bowl, 4¼" Berry	3.00	5.00		Pitcher, 7¾", 68 oz.	135.00		
Bowl, 6½" Nappy	3.50	6.50		Plate, 6" Sherbet	1.25		
Bowl, 8" Large Berry,				Plate, 8½" Luncheon	3.00	5.00	15.00
Handled	7.00	11.50		Saucer (Same as 6" Plate)	1.25		
Bowl, 8" No Handles			30.00	Sherbet	3.50	4.50	
Cup	3.50	4.50		Tumbler, 5", 10 oz. Footed	12.00		35.00

Please refer to Foreword for pricing information

CUBE, "CUBIST"   JEANNETTE GLASS COMPANY, 1929-1933

Colors: Pink, green, crystal, ultramarine

Cube has everything going for it except a dinner plate. A few collectors are put off by patterns without one, but Cube has everything else, including accessory pieces such as candy, butter, shakers and even a powder jar.

Before I get letters, that is a dip in the pitcher rather than a chip. Either the mould didn't completely fill out or the glass "slipped" when it was taken from the mould all those years ago. Today, a flawed piece would be immediately scrapped. Pitchers and tumblers in Cube are hard to find, green ones being more adept at hiding than pink.

This pattern is often mistaken for Fostoria's "American" pattern. The design is similar, but Fostoria's glass is better grade glassware. American pattern listings can be found in my book *Elegant Glassware of the Depression Era*. **The 2" creamer and sugar in crystal Cube are abundant, but seldom collected; but the Cube tray that they rest upon drives novice "American" collectors crazy.** The two trays are shaped differently.

	Pink	Green
Bowl, 4½" Dessert	4.50	5.00
Bowl, 4½" Deep	4.50	5.00
*Bowl, 6½" Salad	6.50	10.50
Butter Dish and Cover	45.00	50.00
Butter Dish Bottom	15.00	17.50
Butter Dish Top	30.00	32.50
Candy Jar and Cover, 6½"	20.00	25.00
Coaster, 3¼"	3.50	4.50
**Creamer, 2"	2.00	
Creamer, 3"	4.50	6.00
Cup	4.50	7.00
Pitcher, 8¾", 45 oz.	135.00	150.00
Plate, 6" Sherbet	1.50	2.00

	Pink	Green
Plate, 8" Luncheon	3.00	4.50
Powder Jar and Cover 3 Legs	12.00	15.00
Salt and Pepper, Pr.	25.00	27.50
Saucer	1.25	1.50
Sherbet, Footed	4.50	6.00
**Sugar, 2"	2.00	
Sugar, 3"	4.50	5.50
Sugar/Candy Cover	6.00	8.00
Tray for 3" Creamer and Sugar, 7½" (Crystal Only)	4.00	
Tumbler, 4", 9 oz.	30.00	35.00

*Ultramarine—$35.00
**Amber—$3.00

"CUPID" PADEN CITY GLASS COMPANY, 1930's

Colors: Pink, green, light blue, black.

Everyone seems to like "Cupid". It's gracefully shaped, artistically etched, and comes in pleasing colors. What more could anyone want from a pattern?

New pieces continue to surface; a black casserole and a blue Samovar are shown here. The Samovar is compliments of Robert McGinnis and Ron Stephens. I have received numerous letters about other items, but the most intriguing is a bottle which looks to be the bottom of tumble-up! Keep me informed and remember a snapshot is worth at least a thousand words. You would be surprised how many people think I can identify a piece of glassware described over the telephone. Believe me, it is nearly impossible!

Most "Cupid" that has surfaced so far are serving pieces or dressy items for the table. Maybe that gives this pattern an "edge" with all collectors. Anyone can blend a piece or two into their table arrangement, be it antique or modern, and derive an aesthetic pleasure from owning a lovely piece of glassware. It isn't necessary to have a whole set of "Cupid", in other words, to obtain an intense satisfaction from it.

The center handled trays were called sandwich trays by Paden City and those handled bowls were called candy trays. Every "sweet tooth" would appreciate your owning (and filling) one of the latter!

	All Colors		All Colors
Bowl, 8½" Oval Footed	32.50	Ice Tub, 4¾"	40.00
Bowl, 9¼" Footed Fruit	35.00	Lamp, Silver Overlay	125.00
Bowl, 9¼" Center Handled	35.00	Mayonnaise, 6" Diameter, Fits on	
Bowl, 11" Console	35.00	8" Plate	40.00
Cake Plate, 11¾"	37.50	Plate, 10½"	25.00
Cake Stand, 2" High, Ftd.	37.50	Samovar	125.00
Candlestick, 5" Wide, Pair	32.50	Sugar, 4¼" Footed	25.00
Candy w/Lid, Footed, 4¾" High	37.50	Sugar, 5" Footed	32.50
Candy w/Lid, 3 Part	47.50	Tray, 10½" Center Handled	27.50
Comport, 6¼"	22.50	Tray, 10⅞" Oval Footed	40.00
Creamer, 4½" Footed	25.00	Vase, 8¼" Elliptical	75.00
Creamer, 5" Footed	32.50	Vase, Fan Shaped	47.50
Ice Bucket, 6"	50.00		

Please refer to Foreword for pricing information

"DAISY", NUMBER 620   INDIANA GLASS COMPANY

Colors: Crystal, 1933; amber, 1940; dark green and milk glass, '60's, '70's.

Daisy, as well as other patterns, can still be found at bargain prices. I just returned from a Depression Glass show in Oregon and talked to a lady who had purchased a complete set for eight for $100.00. This set included cereal bowls, iced teas and all serving pieces except the relish. Has anyone out there got a relish for sell? I've found a customer for you!

The green bowl in the picture is dated 1981 in the bottom, so Indiana still makes these bowls. We're grateful for the date, of course, and I have told you in the past that Indiana had marketed Daisy in avocado green under the name of "Heritage" (not to be confused with Federal's "Heritage" pattern) as late as the '70's. A few collectors are beginning to consider the green, which is fine; just know it's newer glass and pay accordingly.

Few collectors even consider the antique crystal "Daisy"; most prefer the amber made during the war years. In this color, 12 oz. tumblers and cereal bowls are the most difficult pieces to find. (For glass to be considered antique, it must be fifty years old.) By that criteria, a lot of our Depression glass can now be considered truly antique!

	Green, Crystal	Amber		Green, Crystal	Amber
Bowl, 4½" Berry	2.50	6.00	Plate, 9⅜" Dinner	3.00	5.50
Bowl, 4½" Cream Soup	3.00	7.50	Plate, 10⅜" Grill	4.00	10.00
Bowl, 6" Cereal	7.50	20.00	Plate, 11½" Cake or		
Bowl, 7⅜" Deep Berry	4.50	10.00	Sandwich	5.00	9.00
Bowl, 9⅜" Deep Berry	7.50	22.50	Platter, 10¾"	5.00	10.00
Bowl, 10" Oval Vegetable	6.00	12.50	Relish Dish, 8⅜", 3 Part	10.00	20.00
Creamer, Footed	4.50	6.50	Saucer	1.00	1.50
Cup	2.50	4.50	Sherbet, Footed	2.50	7.00
Plate, 6" Sherbet	1.00	2.00	Sugar, Footed	3.00	6.50
Plate, 7⅜" Salad	2.00	5.50	Tumbler, 9 oz. Footed	5.00	12.50
Plate, 8⅜" Luncheon	2.00	4.50	Tumbler, 12 oz. Footed	9.00	25.00

DIANA   FEDERAL GLASS COMPANY, 1937-1941

Colors: Pink, amber, crystal

Diana has found a few avid collectors in recent days, but they are finding that some pieces are not readily available. Tumblers in amber and shakers in all colors are difficult with sherbets being not far behind. (Sherbets are cone-shaped if you find them).

Diana's potential has been overlooked in the past. As you can see from the picture, there are numerous pieces to be found and a quick glance at the price listing will show you that it's still inexpensive, something which can't be said of many Depression glass patterns.

Occasionally, frosted items turn up. In fact, one entire set showed up in pink. Frosted glass, which was made by dipping the glass in camphoric acid, has always found few devotees, however.

	Crystal	Pink	Amber		Crystal	Pink	Amber
*Ash Tray, 3½"	2.00	3.00		Plate, 5½" Child's	2.00	3.50	
Bowl, 5" Cereal	2.50	3.50		Plate, 6" Bread & Butter	1.00	1.50	1.50
Bowl, 5½" Cream Soup	2.50	5.00	6.00	Plate, 9½" Dinner	4.00	5.50	6.50
Bowl, 9" Salad	5.00	6.50	5.50	Plate, 11¾" Sandwich	4.50	5.50	6.50
Bowl, 11" Console Fruit	5.00	6.50	8.00	Platter, 12" Oval	5.00	6.50	7.50
Bowl, 12" Scalloped Edge	4.50	7.50	8.50	Salt and Pepper, Pr.	17.50	40.00	75.00
Candy Jar and Cover, Round	12.00	20.00	25.00	Saucer	1.00	1.50	1.50
Coaster, 3½"	2.00	3.50		Sherbet	2.50	5.00	5.00
Creamer, Oval	2.00	3.50	3.50	Sugar, Open Oval	2.50	3.50	3.50
Cup	2.50	3.50	3.50	Tumbler, 4⅛", 9 oz.	5.00	10.00	13.00
Cup, 2 oz. Demitasse				Junior Set: 6 Cups,			
and 4½" Saucer Set	4.50	12.50		Saucers and Plates with			
				Round Rack	50.00	100.00	

*Green—$3.00

Please refer to Foreword for pricing information

48

DIAMOND QUILTED, "FLAT DIAMOND"   IMPERIAL GLASS COMPANY,

Late '20's-Early '30's.

Colors: Pink, blue, green, crystal, black; some red and amber

Old catalogues only list Diamond Quilted punch bowls in pink. The existence of the actual glass always over-rules whatever was listed by the catalogue. So enjoy this last view of a green one as it now has a new home in Canada.

Blue Diamond Quilted is very attractive and never fails to "sell itself". There are fewer collectors of black, but there is a very limited supply of it. More amber items are surfacing, but not enough, as yet, to be collectible as a set. All three of these colors have increased in price more than pink or green.

Most blue and black Diamond Qulted pieces have the quilting on the inside of the dish. However, you have to turn the black plate over on its face to see the quilting.

Creamers, sugars, cups and saucers have shown up in amber and red, leading one to believe they were probably sold as luncheon sets. All we need find now are plates! You can find an amber mayonnaise pictured, so there has to be a liner for it, also.

According to Imperial files, candle holders were made in two styles. I've only seen the one shown. There should be one with a rolled edge somewhat on the order of those featured below in the old catalogue ad.

Lest you confuse the pattern, Hazel Atlas also made a quilted pitcher and tumblers in cobalt blue, pink and green. The quilting effect stops and becomes a straight line before it reaches the top of the dish. These are a heavier glass, too.

	Pink, Green	Blue, Black		Pink, Green	Blue, Black
Bowl, 4¾" Cream Soup	6.50	15.00	Mayonnaise Set: Ladle,		
Bowl, 5" Cereal	4.50	7.50	Plate, Comport	22.50	45.00
Bowl, 5½" One Handle	5.50	8.50	Pitcher, 64 oz.	35.00	
Bowl, 7" Crimped Edge	5.50	10.00	Plate, 6" Sherbet	2.50	3.50
Bowl, Rolled Edge Console	13.50	30.00	Plate, 7" Salad	4.00	6.50
Cake Salver, Tall 10"			Plate, 8" Luncheon	4.00	10.00
Diameter	27.50		Punch Bowl and Stand	275.00	
Candlesticks (2 Styles), Pr.	9.50	22.50	Plate, 14" Sandwich	8.50	
Candy Jar and Cover,			Sandwich Server,		
Footed	16.50	27.50	Center Handle	15.00	25.00
Compote and Cover, 11½"	37.50		Saucer	2.00	3.50
Creamer	6.00	9.50	Sherbet	4.00	8.50
Cup	4.00	6.00	Sugar	6.00	9.50
Goblet, 1 oz. Cordial	5.50		Tumbler, 9 oz. Water	6.50	
Goblet, 2 oz. Wine	5.50		Tumbler, 12 oz. Iced Tea	7.50	
Goblet, 3 oz. Wine	6.50		Tumbler, 6 oz. Footed	6.00	
Goblet, 6", 9 oz.			Tumbler, 9 oz. Footed	9.50	
Champagne	7.50		Tumbler, 12 oz. Footed	12.50	
Ice Bucket	37.50	55.00	Vase, Fan, Dolphin Handles	22.50	32.50
			Whiskey, 1½ oz.	6.50	

Covered Bowl—6⅜ in. diam., deep round shape with 3 artistic feet, dome cover, fine quality brilliant finish **pot glass**, allover block diamond design, transparent Rose Marie and emerald green. **I C5603**—Asstd. ½ doz. in carton, 20 lbs. **Doz $6.95**

I C989—3 piece set, 2 transparent colors (rose and green), good quality, 10½ in. rolled rim bowl, TWO 3½ in. wide base candlesticks. Asstd. 6 sets in case, 30 lbs. .... **SET (3 pcs) 65c**

Please refer to Foreword for pricing information

DOGWOOD, "APPLE BLOSSOM", "WILD ROSE"   MACBETH-EVANS

GLASS COMPANY, 1929-1932

Colors: Pink, green; some crystal, monax, cremax, yellow.

Dogwood is still in demand. I can not believe how many letters I get ordering 20 piece sets for $1.45 as shown in the 1930's ad in the sixth edition. One lady wanted to know if I would pay the postage if she ordered several sets! (The postage alone would have been more than the money she sent!) In any case, I put these old ads in as I find them and space permits to show how economical (cheap!) this glass really was. Please, no more "orders" for sets at $1.45.

Dogwood always attracts admiration, particularly the pitcher and tumblers which have the silk screened Dogwood design on them. Both pink and green are pictured here. There is a more bulbous pitcher to be found having what collectors refer to as "an American Sweetheart shape". Remember, the pitchers MUST have the Dogwood design, not just SHAPE, to be considered to be Dogwood. These plain pitchers were simply made by the same company.

Pink grill plates come in both styles, all over design or design at the rim only. Green comes only with the rim design. Luncheon plates are **plentiful**. I once sold a dealer 45 at a dollar each. He told me later that it took three years to finally sell all of them! The 10¼" fruit bowl, which is so rarely seen any more, unhappily is the one turning up frosted and drilled through to be used as a lamp shade! I suspect that is one of the reasons why the bowl is so rare. That lamp shade is difficult to sell, but the bowl is greatly in demand.

New collectors should know that PINK cups, creamers and sugars come in both a thick and thin variety, the thin having a slightly rolled edge. Green comes only in the thin shape. Both styles of cups, sugars and creamers are pictured. The platter shown is rarely seen. Fortunately, for those who have been searching for these, a batch of nine were found a few years ago in the town of Charleroi, Pa. I saw that they all got new homes except for one which I kept to photograph. Only a yellow luncheon plate and a cereal bowl have surfaced in that color. The yellow bowl was pictured in a previous edition. There is also a smaller, 11" cake plate in Dogwood like the one pictured in "S" pattern. It has to be considered a rare piece.

There is little demand for the monax Dogwood; those items remain more interesting than desirable. We turned the bowl over in the picture so you could see the design. The monax salver is turning out to be more plentiful than first believed; it makes an excellent decorated cake base. The white background helps "show off" the cake.

The 4¾" stemmed wine goblet was not made by Macbeth-Evans, but it's so close to Dogwood pattern that I wanted collectors to be aware of it.

	Pink	Green	Monax Cremax
*Bowl, 5½" Cereal	14.00	17.50	15.00
Bowl, 8½" Berry	35.00	72.50	39.50
Bowl, 10¼" Fruit	177.50	87.50	67.50
Cake Plate, 11" Heavy Solid Foot	152.50		
Cake Plate, 13" Heavy Solid Foot	62.50	52.50	125.00
Creamer, 2½" Thin	11.00	35.00	
Creamer, 3¼" Thick	13.50		
Cup, Thin or Thick	9.00	15.00	35.00
Pitcher, 8", 80 oz. Decorated	115.00	400.00	
Pitcher, 8", 8 oz. (American Sweetheart Style)	400.00		
Plate, 6" Bread and Butter	4.00	4.00	20.00
*Plate, 8" Luncheon	4.00	4.00	
Plate, 9¼" Dinner	15.00		
Plate, 10½" Grill AOP or Border Design Only	12.50	11.50	
Plate, 12" Salver	18.00		17.50
Platter, 12" Oval (Rare)	225.00		
Saucer	4.00	5.00	15.00
Sherbet, Low Footed	18.00	47.50	
Sugar, 2½" Thin	9.50	35.00	
Sugar, 3¼" Thick	10.50		
Tumbler, 3½", 5 oz. Decorated	157.50		
Tumbler, 4", 10 oz. Decorated	25.00	52.50	
Tumbler, 4¾", 11 oz. Decorated	32.50	62.50	
Tumbler, 5", 12 oz. Decorated	35.00	67.50	
Tumbler, Molded Band	11.00		

*Yellow—$50.00

Please refer to Foreword for pricing information

DORIC   JEANNETTE GLASS COMPANY, 1935-1938

Colors: Pink, green, some delphite, yellow

Doric patterned tumblers are the major concern of collectors in this pattern. You will notice the price jumps in the listing. There have even been a few sold at higher prices to a couple of collectors who had everything else and said, "I'll pay whatever it takes!" Remember, it is you, the collector, who largely determines price, not the dealer. If collectors refuse to pay a high price, the dealer has to re-adjust his pricing strategy; more and more dealers who were out for a quick buck are learning this valuable lesson. The public gets educated much faster in today's world.

Take a good look at the pitchers shown here! That yellow footed and blue delphite pitcher are unique at this writing. Yet, there are bound to be others! Also, the footed green Doric pitcher is something of a wizard at hiding. You will notice that there are two styles of the pink footed pitchers due to a variation at the lip.

One of the major problems in collecting Doric is that many pieces have mould roughness when found. Cereal bowls and footed tumblers are the worst offenders. For those who have difficulty with terminology, look at the picture of pink Doric. The tumbler on the extreme left is the flat 4½", 9 oz.; the other two are the footed tumblers. The heavy ringed base is not as pronounced a foot as with most footed tumblers, but is used in this case to distinguish it from the flat one.

The square Doric dish shown in pink can be found on a metal tray having "two stories" so to speak. It was called a relish tray and comes in two sizes. One was pictured in previous editions.

Sugar dish and candy lids in this pattern do not interchange since the candy lid is taller and has a more traditional, cone (candy lid) shape.

Delphite Doric, though attractive, is hard to find except for sherbets and the three-part candy dish. This is ironic since sherbets in pink and green are "hens teeth" hard to find!

The shaker lids on the pink Doric are original; the green lids are newly made. I point this out merely to let people know that new lids are now being made available for Depression glass shakers. Original lids are preferable unless they're corroded or caved in.

There is a three part, iridized candy dish in Doric pattern that was made as recently as the '70's. It sold in my area at the local dish barn for about 79 cents. If there is a dish barn in your area, it would pay you to go through it from time to time and acquaint yourself with what is available and where some flea market dealers obtain their wares.

	Pink	Green	Delphite		Pink	Green	Delphite
Bowl, 4½" Berry	5.00	5.50	27.50	Plate, 7" Salad	12.50	11.50	
Bowl, 5" Cream Soup		150.00		Plate, 9" Dinner (Serrated 40.00)	7.50	9.50	
Bowl, 5½" Cereal	17.50	22.00		Plate, 9" Grill	7.50	10.00	
Bowl, 8¼" Large Berry	9.50	12.50	77.50	Platter, 12" Oval	11.00	12.00	
Bowl, 9" Two Handled	9.50	9.50		Relish Tray, 4" x 4"	5.00	7.50	
Bowl, 9" Oval Vegetable	11.00	12.50		** Relish Tray, 4" x 8"	6.50	9.50	
Butter Dish and Cover	55.00	67.50		Salt and Pepper, Pr.	24.00	27.50	
Butter Dish Bottom	17.50	25.00		Saucer	2.00	2.50	
Butter Dish Top	37.50	42.50		Sherbet, Footed	7.50	8.50	5.00
Cake Plate, 10", Three Legs	12.00	11.50		Sugar	8.50	9.50	
Candy Dish and Cover, 8"	25.00	25.00		Sugar Cover	9.00	15.00	
* Candy Dish, Three Part	4.50	5.50	4.50	Tray, 10" Handled	7.50	9.50	
Coaster, 3"	9.50	11.00		Tray, 8" x 8" Serving	7.50	8.50	
Creamer, 4"	7.50	8.50		Tumbler, 4½", 9 oz.	27.50	40.00	
Cup	5.50	6.50		Tumbler, 4", 10 oz. Ftd.	20.00	45.00	
Pitcher, 6", 36 oz. Flat	25.00	30.00	500.00	Tumbler, 5", 12 oz., Ftd.	38.00	50.00	
Pitcher, 7½", 48 oz. Footed	250.00	450.00					
(Also in Yellow at $750.00)							
Plate, 6" Sherbet	2.50	3.00					

*Candy in metal holder—$37.50. Iridescent made recently

DORIC AND PANSY   JEANNETTE GLASS COMPANY, 1937-1938

Colors: Ultramarine; some crystal and pink.

In this pattern, there is good news and bad news. The good news is for new collectors of Doric and Pansy; and the bad is for the premier collectors. Since the 6th Edition went to press two years ago, a lot of collectors have gone to England searching for this pattern as I suggested. Evidently, they have had great success as there is now an abundance of this pattern on the market, and prices have begun to steadily decline on all the once hard to find items! Older collectors do not like to see this, but the fact that there are few new collectors of items such as butter dishes or salt and pepper shakers make these more plentiful than the demand at present. One of the major reasons new people in Depression glass do not item collect (i.e. shakers or butters) is that the cost is prohibitive. There are a few beginning collectors of sugar and creamers, and with the supply of Doric and Pansy sugar and creamers now available, there should be a few new homes for these in the next few years.

Many Doric and Pansy shakers are weakly patterned, they need to have SOME pattern design to be called Doric and Pansy, however. I've seen a few that had the shape and color only. These really can't be called Doric and Pansy shakers.

Ultramarine Doric and Pansy doesn't always "match". Due to the unstable ways of heating the glass back then, there were varing shades of ultramarine from one batch to the next.

Only berry sets and children's sets have been found in pink.

Remember, I am reporting to you, my readers, the facts as I become aware of them. Please keep me informed of your finds. Maybe a warehouse of Depression glass will turn up in Hawaii, and we can all make a trip to pick some out for our collections. (That did happen for "Occupied Japan" collectors!)

	Green, Teal	Pink Crystal		Green, Teal	Pink, Crystal
Bowl, 4½" Berry	9.50	6.00	Plate, 6" Sherbet	7.00	6.00
Bowl, 8" Large Berry	57.50	17.50	Plate, 7" Salad	25.00	
Bowl, 9" Handled	22.50	9.50	Plate, 9" Dinner	17.50	5.00
Butter Dish and Cover	500.00		Salt and Pepper, Pr.	325.00	
Butter Dish Bottom	100.00		Saucer	3.00	2.25
Butter Dish Top	400.00		Sugar, Open	120.00	57.50
Cup	15.00	7.50	Tray, 10" Handled	15.00	
Creamer	125.00	57.50	Tumbler, 4½", 9 oz.	35.00	

DORIC AND PANSY
"PRETTY POLLY PARTY DISHES"

	Teal	Pink		Teal	Pink
Cup	25.00	20.00	Creamer	27.50	22.50
Saucer	4.00	3.00	Sugar	27.00	22.50
Plate	7.00	5.00	14 Piece Set	185.00	150.00

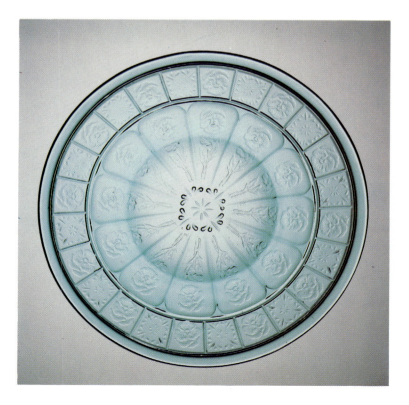

ENGLISH HOBNAIL   WESTMORELAND GLASS COMPANY, 1920's-1970's

Colors: Crystal, pink, amber, turquoise, cobalt, green, blue, red.

This is a beautiful pattern which has had tremendous longevity, meaning there is much old to be found and much new! For instance, red English Hobnail was causing quite a stir in collecting circles until Westmoreland made 17 pieces, including the pitcher, for Levay Distributing Company in the late '70's. However, Westmoreland is no more! All of the glass and the moulds have been sold through auction. Only time will tell if English Hobnail will be made by some other company. I have not been able to find out where the moulds for this pattern went, so be sure to subscribe to a monthly publication to keep abreast of current news in the glass world.

Pink is about the only COLOR you can hope to collect an entire set of, and there are at least two different shades of that. There are three distinct greens, two ambers (the lighter version being made in the 1960's), two turquoise, and a number of fired-on colors, plus round and squared shapes. No, I'm not trying to put you off collecting this, just letting you know what you'd be in for once you decide to collect it.

Crystal appears frequently. It's relatively inexpensive now. Some of the crystal comes with black bases or trims.

This is another pattern that you can enjoy owning an occasional piece of without coveting an entire set. Many people buy the candy dishes or cologne bottles, a lamp or serving tray, a pitcher or shakers just to add color to a room or set of china. One man told me he enjoyed being served his egg in his fancy English Hobnail egg cup!

To help new collectors distinguish English Hobnail from Miss America, I offer the following observations. English Hobnail pieces have center rays of varying distance; the hob tips are more rounded giving it a smoother "feel"; and the goblets have rims that flair slightly plus moving directly from the hobs to the plain glass rim. Miss America rays flair equidistant from the center; the hobs are sharp to touch and the goblets don't flair at the rim and have three sets of rings above the hobs before entering a plain glass rim.

	Cobalt, Amber, Turquoise*, Pink, Green		Cobalt, Amber, Turquoise*, Pink, Green
**Ash Tray, Several Shapes	18.50	Goblet, 5 oz. Claret	13.50
Bowls, 4½", 5" Square		** Goblet, 6¼", 8 oz.	17.50
and Round	9.50	Grapefruit, 6½" Flange Rim	13.50
Bowl, Cream Soup	13.50	Lamp, 6¼" Electric	50.00
Bowls, 6" Several Styles	10.00	** Lamp, 9¼"	100.00
Bowls, 8" Several Styles	16.00	Lampshade, 17" Diameter	
**Bowls, 8" Footed and		(Crystal)	117.50
Two Handled	37.50	Marmalade and Cover	32.50
**Bowls, 11" and 12"		Pitcher, 23 oz.	125.00
Nappies	35.00	Pitcher, 39 oz.	130.00
Bowls, 8", 9" Oval Relish	15.00	Pitcher, 60 oz.	150.00
Bowl, 12" Oval Relish	17.50	Pitcher, ½ Gal. Straight	
Candlesticks, 3½" Pair	25.00	Sides	175.00
Candlesticks, 8½" Pair	45.00	**Plate, 5½", 6½" Sherbet	3.50
Candy Dish, ½ lb.		Plate, 7¼" Pie	4.00
Cone Shaped	45.00	** Plate, 8" Round or Square	7.50
Candy Dish and Cover,		Plate, 10" Dinner	20.00
Three Feet	57.50	Salt and Pepper, Pair,	
Celery Dish, 9"	16.50	Round or Square Bases	67.50
Celery Dish, 12"	20.00	Salt Dip, 2" Footed and	
**Cigarette Box	22.50	with Place Card Holder	16.50
**Cologne Bottle	25.00	Saucer	3.50
Creamer, Footed or Flat	15.00	** Sherbet	12.50
Cup	15.00	Sugar, Footed or Flat	15.00
Decanter, 20 oz. with		Tumbler, 3¾", 5 oz. or 9 oz.	12.50
Stopper	57.50	Tumbler, 4", 10 oz. Iced Tea	14.50
Demitasse Cup and Saucer	30.00	Tumbler, 5", 12 oz. Iced Tea	17.50
Egg Cup	25.00	Tumbler, 7 oz. Footed	13.50
Goblet, 1 oz. Cordial	16.00	Tumbler, 9 oz. Footed	14.50
Goblet, 2 oz. Wine	13.50	Tumbler, 12½ oz. Footed	18.50
Goblet, 3 oz. Cocktail	15.00	Vase	75.00
		Whiskey, 1½ oz. and 3 oz.	16.50

*Add about 50% more for Turquoise
**Cobalt double price listed

Please refer to Foreword for pricing information

FIRE-KING DINNERWARE "ALICE", "JANE RAY", "SQUARE"

ANCHOR HOCKING GLASS CORPORATION, 1940's-1960's

Colors: Jade-ite, blue, white w/trims.

I am combining these three patterns into one grouping for now. Strictly speaking, these were made later than Depression glass, but many collectors are turning to these because they are readily available and inexpensive. As is the case in other patterns, demand creates a rise in price, but there is still an abundance of this glassware commonly called "Oatmeal" glass in many areas. It was packed in Mother's Oats and before instant and cold cereals were available, everyone (seemingly) ate oatmeal.

The dinner plates in "Alice" are in shorter supply than any other piece. I suspect this is because they were a little large to fit in boxes of oats and had to be purchased.

"Alice" is pictured below, "Jane Ray" top right and "Square" bottom right.

"Alice" price*

	Jade-ite
* Cup	1.00
** Plate, 8½"	3.75
*** Saucer	.50

*Add $1.50 for White w/Trim **Add 25¢ for White w/Trim ***Add 50¢ for White w/Trim

"Square" prices

	All Colors
Bowl, 4¾", Dessert	2.50
Bowl, 7⅜", Salad	5.00
Cup	2.00
Plate, 8⅜", Luncheon	2.75
Plate, 9¼", Dinner	3.50
Saucer	.50

"Jane Ray" prices

	Jade-ite
Bowl, 4⅞", Dessert	1.00
Bowl, 5⅞", Oatmeal	1.75
Bowl, 7⅝", Soup	2.00
Bowl, 8¼", Vegetable	3.50
Cup	1.00
Creamer	2.00
Plate, 7¾", Salad	1.50
Plate, 9⅛", Dinner	2.50
Platter, 12"	3.50
Saucer	.50
Sugar	1.50
Sugar Cover	2.00

FIRE-KING DINNERWARE, "PHILBE"   HOCKING GLASS COMPANY,

1937-1938

Colors: Blue, green, pink, crystal.

I get more letters from people wanting to know where they can find "Philbe" pattern than any other in the book. If I knew where to find it, you had better believe I would be there very quickly.

Does anyone have a green candy top? I found a candy bottom, a water tumbler in green and a couple of 6" plates in blue recently. Whether you collect this pattern or not, you need to be familiar with it lest you stumble onto some and miss an opportunity to make a profit.

The picture of the blue cookie jar is courtesy of Anchor Hocking. I had one years ago in green which I allowed a "friend" to talk me out of for the $10.00 I had in it because they were "collecting" it. I later found they "collected" it only long enough to sell it for the tidy sum I knew it to be worth.

If any pieces of this pattern are "commonly found", you'd have to say green grill plates, pink oval bowls and the blue 6½" footed iced teas fit that group. The pitchers shown, plus one other pink juice, are all that have turned up so far. Keep looking. There are bound to be more.

Many of the dinnerware pieces have shapes similar to Cameo, another Hocking pattern. So, if you see a Cameo-shaped blue pitcher which turns out not to be Cameo, chances are you've found a rare Fire-King Dinnerware pitcher!

Help keep me informed of any new finds in this pattern. My address is in the front of the book.

	Crystal	Pink Green	Blue
Bowl, 5½" Cereal	10.00	30.00	40.00
Bowl, 7¼" Salad	15.00	40.00	60.00
Bowl, 10" Oval Vegetable	15.00	37.50	75.00
Candy Jar, 4" Low, with Cover	75.00	200.00	275.00
Cookie Jar with Cover	100.00	300.00	400.00
Creamer, 3¼" Footed	25.00	37.50	57.50
Cup	20.00	52.50	100.00
Goblet, 7¼", 9 oz. Thin	37.50	117.50	150.00
Pitcher, 6", 36 oz. Juice	150.00	300.00	550.00
Pitcher, 8½", 56 oz.	250.00	350.00	650.00
Plate, 6" Sherbet	10.00	25.00	35.00
Plate, 8" Luncheon	12.00	17.50	30.00
Plate, 10" Heavy Sandwich	15.00	20.00	35.00
Plate, 10½" Salver	15.00	20.00	35.00
Plate, 10½" Grill	12.00	17.50	30.00
Plate, 11⅝" Salver	12.00	17.50	32.50
Platter, 12" Closed Handles	15.00	27.50	50.00
Saucer, 6" (Same as Sherbet Plate)	10.00	25.00	35.00
Sugar, 3¼" Footed	25.00	45.00	65.00
Tumbler, 4", 9 oz. Flat Water	25.00	100.00	125.00
Tumbler, 3½" Footed Juice	30.00	90.00	125.00
Tumbler, 5¼", 10 oz. Footed	20.00	65.00	50.00
Tumbler, 6½", 15 oz. Footed Iced Tea	25.00	45.00	40.00

FIRE-KING OVEN GLASS   ANCHOR HOCKING GLASS CORPORATION,

1941-1950's

Colors: Pale blue, crystal; some ivory and jade-ite.

Fire-King is the least favorite pattern of our photographer for this book. When he sees us unpacking it, he groans and says, "Not that (censored) blue stuff again!" It is very difficult to get the blue color to show under strong studio lights; so if you see color as blue, know it has not been easy. All he asks is that I find some more pieces with orange labels for the next book. . .!

We again owe thanks to Anchor Hocking for the picture of the blue skillet and nipple cover. Now that we know these items were made, possibly our search will prove more fruitful! The jade-ite skillet was pictured in the 2nd edition *Kitchen Glassware of the Depression Years*. Only a few of those skillets have turned up.

Handles on the large roaster sit opposite rather than atop each other so as to create a larger gripping surface. (The "tabs" are to keep the handles from sliding on each other.) These work best if you think of a clock with the tabs at three and nine as shown in the picture.

The one cup measure without a spout is called a "dry" measure and is rare.

The child's bake set ("Sunny Suzy Glass Baking Set") pictured in the 4th edition is bringing $35.00-40.00 in its original box.

I have re-listed the 4⅜" individual pie plate and the 5⅜" deep dish pie plate (as listed by Anchor Hocking) under "bowls" since I had so many calls and inquiries regarding these. These are shown on the left beside the mug and one spout measuring cup. The smaller of these "bowls" is hard to find.

Novice collectors should know there are four different custard cups; and the mugs come in a thick and thicker version.

Uncovered casseroles were called "bakers" while those sold with lids were called "casseroles".

	Blue		Blue
Baker, 1 pt., Round or Square	3.50	Custard Cup, 5 oz.	3.00
Baker, 1 qt.	4.50	Custard Cup, 6 oz., 2 Styles	3.50
Baker, 1½ qt.	8.50	Loaf Pan, 9⅛" Deep	15.00
Baker, 2 qt.	10.00	Measuring Bowl, 16 oz.	15.00
Bowl, 4⅜", Individual Pie Plate	8.50	Nurser, 4 oz.	10.00
Bowl, 5⅜", Cereal or Deep Dish Pie		Nurser, 8 oz.	15.00
Plate	8.50	Pie Plate, 8⅜"	7.00
Cake Pan (Deep), 8¾" (Roaster)	14.00	Pie Plate, 9"	8.00
Casserole, 1 pt., Knob Handle Cover	10.00	Pie Plate, 9⅝"	9.00
Casserole, 1 qt., Knob Handle Cover	10.00	Pie Plate, 10⅜" Juice Saver	45.00
Casserole, 1½ qt., Knob Handle Cover	12.00	Perculator Top, 2⅛"	3.50
Casserole, 2 qt., Knob Handle Cover	15.00	Refrigerator Jar & Cover, 4½" x 5"	7.50
Casserole, 1 qt., Pie Plate Cover	12.50	Refrigerator Jar & Cover, 5⅛" x 9⅛"	15.00
Casserole, 1½" qt., Pie Plate Cover	15.00	Roaster, 8¾"	27.50
Casserole, 2 qt., Pie Plate Cover	18.00	Roaster, 10⅜"	45.00
Casserole, 10 oz., Tab Handle Cover	12.00	Table Server, Tab Handles (Hot Plate)	10.00
Coffee Mug, 7 oz., 2 Styles	17.50	Utility Bowl, 6⅞"	7.50
Cup, 8 oz., Dry Measure, No Spout	35.00	Utility Bowl, 8⅜"	8.50
Cup, 8 oz. Measuring, 1 Spout	10.00	Utility Bowl, 10⅛"	12.00
Cup, 8 oz., Measuring, 3 Spout	16.00	Utility Pan, 8⅛" x 12½"	12.00

Please refer to Foreword for pricing information

FIRE-KING OVEN WARE TURQUOISE BLUE ANCHOR HOCKING GLASS
CORPORATION, 1950's

Color: Turquoise blue.

Turquoise Blue is the name found on original labels. This glass is also marked "Heat-Proof" on the label and the back is embossed "Oven Ware". You will find that it even works in the microwave. We have been using this pattern for our every day dishes for several years. It wears well except if your son slams the dishwasher door on the rolled out dish rack. This type action destroyed seven plates at one time at our house and made dealers at the next few shows I attended happy to see me . . . at least those who had Turquoise Blue stocked.

The tear-shaped mixing bowls were issued as "Swedish Modern" in 1957, and the round ones were advertised as "Splash Proof". I can attest to the fact that the oval shaped bowls are easy to pour from when using.

The smaller plates, 6⅛" and 7", are both more difficult to find than the 9" dinner plates, and the soup/salad bowls are an extremely useful size! Our first one came as a gift from a sweet lady who heard we were using this but had never seen bowls this size. Believe me, that prompted us to look harder for them. They're great!

	Blue		Blue
Bowl, 4½", Berry	2.25	Creamer	3.00
Bowl, 5", Cereal	3.25	Cup	1.50
Bowl, 6⅝", Soup/Salad	3.75	Mug, 8 oz.	4.00
Bowl, 8", Vegetable	5.50	Plate, 6⅛"	2.00
Bowl, tear, Mixing, 1 pt.	3.50	Plate, 7"	3.00
Bowl, tear, Mixing, 1 qt.	4.50	Plate, 9"	2.25
Bowl, tear, Mixing, 2 qt.	5.50	Plate, 9", w/cup indent	3.50
Bowl, tear, Mixing, 3 qt.	6.50	Plate, 10"	4.00
Bowl, Round, Mixing, 1 qt.	3.50	Relish, 3 part	5.00
Bowl, Round, Mixing, 2 qt.	4.50	Saucer	.50
Bowl, Round, Mixing, 3 qt.	5.50	Sugar	3.00
Bowl, Round, Mixing, 4 qt.	6.50		

FIRE-KING OVEN WARE "SWIRL" ANCHOR HOCKING GLASS
CORPORATION, 1955-1960's

Colors: Blue, pink, white w/gold trim, ivory w/trims, Jade-ite.

"Swirl" and Turquoise Blue pieces are all embossed Oven Ware. Each color had its own name. The blue is "Azur-ite"; pink is "Pink"; white is "22K-Gold" as evidenced by labels on these colors. The ivory trimmed red was found on our way to the photography session and had been well abused with paint and other dirt on the inside. Needless to say, the labels for it were long gone, so, if you find a piece with a label, let me know what it is called.

As with the other Fire-King patterns, this is not actually Depression glass, but it is being collected by Depression glass collectors, many of whom are using it as we do, for everyday dishes.

There may be a slightly higher price for the blue in some areas, but most other colors seem to be selling about the same price. The 22k gold on the white even brings its price in line with the other colors.

	Jade-ite	Other Colors
Bowl, Berry, 4⅞"	1.75	2.50
Creamer	2.00	3.50
Cup	1.75	2.50
Plate, 6⅞", Salad	1.25	1.75
Plate, Dinner, 9⅛"	2.25	3.50
Platter, 12"	6.50	9.50
Saucer	.50	.75
Sugar	1.50	2.00
Sugar Cover	1.50	2.00

Please refer to Foreword for pricing information

FLORAGOLD, "LOUISA"   JEANNETTE GLASS COMPANY, 1950's

Colors: Iridescent, some shell pink, ice blue, crystal

Floragold is a pattern that you either like or can not stand at all. For example, on our way back from a speaking engagement last fall, my wife and I stopped at a roadside Flea Market where I found a Floragold cereal bowl priced at $5.00. As I picked it up, I was informed that the Florence "book" price for that was $17.50, but if I wanted that ugly bowl, $4.00 would buy it. So, I bought it. Now, if anyone else has glass at 20% to 25% of the price I quote, save booth rental at the Flea Market and give me a call.

There is a pattern in Carnival glass very similar to this which is known as "Louisa", hence the crossed nomenclature.

The smaller butter dish (5½" x 3" tall) with the squashed knob pictured beside the normal (6¼" x 3½" tall) butter remains a unique find at present. That small butter now resides in a Midwestern collection.

I have been asked time and again what the difference is between the 10 and 11 ounce tumblers. One ounce is obvious. The 10 ounce has a narrow band around the top which the 11 ounce does not have. The 15 ounce tumbler is very hard to find except in crystal where they sell in the $6.00-7.00 range.

There is a tid-bit in Floragold made from two ruffled bowls rather than the usual plate type. These are set around a white, wooden post.

Cups were sold with that large bowl or a pitcher and called "egg nog" sets. Therefore, cups are much more plentiful than saucer/sherbet plates.

That is a squared bowl in the picture next to the plate. Depth is lost at this camera angle.

Please don't write me about the oblong, footed, scalloped edge candy dish! There were TWO pictured in the 5th Edition. It's a commonly found item. I just couldn't turn one up in time for this picture! (It looks like the ¼ lb. butter cover turned upside down and having scalloped edges and four feet).

The salt and pepper can also be found with brown lids. Both white and brown are plastic and crack when over tightened.

The vase looks like a large tumbler whose top was inwardly scalloped. This is shown in the pattern shot.

	Iridescent		Iridescent
Bowl, 4½" Sqaure	3.50	Coaster/Ash Tray, 4"	4.50
Bowl, 5½" Round Cereal	17.50	Creamer	5.50
Bowl, 5½" Ruffled Fruit	3.50	Cup	4.00
Bowl, 8½" Ruffled Fruit	4.00	Pitcher, 64 oz.	22.50
Bowl, 8½" Square	9.50	Plate, 5¾" Sherbet	5.00
Bowl, 9½" Deep Salad	25.00	Plate, 8½" Dinner	16.00
Bowl, 9½" Ruffled	6.50	Plate or Tray, 13½"	12.50
Bowl, 12" Ruffled Large Fruit	6.50	Indent on 13½" Plate	25.00
Butter Dish and Cover, ¼ lb.		Platter, 11¼"	13.50
Oblong	15.00	*Salt and Pepper, Plastic Tops	35.00
Butter Dish and Cover, Round	35.00	Saucer, 5¼" (No Ring)	5.00
Butter Dish Bottom	12.00	Sherbet, Low Footed	8.00
Butter Dish Top	23.00	Sugar	5.00
Candlesticks, Double Branch Pr.	30.00	Sugar Lid	7.50
Candy or Cheese Dish and Cover,		Tumbler, 10 oz. Footed	10.00
6¾"	35.00	Tumbler, 11 oz. Footed	11.00
Candy, 5¼" Long, 4 Feet	4.50	Tumbler, 15 oz. Footed	45.00
Candy Dish, 1 Handle	4.50	Vase or Celery	97.50

*Tops $7.50 each.

FLORAL, "POINSETTIA"   JEANNETTE GLASS COMPANY, 1931-1935

Colors: Pink, green, delphite, jadite, crystal, amber, red, yellow.

Floral keeps turning up in England, and many pieces are being shipped back in freight containers purchased in lots by dealers. So, it's not only the furniture, but the glass, you need to check out in exclusive European shops.

I can say for a fact that if you are looking for Floral lemonade pitchers, go to the Northwest. In two recent trips to Seattle and Eugene, I saw four green and eleven pink. There is glass in that area and some of it in quantity!

There have been a few new discoveries in Floral since the last edition. You may notice the first picture of a pink Floral cream soup although I have had reports on one before. Two turned up at an Indianapolis show; I kept the one with a cracked handle to show and photograph. An opaque, red/yellow bowl like the cremax one shown (with the pink) has been found recently. The dealer who bought it was told that it was Cambridge glass. You never know what will be found!

A pair of octagonal vases (one is pictured) in Floral came from England and were sold at auction in June, 1983, for $150.00 each! Bargains do still turn up. It pays to be educated. The Floral pattern is around the base of these vases.

The dresser set pictured is the only one of those to be found thus far. One powder dish measures 3″ and the other 4¼″. Several dresser trays have been found, however, so there must be other powder jars.

Lids to the sugar and candy are interchangeable.

The 11″ platter comes with scalloped indentations reminiscent of the Cherry Blossom platter. The normally found platter has smooth sides.

Unusual items in Floral (so far) include the following:
  a) an entire set of DELPHITE Floral
  b) a YELLOW, two part relish dish
  c) an AMBER plate, cup and saucer
  d) green and crystal JUICE PITCHERS w/ground bottoms (shown)
  e) footed vases in green and crystal, flared at the rim (shown); some hold flower frogs with THE PATTERN ON THE FROGS (shown)
  f) a crystal lemonade pitcher
  g) lamps (shown in green and pink)
  h) a green GRILL plate
  i) an octagonal vase with a patterned, round foot (shown)
  j) a RUFFLED EDGED berry and master berry bowl
  k) pink and green Floral ICE **tubs** (shown)
  l) oval vegetable with cover
  m) a rose bowl (shown)
  n) a 9″ comport in pink and green (shown)
  o) 9 oz. flat tumblers in green (shown)
  p) 3 oz. ftd. tumblers in green (shown)
  q) 8″ round bowl in cremax (shown) and opaque red
  r) CARAMEL colored dinner plate
  s) cream soups (shown in pink)
  t) cremax creamer and sugar

See page 72 for prices.

FLORAL, "POINSETTIA" (Con't.)

	Pink	Green	Delphite	Jadite
Bowl, 4″ Berry (Ruffled 45.00)	8.50	9.00	25.00	
Bowl, 5½″ Cream Soup	600.00	600.00		
*Bowl, 7½″ Salad (Ruffled 65.00)	9.50	11.00	45.00	
Bowl, 8″ Covered Vegetable	22.50	25.00	37.50 (no cover)	
Bowl, 9″ Oval Vegetable	10.00	12.00		
Butter Dish and Cover	67.50	72.50		
Butter Dish Bottom	17.50	20.00		
Butter Dish Top	50.00	52.50		
Canister Set: Coffee, Tea, Cereal Sugar, 5¼″ Tall, Each				25.00
Candlesticks, 4″ Pr.	45.00	62.50		
Candy Jar and Cover	27.50	30.00		
Creamer, Flat (Cremax $30.00)	8.00	9.50	57.50	
Coaster, 3¼″	7.50	8.00		
Comport, 9″	275.00	300.00		
***Cup	7.50	8.50		
Dresser Set (As Shown)		950.00		
Frog for Vase (Also Crystal $400.00)		575.00		
Ice Tub, 3½″ High Oval	500.00	500.00		
Lamp	117.50	117.50		
Pitcher, 5½″, 23 or 24 oz.		450.00		
Pitcher, 8″, 32 oz. Footed Cone	22.50	26.50		
Pitcher, 10¼″, 48 oz. Lemonade	145.00	170.00		
Plate, 6″ Sherbet	3.50	3.50		
Plate, 8″ Salad	6.50	7.00		
**Plate, 9″ Dinner	9.00	10.00	95.00	
Plate, 9″ Grill		50.00		
Platter (Like Cherry Blossom)	40.00	40.00		
Platter, 10¾″ Oval	11.00	12.50	95.00	
Refrigerator Dish and Cover, 5″ Square		45.00		12.50
***Relish Dish, Two Part Oval	9.50	9.50		
Salt and Pepper, 4″ Footed Pair	35.00	40.00		
Salt and Pepper, 6″ Flat	35.00			
***Saucer	6.00	6.50		
Sherbet	8.50	9.50	65.00	
Sugar (Cremax $30.00)	7.50	8.50	50.00 (open)	
Sugar/Candy Cover	9.50	12.50		
Tray, 6″ Square, Closed Handles	9.50	12.00		
Tumbler, 4½″, 9 oz. Flat		157.50		
Tumbler, 3½″, 3 oz. Footed		87.50		
Tumbler, 4″, 5 oz. Footed Juice	12.00	15.00		
Tumbler, 4¾″, 7 oz. Footed Water	12.00	15.00	125.00	
Tumbler, 5¼″, 9 oz. Footed Lemonade	30.00	30.00		
Vase, 3 Legged Rose Bowl		350.00		
Vase, 3 Legged Flared (Also in Crystal)		350.00		
Vase, 6⅞″ Tall (8 Sided)		350.00		

*Cremax $100.00
**These have now been found in amber and red.
***This has been found in yellow.

FLORAL AND DIAMOND BAND   U.S. GLASS COMPANY, Late 1920's

Colors: Pink, green; some iridescent, black and crystal.

Demand for Floral and Diamond has suffered due to a lack of new butter dish and pitcher collectors. As discussed previously, there are more of these items looking for homes than there are collectors looking for them.

As is true of other patterns made by this company, there are no cups and saucers. This has always been a "turn off" to new collectors.

In the old advertisements below, notice that one calls this "floral and diamond" while the other two reverse that to "diamond and floral".

Iridized pieces are known to Carnival glass collectors as "Mayflower" (which is not to say they are, in fact, Carnival glass, you understand). Whatever the pattern is called, it is more like earlier Pattern glass than your usual Depression glass patterns. It's heavier and has bolder designs.

There appears to be more green available than pink; yet the shade of green often varies due to the less than precise methods of firing glass back then. Some of the green has a blue cast making pieces more aqua than green.

Small sugars and creamers have turned up in black.

Sugar lids, iced tea glasses and luncheon plates are the most difficult items to find. The iridized butter is the rarest piece in Floral and Diamond. Mould roughness is considered "normal" for this pattern.

	Green	Pink			Green	Pink
Bowl, 4½" Berry		5.00	4.50	*Pitcher, 8", 42 oz.	60.00	55.00
Bowl, 5¾" Handled Nappy		7.00	6.50	Plate, 8" Luncheon	15.00	12.00
Bowl, 8" Large Berry		9.50	8.50	Sherbet	4.50	4.00
* Butter Dish and Cover		75.00	85.00	Sugar, Small	6.50	6.00
Butter Dish Bottom		42.50	52.50	Sugar, 5¼"	8.50	8.00
Butter Dish Top		32.50	32.50	Sugar Lid	25.00	20.00
Compote, 5½" Tall		9.50	7.50	Tumbler, 4" Water	11.50	10.00
Creamer, Small		6.50	6.00	Tumbler, 5" Iced Tea	15.00	14.00
Creamer, 4¾"		10.00	10.00			

*Iridescent—$125.00
Crystal—$100.00

Seven-Piece Berry Set

You'll really be most satisfied with the purchase of this set. It's very attractive, and affords a fitting and stylish addition to your present pieces. In green pressed glass, with diamond and floral design. Large bowl, 8 inches in diameter, and six sauce dishes to match, 4½ inches in diameter.
35N6838—Weight, packed, 7 pounds. Per set...... **68c**

Five-Piece Table Set

Heavy pressed glass in light green, with pressed diamond and floral design. Creamer, covered sugar bowl and covered butter dish. Weight, packed, 9 pounds.
35N6836........ **65c**

Seven-Piece   Water Set

Made from green pressed glass, with a floral and diamond design. You'll find that the sparkling scintillating pitcher and glasses are a set you'll be mighty proud to own when serving cold drinks. 3-pint pitcher. Six 8-ounce tumblers.
35N6837—Weight, packed, 12 pounds. Per set. **$1.18**

Please refer to Foreword for pricing information

FLORENTINE NO. 1, " OLD FLORENTINE", "POPPY NO. 1" HAZEL

ATLAS GLASS COMPANY, 1932-1935

Colors: Pink, green, crystal, yellow, cobalt.

Since there are two Florentine patterns, both made by this company, beginners often have trouble distinguishing between the two. It helps to know that Florentine No. 1 was originally advertised as "Florentine Hexagonal" as opposed to "Florentine Round" or Florentine No. 2. Florentine No. 1 tumblers are all footed, with the foot having the same gently serrated edges as the plate shown in detail in the pattern shot. All footed items in Florentine No. 1 will have the serrated edges as will all flat pieces.

There are at least two extremely rare, cobalt blue, Florentine No. 1 pitchers. I saw one at a show in Denver, and a letter from California informed me of another. Several cobalt cups have surfaced, also, although I have not heard of any saucers. Keep looking. You know the company made others!

No, I do not know who decorated the crystal plate with the yellow and red bands. My only comment is that it stands out in the picture where a normal crystal one would have disappeared.

Due to lack of collectors for pink and fewer new butter dish collectors, the price on the pink butter has dipped. Lack of demand and scarcity of pink combined make for a lackadaisical market in pink Florentine at present.

	Crystal, Green	Yellow	Pink	Blue
Ash Tray, 5½″	16.50	25.00	24.00	
Bowl, 5″ Berry	6.50	10.00	8.50	13.50
Bowl, 6″ Cereal	9.50	12.50	12.50	
Bowl, 8½″ Large Berry	15.00	20.00	22.50	
Bowl, 9½″ Oval Vegetable & Cover	32.50	37.50	37.50	
Butter Dish and Cover	100.00	135.00	100.00	
Butter Dish Bottom	40.00	55.00	40.00	
Butter Dish Top	60.00	80.00	60.00	
Coaster/Ash Tray, 3¾″	12.50	15.00	20.00	
Creamer	7.50	10.00	10.00	
Creamer, Ruffled	22.00		25.00	45.00
Cup	6.00	7.00	6.50	57.50
Pitcher, 6½″, 36 oz. Footed	30.00	40.00	37.50	500.00
Pitcher, 7½″, 48 oz. Flat, Ice Lip or None	40.00	137.50	80.00	
Plate, 6″ Sherbet	3.00	4.00	3.50	
Plate, 8½″ Salad	5.50	9.50	9.00	
Plate, 10″ Dinner	10.00	15.00	15.00	
Plate, 10″ Grill	7.50	10.00	11.00	
Platter, 11½″ Oval	9.50	13.50	15.00	
Salt and Pepper, Footed	30.00	42.50	45.00	
Saucer	2.00	3.00	3.00	
Sherbet, 3 oz. Footed	5.50	8.50	8.50	
Sugar	7.50	9.50	9.50	
Sugar Cover	11.00	13.50	12.00	
Sugar, Ruffled	20.00		22.00	40.00
Tumbler, 3¼″, 5 oz. Footed	10.00			
Tumbler, 3¾″, 5 oz. Footed Juice	10.00	15.00	13.00	
Tumbler, 4¾″, 10 oz. Footed Water	17.00	15.00	15.00	
Tumbler, 5¼″, 12 oz. Footed Iced Tea	20.00	20.00	20.00	
Tumbler, 5¼″, 9 oz. Lemonade (Like Floral)			50.00	

Please refer to Foreword for pricing information

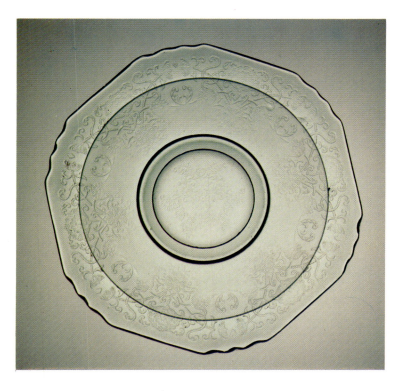

FLORENTINE NO. 2, "POPPY NO. 2"   HAZEL ATLAS GLASS COMPANY,

1934-1937

Colors: Pink, green, crystal; some cobalt, amber, ice blue

I get several letters a year about the jello or custard cup in Florentine No. 2. The cup is shown in green next to a yellow indented liner in the foreground of the photograph. These cups are few and far between, hence, the trouble in identifying them.

Fired-on pieces keep turning up in this pattern. That red saucer in the back is the most recent example.

Yellow is still the predominate color collected; green has a few devotees. Of course, everyone wants cobalt blue tumblers, but there is little else to go with them in this pattern.

Several pieces of dark amber have surfaced, namely three tumblers (4½", ftd., 9 oz; 4" flat, 9 oz.; 5" flat, 12 oz.), a cup, saucer and sherbet.

The pattern shot was taken of a Federal "Madrid" shaped sherbet having a Hazel Atlas Florentine No. 2 design. This came from a Mexican flea market.

Lidless candies are NOT mayonnaise dishes although I have seen some labeled as such. How you use them is entirely your business. One ingenious dealer had even found a ladle to put in his candy bottom. Granted, lids are hard to find.

Tops to butter dishes and oval vegetable bowls are interchangeable between respective pieces of the two Florentine patterns.

	Crystal, Green	Pink	Yellow	Blue		Crystal, Green	Pink	Yellow	Blue
Bowl, 4½" Berry	8.00	9.00	12.00		Pitcher, 7½", 48 oz.	40.00	97.50	130.00	
Bowl, 4¾" Cream Soup	9.50	9.00	12.00		Pitcher, 8", 76 oz.	72.50	197.50	177.50	
Bowl, 5" Cream Soup, or Ruffled Nut		9.50		30.00	Plate, 6" Sherbet	2.50		4.00	
Bowl, 5½"	20.00		25.00		Plate, 6¼" with Indent	13.50		22.50	
Bowl, 6" Cereal	12.50	14.50	22.50		Plate, 8½" Salad	5.00	6.00	7.00	
Bowl, 7½" Shallow			50.00		Plate, 10" Dinner	9.50	12.00	11.00	
Bowl, 8" Large Berry	14.50	16.50	16.50		Plate, 10¼" Grill	6.50		8.00	
Bowl, 9" Oval Vegetable and Cover	32.50		42.50		Platter, 11" Oval	10.00	11.00	11.00	
Bowl, 9" Flat	16.50				Platter, 11½" for Gravyboat			30.00	
Butter Dish and Cover	82.50		125.00		Relish Dish, 10", 3 Part or Plain	12.00	15.00	16.00	
Butter Dish Bottom	22.50		37.50		** Salt and Pepper, Pr.	35.00		40.00	
Butter Dish Top	60.00		80.00		Saucer (Amber 15.00)	2.50		3.50	
Candlesticks, 2¾" Pair	32.50		45.00		Sherbet, Footed (Amber 39.50)	6.00		7.50	
Candy Dish and Cover	75.00	100.00	125.00		Sugar	6.00		8.50	
Coaster, 3¼"	9.00	13.50	16.50		Sugar Cover	10.00		14.50	
Coaster/Ash Tray, 3¾"	12.50		15.00		Tray, Condiment for Shakers, Creamer and Sugar (Round)			52.50	
Coaster/Ash Tray, 5½"	15.00		27.50		Tumbler, 3½", 5 oz. Juice	9.00	6.00	16.00	
Comport, 3½" Ruffled	12.50	6.50	17.50	45.00	Tumbler, 3½", 6 oz. Blown	8.50			
Creamer	6.50		8.50		*** Tumbler, 4", 9 oz. Water	10.00	7.00	15.00	50.00
Cup (Amber 35.00)	5.50		7.00		**** Tumbler, 5", 12 oz. Iced Tea	20.00		28.00	
Custard Cup or Jello	42.50		62.50		Tumbler, 3¼", 5 oz. Footed	10.00		9.00	
Gravy Boat			35.00		Tumbler, 4", 5 oz. Footed	10.00		10.00	
Pitcher, 6¼", 24 oz. Cone Footed			85.00		Tumbler, 4½", 9 oz. Footed	14.00		20.00	
*Pitcher, 7½", 28 oz. Cone Footed	20.00		20.00		Vase or Parfait, 6"	20.00		45.00	

*Blue—$400.00
**Fired-On Orange or Blue, Pr.—$35.00
***Amber—$47.50
****Amber—$60.00

FLOWER GARDEN WITH BUTTERFLIES, "BUTTERFLIES AND ROSES" U.S. GLASS COMPANY, Late 1920's

Colors: Pink, green, blue-green, canary yellow, crystal, amber, black.

Prices for Flower Garden with Butterflies have flitted out of sight along with the butterflies on some pieces. This has become a pattern collected by only a few due to price. A new collector has trouble starting a set unless he has a strong pocketbook or a great credit rating at the bank.

My wife has always had a fondness for the green, and we both like the blue. We do have a few other pieces such as the Canary yellow heart-shaped candy, because we like the piece!

Thanks to Frank and Sherry McClain, you can see a large collection of black on P. 83 and an assortment of colors on p. 81. Frank found out how much "fun" we have taking photos for the book when he took these pictures. We hope you appreciate all his efforts! I certainly do!

Many new discoveries are listed and priced. I would like to point out the crystal tumbler in front of the amber candy on the opposite page since that is the first of those to appear. I found most intriguing the black 6" candlestick having a 6½" black GLASS CANDLE with the pattern on it! Now, that is neat! The other interesting piece is the "flying saucer" shaped covered bowl in the foreground on the left. This measures 4⅞" high and 7¼" wide.

	Amber Crystal	Pink Green Blue-Green	Blue Canary Yellow
Ash Tray, Match-Pack Holders	175.00	185.00	195.00
Candlesticks, 4" Pair	45.00	57.50	85.00
Candlesticks, 8" Pair	85.00	95.00	125.00
Candy w/Cover, 6", Flat	125.00	150.00	
Candy w/Cover, 7½" Cone Shaped	100.00	115.00	150.00
Candy w/Cover, Heart Shaped		325.00	450.00
*Cologne Bottle w/Stopper, 7½"		165.00	200.00
Comport, 2⅞"h.		20.00	25.00
Comport, 3" h. fits 10" Plate	17.50	20.00	25.00
Comport, 4¼" h. x 4¾" w.			45.00
Comport, 4¾" h. x 10¼" w.	45.00	60.00	75.00
Comport, 5⅞"h. x 11" w.	50.00		85.00
Comport, 7¼"h. x 8¼"w.	55.00	75.00	
Creamer		67.50	
Cup		65.00	
Mayonnaise, ftd. 4¾"h. x 6¼" w., w/7" Plate & Spoon	75.00	85.00	110.00
Plate, 7"	15.00	20.00	25.00
Plate, 8", Two Styles	13.50	16.50	22.50
Plate, 10"		32.50	42.50
Plate, 10", Indent for 3" Comport	35.00	40.00	50.00
Powder Jar, 3½", Flat		45.00	
Powder Jar, Ftd., 6¼" h.	65.00	82.50	125.00
Powder Jar, Ftd., 7½" h.	75.00	95.00	150.00
Sandwich Server, Center Handle	50.00	65.00	75.00
Saucer		25.00	
Sugar		62.50	
Tray, 5½" x 10", Oval	47.50		
Tray, 11¾" x 7¾", Rectangular	47.50	57.50	77.50
Tumbler, 7½ oz.	100.00		
Vase, 6¼"	67.50	87.50	107.50
Vase, 10½"		100.00	150.00

*Stopper, if not broken off, ½ price of bottle

Please refer to Foreword for pricing information

FLOWER GARDEN WITH BUTTERFLIES, "BUTTERFLIES AND ROSES", (Con't.)

PRICE LIST FOR BLACK ITEMS ONLY

Bon Bon w/Cover, 6⅝″ diameter	250.00
Bowl, 7¼″, w/Cover, "flying saucer"	350.00
Bowl, 8½″, Console, w/Base	150.00
Bowl, 9″ Rolled Edge, w/Base	200.00
Bowl, 11″ Ftd. Orange	225.00
Bowl, 12″ Rolled Edge Console w/Base	200.00
Candlestick, 6″ w/6½″ Candle, Pair	375.00
Candlestick, 8″, Pair	225.00
Cheese and Cracker, Ftd., 5⅜″h. x 10″ w.	350.00
Comport and Cover, 2¾″ h. (Fits 10″ Indented Plate)	200.00
Cigarette Box & Cover, 4⅜″ long	195.00
Comport, Tourraine, 4¼″h. x 10″w.	225.00
Comport, Ftd., 5⅝″h. x 10″w.	225.00
Comport, Ftd., 7″h.	175.00
Plate, 10″, Indented	100.00
Sandwich Server, Center Handled	100.00
Vase, 6¼″, Dahlia, Cupped	175.00
Vase, 8″, Dahlia, Cupped	225.00
Vase, 9″, Wall Hanging	300.00
Vase, 10″, 2 Handled	250.00
Vase, 10½″, Dahlia, Cupped	275.00

Please refer to Foreword for pricing information

FOREST GREEN   ANCHOR HOCKING GLASS COMPANY CORPORATION, 1950-1957

Colors: Forest green

It is amazing what new collecting blood can do to prices. A Forest Green platter for $20.00 would have made a dealer fall over in laughter years ago. Really, they are selling for that now, and dealers can not keep them at that price. The dinner plates are the only other hard-to-find item in this pattern; many collectors are settling for the luncheon plates instead.

Younger collectors are gathering sets of this while it is relatively inexpensive. Dealers report that it's a steadily selling glass year around, but it becomes an increasingly "hot" item at Christmas time, particularly the punch bowl, stand and cups.

Pitchers and tumblers are plentiful; they often sport some "scene" in white.

The "Bubble" creamer and sugar where placed in the picture to remind you that another pattern is available in this color. There are kitchenware items as well. Notice the mixing bowls at the back.

This isn't Depression glass per se, being manufactured much later. However, since so many are collecting Forest Green, I included it.

	Green		Green
Ash Tray	3.00	Plate, 10" Dinner	8.50
Batter Bowl	8.00	Platter, Rectangular	12.00
Bowl, 4¾" Dessert	3.50	Punch Bowl w/Stand	20.00
Bowl, 6" Soup	6.50	Punch Cup	1.75
Bowl, 7⅜" Salad	6.50	Saucer	1.25
Creamer, Flat	4.50	Sugar, Flat	4.50
Cup	2.50	Tumbler, 5 oz.	2.00
Mixing Bowl Set, 3 Piece	20.00	Tumbler, 10 oz.	4.00
Pitcher, 22 oz.	12.50	Vase, 4" Ivy	3.00
Pitcher, 3 qt. Round	20.00	Vase, 6⅜"	3.50
Plate, 6⅝" Salad	2.00	Vase, 9"	5.00
Plate, 8⅜" Luncheon	4.00		

FORTUNE   HOCKING GLASS COMPANY, 1937-1938

Colors: Pink, crystal.

There are fewer pieces in this picture than were shown previously, but the color shows truer here. This pattern is a little hard to come by, particularly in plates, cups and saucers. It's an inexpensive pattern. Due to its short run at the factory, there are so few pieces to be found that collectors virtually ignore it.

Bowls appear more frequently than other items, so, if you'd like some pretty pink Depression bowls to use occasionally, you could probably soon find enough to allow you to enjoy the pattern.

Candy dish collectors latch onto them; that's probably the best piece to own in the entire pattern.

	Pink, Crystal		Pink, Crystal
Bowl, 4" Berry	2.50	Cup	3.00
Bowl, 4½" Dessert	3.50	Plate, 6" Sherbet	2.00
Bowl, 4½" Handled	3.50	Plate, 8" Luncheon	5.00
Bowl, 5¼" Rolled Edge	4.00	Saucer	2.00
Bowl, 7¾" Salad or Large Berry	8.00	Tumbler, 3½", 5 oz. Juice	3.50
Candy Dish and Cover, Flat	15.00	Tumbler, 4", 9 oz. Water	4.50

Please refer to Foreword for pricing information

FRUITS   HAZEL ATLAS AND OTHER GLASS COMPANIES, 1931-1933

Colors: Pink, green; some crystal and iridized.

"Fruits" 8″ berry bowls are hard to find in pink or green. Both are pictured, but the green one was set up in the back on the right and looks like a plate.

"Fruits" is a name given glass manufactured by several different companies whose designs encompassed some variety of fruit. You'll find tumblers with pears, and some with cherries; some are iridized. There are pieces that have several fruits on the same dish (i.e. pears, grapes, cherries, etc). It's the "cherries only" tumblers that are more highly prized by collectors simply because they go with the "Fruits" pitcher which, so far, has only been found in green and crystal. Maybe a pink one will surface some day.

A 5″, 12 oz. flat tumbler in green, mentioned in the last book, has not called forth any others. There's got to be more than one!

	Green	Pink		Green	Pink
Bowl, 5″ Cereal	12.00	10.50	Sherbet	6.00	5.50
Bowl, 8″ Berry	32.50	30.00	Tumbler, 3½″ Juice	7.50	7.00
Cup	4.50	4.00	Tumbler, 4″ (One Fruit)	8.00	7.50
Pitcher, 7″ Flat Bottom	40.00		Tumbler, 4″ (Combination		
Plate, 8″ Luncheon	4.00	4.00	of Fruits)	11.00	8.00
Saucer	2.50	2.50	Tumbler, 5″, 12 oz.	40.00	25.00

HARP   JEANNETTE GLASS COMPANY, 1954-1957

Colors: Crystal, crystal with gold trim, some shell pink and ice blue.

Harp is a much later pattern than Depression glass, of course, but there are few pieces of it to collect. However, it does boast those cake stands which are reminiscent of Pattern glass, a glass that is even older than Depression! The design is on the foot of the pink and blue cake stands. There are two contrasting styles of cake stands, so don't let that throw you.

What has amazed me recently is the number of folks looking for cups, saucers and plates. I knew the two handled tray was hard to find because I had difficulty finding one for a picture. Consider Harp for a bridge set.

Demand is forcing prices up in this pattern. Yet, it is still an inexpensive set to collect.

	Crystal		Crystal
Ash Tray/Coaster	3.50	Plate, 7″	4.00
Coaster	2.00	Saucer	2.00
Cup	5.50	Tray, 2 Handled Rectangular	17.50
*Cake Stand, 9″	15.00	Vase, 6″	9.50

*Ice blue or shell pink—$17.50

GEORGIAN, "LOVEBIRDS"   FEDERAL GLASS COMPANY, 1931-1936

Colors: Green, crystal

Plenty of Georgian is still being found although there are hard-to-find pieces in the pattern. It is not as easily sold today as it was a few years ago when everyone was collecting it. Much impetus toward collecting Georgian was given in 1977 when the Peach State Depression Glass Club arranged for a setting of it to be given to the Smithsonian Institution in President Jimmy Carter's name. Needless to say, much publicity was gained for the glass and a step toward preserving American-made glassware was taken. (For a picture of "The President's Table" and a more detailed account of this club's coup, see the 4th edition of this book). For a time after this, Georgian was relatively scarce.

Beginning collectors tend to confuse this pattern with "Parrot". Georgian has round shaping and alternates birds with baskets of flowers in the design. "Parrot" is square shaped and has only birds and palm trees.

Dinner plates were made in two designs. One is like the pattern shot showing a full design, the other type has only the center motif and the garland.

Tumblers have only BASKETS in their design. Many people have missed owning tumblers because they were looking for the birds!

There are two styles of sugar bowls and unfortunately, the sugar lids are not interchangeable should you get so lucky as to find a lid. The lid to the large sugar is extremely difficult to find. There are no birds on the sugar lids.

The 6½" bowl, with straighter sides, is hard to find. It is pictured on the left behind the creamer and sugar.

There's a giant, walnut lazy susan ("cold cuts server") which comes with this Georgian design.

The "conversation" piece most recently discovered in this pattern is a "mug". It was likely a creamer-to-be whose spout wasn't made. Nonetheless, it isn't "spouted", so it's touted as a mug.

	Green		Green
Bowl, 4½" Berry	4.00	Plate, 6" Sherbet	2.50
Bowl, 5¾" Cereal	12.00	Plate, 8" Luncheon	5.00
Bowl, 6½" Deep	42.50	Plate, 9¼" Dinner	16.50
Bowl, 7½" Large Berry	35.00	Plate, 9¼" Center Design Only	15.00
Bowl, 9" Oval Vegetable	42.00	Platter, 11½" Closed Handled	42.50
Butter Dish and Cover	65.00	Saucer	2.00
Butter Dish Bottom	40.00	Sherbet	6.50
Butter Dish Top	25.00	Sugar, 3", Footed	6.50
Cold Cuts Server, 18½" Wood with		Sugar, 4", Footed	8.00
Seven 5" Openings for 5" Coasters	500.00	Sugar Cover for 3"	20.00
Creamer, 3", Footed	7.50	Sugar Cover for 4"	50.00
Creamer, 4", Footed	8.50	Tumbler, 4", 9 oz. Flat	32.50
Cup	7.00	Tumbler, 5¼", 12 oz. Flat	65.00
*Hot Plate, 5" Center Design	30.00		

*Crystal—$18.50

89

HERITAGE   FEDERAL GLASS COMPANY, Late 1930's-1960's

Colors: Crystal; some pink, blue, green, cobalt.

Heritage is a pattern that deserves some attention by new collectors since it is still relatively inexpensive, extremely attractive, fairly easy to find, and has few enough pieces that you can find an entire set in crystal.

This crystal pattern "dresses" a table too. It doesn't disappear, rather it commands attention, something new collectors respond to quite naturally.

If you find any of those colored berry sets, latch onto them! Many Heritage collectors will be GLAD to take them off your hands! A lady in California wrote recently to tell me her mother had given her a pink Heritage bowl that she'd gotten at a bazaar for 50 cents in 1955! No, she didn't wish to sell it for a profit!

	Crystal	Pink	Blue Green
Bowl, 5" Berry	4.50	15.00	30.00
Bowl, 8½" Large Berry	12.50	40.00	75.00
Bowl, 10½" Fruit	10.00		
Cup	3.50		
Creamer, Footed	12.50		
Plate, 8" Luncheon	4.50		
Plate, 9¼" Dinner	6.50		
Plate, 12" Sandwich	8.50		
Saucer	1.75		
Sugar, Open Footed	9.50		

HEX OPTIC, "HONEYCOMB"   JEANNETTE GLASS COMPANY, 1928-1932

Colors: Pink, green, iridescent in 1950's

Kitchenware collectors are creating more demand for some of the Hex Optic items than there are collectors for the pattern itself. Particularly attractive to them are the stacking refrigerator sets and the bucket reamer. Two of these reamers are pictured in the 2nd edition of the Kitchenware book. Hex Optic was probably intended for kitchen use all along, and today, it is more in demand for this utilitarian aspect.

A sunflower motif is a typical Jeannette marking for kitchenware items and can be seen in the 5", 32 ounce pitcher in Hex Optic. The taller pitcher is footed, cone shaped and similar in shape to the Floral lemonade pitcher.

Scarce and higher priced items include the sugar shaker, rectangular butter, whiskey, stacking refrigerator sets, bucket reamer and larger pitcher.

Iridized tumblers, oil lamps, and pitchers were made after 1950. The teal colored tumbler may possibly date with the "Doric and Pansy" era.

	Pink, Green		Pink, Green
Bowl, 4¼" Ruffled Berry	2.50	Plate, 6" Sherbet	1.50
Bowl, 7½" Large Berry	5.00	Plate, 8" Luncheon	4.50
Bowl, 7¼" Mixing	10.00	Platter, 11" Round	5.00
Bowl, 8¼" Mixing	14.00	Refrigerator Dish, 4" x 4"	7.00
Bowl, 9" Mixing	15.00	Refrigerator Stack Set, 3 Pc.	35.00
Bowl, 10" Mixing	18.00	Salt and pepper, Pr.	17.50
Bucket Reamer	40.00	Saucer	1.50
Butter Dish and Cover, Rectangular 1 lb. Size	45.00	Sugar, 2 Styles of handles	4.00
		Sugar Shaker	60.00
Creamer, 2 Style Handles	4.00	Sherbet, 5 oz. Footed	3.50
Cup, 2 Style Handles	2.50	Tumbler, 3¾", 9 oz.	3.50
Ice Bucket, Metal Handle	12.50	Tumbler, 4¾", 7 oz. Footed	6.50
Pitcher, 5", 32 oz. Sunflower Motif in Bottom	15.00	Tumbler, 5¾" Footed	4.50
		Tumbler, 7" Footed	7.50
Pitcher, 9", 48 oz. Footed	30.00	Whiskey, 2", 1 oz.	3.50

Please refer to Foreword for pricing information

HOBNAIL   Hocking Glass Company, 1934-1936

Colors: Crystal, crystal w/red trim, pink.

I have been seeing more of this in my travels than I used to see. While there is not a tremendous demand for it, there does seem to be more interest than there was heretofore. One collector said she discovered Hobnail after noticing that it had many of the same shapes that her Moonstone had. Since that pattern was introduced in 1941 and this one was out of the company catalogues by 1937, it is likely that the Hobnail molds were reworked and used again for Moonstone, thereby saving the company money.

All items shown are made by Hocking. Many companies made patterns with a hobnail design. This is a very attractive glassware. However, you still don't see a lot of it at shows, so, if you are collecting it, you will probably have to specifically ask dealers for it. This is one of the patterns they tend to leave in the shop instead of carrying it to shows.

I've had numerous collectors ask me to help them find the red trimmed items. They are eye catching, aren't they! Sugars and creamers are particularly difficult to find with the trim.

Collectors of pink should be aware that there is a pink Hobnail pitcher and tumblers made by another company that will serve you well. It was pictured in the 5th edition. It's so alike that few would know the difference if you didn't point it out to them!

	Pink	Crystal
Bowl, 5½″ Cereal		2.50
Bowl, 7″ Salad		2.00
Cup	2.00	2.00
Creamer, Footed		2.50
Decanter and Stopper, 32 oz.		15.00
Goblet, 10 oz. Water		4.50
Goblet, 13 oz. Iced Tea		5.00
Pitcher, 18 oz. Milk		12.50
Pitcher, 67 oz.		17.50
Plate, 6″ Sherbet	1.50	1.00
Plate, 8½″ Luncheon	2.00	2.00
Saucer (Sherbet Plate in Pink)	1.50	1.00
Sherbet	2.50	2.00
Sugar, Footed		2.50
Tumbler, 5 oz. Juice		3.00
Tumbler, 9 oz., 10 oz. Water		4.00
Tumbler, 15 oz. Iced Tea		5.00
Tumbler, 3 oz. Footed Wine		4.50
Tumbler, 5 oz. Footed Cordial		4.00
Whiskey, 1½″ oz.		4.00

HOLIDAY, "BUTTONS AND BOWS"   JEANNETTE GLASS COMPANY,
1947-1949

Colors: Pink, iridescent; some shell pink opaque and crystal.

The popularity of Holiday remains constant; thus, the harder-to-find pieces continue their upward spiral. Iced tea tumblers, candlesticks and the milk pitcher lead the way. There are three other pieces that are in short supply--console bowls, cake and chop plates. None of these six pieces will ever stand a surge of collecting in Holiday. I do not think you will ever see these items lower in price than now; so if you have been putting off purchasing any of the above, my suggestion is to buy them as soon as you can.

Holiday is one of those patterns that is not Depression glass per se since the pattern was made later than many in this book. My mother likes this pattern. I still remember buying her six iced tea tumblers in the early '70's for $10.00 each and worrying that I'd paid too much for them! I could certainly sell all I could find in that price range today!

Iridizing glass to give it a more "Carnival" glass look was a common procedure in the early '50's. Some Holiday pieces were iridized, namely the platter, footed juice and small milk pitcher. An opaque, shell pink, console bowl was made in the late '50's. Iridized items are more novel than rare as few collectors desire them.

You should know that there are two styles of cups and saucers. The cups which have rayed bottoms fit saucers having those same rays. Plain bottomed cups require saucers which have a plain center. You can not mix these. The cups will not fit the wrong saucers because of cup ring size differences.

One of the major problems to be aware of is the points which chip because they protrude so abundantly on this pattern. Never buy a damaged piece for top price. There is still plenty of Holiday available, but it is not all in mint condition.

	Pink		Pink
Bowl, 5⅛" Berry	7.00	Pitcher, 6¾", 52 oz.	22.50
Bowl, 7¾" Soup	24.00	Plate, 6" Sherbet	2.50
Bowl, 8½" Large Berry	14.50	Plate, 9" Dinner	8.50
Bowl, 9½" Oval Vegetable	12.00	Plate, 13¾" Chop	57.50
Bowl, 10¾" Console	65.00	Platter, 11⅜" Oval	9.00
Butter Dish and Cover	30.00	Sandwich Tray, 10½"	9.00
Butter Dish Bottom	10.00	Saucer, Two Styles	3.00
Butter Dish Top	20.00	Sherbet	5.00
Cake Plate, 10½", 3 Legged	55.00	Sugar	6.00
Candlesticks, 3" Pair	55.00	Sugar Cover	8.50
Creamer, Footed	6.00	Tumbler, 4", 10 oz. Flat	15.00
Cup, Two Sizes	5.00	Tumbler, 4" Footed	24.00
Pitcher, 4¾", 16 oz. Milk	45.00	Tumbler, 6" Footed	60.00

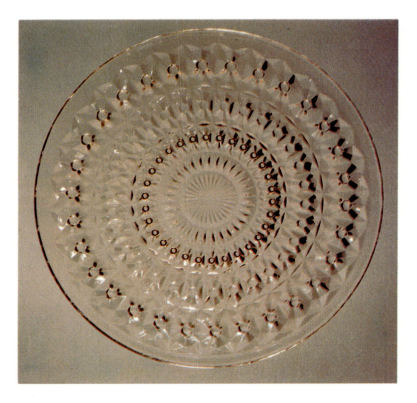

HOMESPUN, "FINE RIB"   JEANNETTE GLASS COMPANY, 1939-1940

Colors: Pink, crystal

One thing that has come to my attention recently is that there are two styles of footed tumblers in Homespun. Some of the tumblers have lines that go all the way to the top while others have lines that stop and form a clear band around the top. I have no idea which type is predominate, but I thought this discrepancy might interest you.

Further, close examination of the 96 oz. pitcher (which doesn't contain the waffle design) and Hazel Atlas's "Fine Rib" cobalt pitcher and tumblers shows them to be identical as far as I'm concerned.

By the way, I have the teapot that fits under that child's teapot lid pictured. The lid got packed, unfortunately, the teapot stayed at home on the shelf!

The footed, 4", 5 oz. tumblers (with platters) have turned up in lists as juices or cocktail **sets**. These must have been heavily promoted by someone long ago since the abundance of footed juices is almost legendary. They compare with the Sunflower cake plate, Dogwood luncheon plates and amber Patrician dinner plates in availability today. There are no sugar lids, but there is a pink (and a green) powder jar with the wrong type knob whose lid will fit the sugar. It's another "cousin". Catalogue listings plainly show these sugars never had lids; further, they never made Homespun in green!

I repeat an explanation from the 6th Edition. We were setting up the glass for this Homespun shot at the photographers and I started to set in the "Homespun" crystal butter dish which I'd pictured before. It had the same knob and the same waffle design in the bottom and top. What it did NOT have was fine ribbing; I was startled to see minute little squares. The crystal may be a first cousin to Homespun, but it really isn't Homespun! Thus, I have to conclude that the only pieces made in crystal are the child's dishes, and even that set doesn't seem to have a teapot and lid! They were rather stingy with their crystal for this pattern.

	Pink, Crystal		Pink, Crystal
Bowl, 4½", Closed Handles	4.50	Platter, 13", Closed Handles	8.50
Bowl, 5" Cereal	7.50	Saucer	2.00
Bowl, 8¼" Large Berry	8.50	Sherbet, Low Flat	6.50
Butter Dish and Cover	40.00	Sugar, Footed	6.00
Coaster/Ash Tray	5.00	Tumbler, 4", 9 oz. Water	10.00
Creamer, Footed	6.50	Tumbler, 5¼", 13 oz. Iced Tea	14.00
Cup	4.00	Tumbler, 4", 5 oz. Footed	4.00
Pitcher, 96 oz.	27.05	Tumbler, 6¼", 9 oz. Footed	12.00
Plate, 6" Sherbet	2.00	Tumbler, 6½", 15 oz. Footed	15.00
Plate, 9¼" Dinner	9.50		

HOMESPUN CHILD'S TEA SET

	Pink	Crystal
Cup	22.50	15.00
Saucer	6.25	4.50
Plate	8.75	6.50
Tea Pot	21.50	
Tea Pot Cover	35.00	
Set: 14 Pieces	200.00	
Set: 12 Pieces		105.00

INDIANA CUSTARD, "FLOWER AND LEAF BAND"   INDIANA GLASS

COMPANY, 1930's; 1950's

Colors: Ivory or custard, early 1930's; white, 1950's

Indiana Custard gets little respect from most Depression era collectors, but if you advertise cup and saucers too cheaply, the phone will ring off the wall for days on end. Usually, a price that was low and jumps dramatically brings droves of that item out of the woodwork, but that has not been true here. Cup and saucers were hard to find at $5.00 a set, and they are even more difficult at today's prices.

Many collectors don't have sherbets (including item collectors). Except in this pattern, sherbets are good "items" to collect in Depression glass. Most will even fit into the child's allowance limitations and many people prefer having one of everything rather than having to limit themselves to a single pattern.

I finally got the white plates pictured with the correct pattern this time. These decorated plates sell around $5.00 each; most of the white is hard to give away at any price. Figure white prices at 20% of the custard prices except for the cup and saucer which sells at $3.00 a set.

	French Ivory		French Ivory
Bowl, 4⅞" Berry	5.50	Plate, 5¾" Bread and Butter	4.50
Bowl, 5¾" Cereal	12.50	Plate, 7½" Salad	8.50
Bowl, 7½" Flat Soup	16.50	Plate, 8⅞" Luncheon	8.50
Bowl, 8¾" Large Berry	20.00	Plate, 9¾" Dinner	13.50
Bowl, 9½" Oval Vegetable	20.00	Platter, 11½" Oval	22.50
Butter Dish and Cover	52.50	Saucer	6.00
Cup	29.00	Sherbet	67.50
Creamer	12.50	Sugar	8.50
		Sugar Cover	13.50

Please refer to Foreword for pricing information

IRIS, "IRIS AND HERRINGBONE" JEANNETTE GLASS COMPANY,

1928-1932; 1950's; 1970's

Colors: Crystal, iridescent; some pink; recently, bi-colored red/yellow and blue/green combinations and white.

Iris sells so fast in the south that we have trouble keeping it when we set up at Southern shows. It never seems to sell quite so well in other locations. Many collectors in the Tenneessee area say that it is because Iris is the state flower, but it also sells well in the Carolinas where it isn't the state flower. Oh well, regional differences are what makes this an entertaining hobby.

First, let me point out an error in sizes that was mentioned to me by an avid collector. The straight sided cereal bowl (shown here between the sugar and creamer) which has always been listed as 6 inches, is, in reality, only 5 inches across. This bowl is not quite as hard to find as the soup, but nearly so. Some collectors, in fact, have never seen one. Small beaded edged bowls are hard to find anywhere except, perhaps, in the Northwest. The 8" beaded bowl is elusive all over.

One thing I should mention is that iridized wines have plain, non-rayed bottoms. These have **not** been reproduced! There are more and more iridized water goblets showing up, but not enough to satisfy all collectors who want them.

All in all, Iris pattern has defied the economy and surged ahead in price. Even nut and fruit bowl sets and lamp shades are being swept from the market (when found in the $20.00 to 25.00 range). Those priced higher seem to remain with the owner until the price is reduced.

You will find some pieces that have been acid treated, giving them a satin-like appearance. Collectors pay very little attention to these, including the rarely seen 8" plate! Also, some newly made, bi-colored vases and candy bottoms have been made with the color having been sprayed on over crystal. These don't have the rayed bottoms of the old candy dishes, so, there is no difficulty encountered there. Milk glass Iris vases are a product of the '70's and are selling for $2.00 to $3.00. Some of these have green or pink painted exteriors.

I thought you might like to see a rare demitasse saucer. This one is unusual in the fact that it has painted flowers! The lack of the demitasse saucers was explained when I ran into a 1947 magazine ad showing the cups on plain copper saucers for "al fresco dining". Notice the unusual pink vase. I recently had a report of a green sugar in California, but I have not confirmed that at this time. Don't pass by ANY crystal coasters without checking them for Iris pattern. One of my readers found eight for a dollar at a flea market! She was so shaken she called to ask if someone was making them again.

	Crystal	Iridescent		Crystal	Iridescent	Pink, Green
Bowl, 4½" Berry, Beaded Edge	25.00	6.50	Fruit or Nut Set	30.00		
Bowl, 5" Ruffled Sauce	5.50	5.00	Goblet, 4" Wine	12.00	15.00	
Bowl, 5" Cereal	25.00		Goblet, 4¼", 3 oz., Cocktail	15.00		
Bowl, 7½" Soup	75.00	20.00	Goblet, 4½" Wine	12.50		
Bowl, 8" Berry, Ruffled	9.50	8.50	Goblet, 5¾", 4 oz.	16.00		
Bowl, 8" Berry, Beaded Edge	47.50	9.50	Goblet, 5¾", 8 oz.	15.00	30.00	
*Bowl, 9½" Salad	8.50	8.00	Lampshade	27.50		
Bowl, 11" Ruffled Fruit	8.50	6.00	Pitcher, 9½" Footed	20.00	25.00	
Bowl, 11" Fruit, Straight Edge	30.00		Plate, 5½" Sherbet	6.50	5.00	
Butter Dish and Cover	25.00	27.50	Plate, 8" Luncheon	35.00		
Butter Dish Bottom	5.00	7.50	Plate, 9" Dinner	30.00	17.50	
Butter Dish Top	20.00	20.00	Plate, 11¾" Sandwich	12.00	11.00	
Candlesticks, Pr.	17.50	22.50	Saucer	5.00	3.50	
Candy Jar and Cover	65.00		Sherbet, 2½" Footed	14.00	9.00	
Coaster	30.00		Sherbet, 4" Footed	10.00		
Creamer, Footed	7.00	8.00	Sugar	6.00	6.00	
Cup	7.50	7.50	Sugar Cover	6.50	6.00	
**Demitasse Cup	15.00	50.00	Tumbler, 4" Flat	47.50		
**Demitasse Saucer	35.00	60.00	Tumbler, 6" Footed	10.00	9.00	
			Tumbler, 7" Footed	12.50		
			Vase, 9"	15.00	14.00	45.00

*Pink—$40.00
**Ruby, Blue, Amethyst priced as Iridescent

Please refer to Foreword for pricing information

JUBILEE   LANCASTER GLASS COMPANY, Early 1930's

Colors: Yellow, pink.

Jubilee was included in the 5th Edition as a new pattern and since that time the acceptance by collectors has been nothing short of phenomenal. The TRUE pattern has 12 petals to the flower and is open in the center. There are usually sharp points on the petals, but some are rounded. There are no small petals in between each of the larger petals. Now having said that, I must add that Lancaster made a multitude of patterns LIKE Jubilee, and most collectors are willing to substitute these look-alikes in their sets when they can not find the real thing. However, there are a few purists out there, and if you advertise it as Jubilee, you had better make sure that it is Jubilee.

You will note some new pieces and a new listing of a footed juice. A reader sent me one, and a few days later I found nine for $7.50 each, and the very next day I found some for $5.00! That was over a year ago, and I have not seen another. That's frequently the way things occur in collecting. You never see a piece, then, it seems to "rain" them, and then there's a "drought". (If the reader who sent the juice will contact me again, I will send him a check! As happens when you get 400 to 500 letters a month, addresses sometimes go astray).

I'd heard reports of pink Jubilee, so I was delighted to find the pink sugar to confirm what I'd heard.

One new piece of Jubilee is the candle holder, which was found in an antique mall just as my wife and I were leaving. We were looking for quilts for Cathy's book and had purchased several items. As we were going out the door, a lady asked for a jewelry case near the door to be opened. I glanced over, having never noticed the case, and there sat the candlestick!

New collectors should know that there are three different goblets. One is 6″ and holds 10 ounces. Another is a more bulbous 6⅛″, but it holds 12½ ounces. So far, I've only encountered three of the larger ones, so they must be scarce. The newly listed juice is 5″ and holds 6 ounces.

Serving pieces are very elusive in Jubilee. The mayonnaise has really escalated in price, but collectors are paying that price when they can find one.

	Yellow		Yellow
Bowl, 9″ Handled Fruit	37.50	Plate, 7″ Salad	6.50
Candlestick, Pr.	50.00	Plate, 8¾″ Luncheon	8.50
Cheese & Cracker Set	45.00	Plate, 13″ Sandwich	25.00
Creamer	15.00	Saucer	3.00
Cup	10.00	Sherbet/Champagne, 4¾″	20.00
Goblet, 5″, 6 oz.	30.00	Sugar	15.00
Goblet, 6″, 10 oz.	22.50	Tray, 11″, 2 Handled Cake	27.50
Goblet, 6⅛″, 12½ oz.	50.00	Tray, Center Handled Sandwich	40.00
Mayonnaise & Plate	87.50		
w/Original Ladle	100.00		

LACE EDGE, "OPEN LACE"   HOCKING GLASS COMPANY, 1935-1938

Colors: Pink, some crystal

Lace Edge is a pattern that causes me to get numerous letters about new finds and new colors. Most of these can be summed up by saying the following: Many companies manufactured a laced-type pattern (see "Laced Edge" by Imperial), however, Hocking made this Lace Edge pattern in pink and crystal. Therefore, if you find similar pieces in green, blue, yellow or black, you have found a piece made by some other glass firm. That should clear up all except the pink. Hocking's pink Lace Edge is cheap glass. If you hit the edge with your finger, it goes "thunk". Most other pink lacy patterns similar to Lace Edge will have a truer, prettier pink color and "ring" when you give it the finger test. (By the way, I might add that an antique dealer who handles glassware might consider doing you bodily harm if you do that to HIS glassware. I advocate this test ONLY for Lace Edge which belongs to you!)

For those who have asked over the years, I have included a Lace Edge vase. This one has been "satinized", a process which turns more people off than on, but, at least you'll know what the 7" vase looks like. A console bowl and candlesticks can also be found "frosted". You will occasionally see high prices placed on these pieces, but they hold little appeal for collectors and should bring considerably less than those same pieces without the frosting process. (That's why you see this vase. I found someone who felt the same as I.)

The 9" comport shown in the pattern shot is an extremely rare find. Please don't pass any of these by since the last report I had on this one had it selling for twice the price of an ounce of gold!

There are several items in Lace Edge that even dealers confuse with other Depression patterns. First, there is the tumbler previously discussed under Coronation. You will notice that the rays on the Lace Edge tumbler climb only a third of the way up the glass. We left the saucer from under the cup so that you could see clearly what a short distance the rays travel up Lace Edge cups. On Queen Mary cups (the pattern with which these cups are confused), the rays climb nearly to the top of the cup.

Novices should be aware that the 7¾" salad bowl and the butter bottom are one in the same. Both are pictured in the foreground. Because of the open area lacing in the design, this pattern damages easily. That is not to say the laces break off, rather, they chip and crack through from edge to edge within the single laces. Therefore, it is imperative that you examine each lace of a piece before paying a mint price for it.

In the back of the picture at either side you can see a 7½", three part relish and a 7¾" ribbed salad bowl. Demand for both of these has spiraled and the price has reacted upward. The larger ribbed bowl is plentiful, but that is not the case with 7¾" version!

	Pink*		Pink*
**Bowl, 6⅜" Cereal	12.50	Fish Bowl, 1 gal. 8 oz.	
Bowl, 7¾" Ribbed	32.00	(Crystal Only)	15.00
Bowl, 7¾" Salad	13.50	Flower Bowl, Crystal Frog	16.50
Bowl, 8¼" (Crystal)	5.00	Plate, 7¼" Salad	12.50
Bowl, 9½" Plain or Ribbed	12.00	Plate, 8¾" Luncheon	12.00
***Bowl, 10½", 3 Legs, (Frosted, $25.00)	120.00	Plate, 10½" Dinner	17.50
Butter Dish or Bon Bon		Plate, 10½" Grill	11.50
with Cover	42.50	Plate, 10½", 3 Part Relish	17.50
Butter Dish Bottom	12.50	Plate, 13", 4 Part Solid Lace	17.50
Butter Dish Top	30.00	Platter, 12¾"	17.50
***Candlesticks, Pr. (Frosted $40.00)	120.00	Platter, 12¾", 5 Part	16.50
Candy Jar and Cover, Ribbed	32.50	Relish Dish, 7½", 3 Part Deep	40.00
Comport, 7"	15.00	Saucer	6.50
Comport, 7" and Cover, Footed	27.50	***Sherbet, Footed	47.50
Comport, 9"	500.00	Sugar	14.50
Cookie Jar and Cover	40.00	Tumbler, 3½", 5 oz. Flat	7.00
Creamer	15.00	Tumbler, 4½", 9 oz. Flat	9.00
Cup	15.00	Tumbler, 5", 10½ oz. Footed	42.00
		Vase, 7", (Frosted $35.00)	225.00

*Satin or frosted items 50% lower in price
**Officially listed as cereal or cream soup
***Price is for absolute mint condition

Please refer to Foreword for pricing information

Monday - Saturday 10:00
Note: Jan – March we are closed on Wednesdays

LACED EDGE, "KATY BLUE",   IMPERIAL GLASS COMPANY, Early 1930's

Colors: Blue w/opalescent edge; green w/opalescent edge.

This is an attractive pattern, but there is not much of it around. The blue color (that 40% of the American public prefer) combined with a white edge and an open work design make it a collector's dream!

Imperial called the new white edging technique "Sea Foam" and added this opalescent type edging to many of its blue, green and pink lines of glass.

Serving pieces in this are not easily found, and very little of the green Laced Edge has turned up to date. A couple of cups and saucers were all I could find.

Laced Edge is a prime example of why Depression glass has suffered some doldrums in recent months. In the early years of collecting, dealers soon realized that a gradual increase in Depression glass prices was inevitable. They bought hoping to double or triple their initial investments, and many did! However, they became "spoiled" by these easy profits and very impatient with the recent slower profits due to the slowdown of the economy and due to the collector having more knowledge of prices. So, they started playing pricing games. They would advertise items at huge price increases over booked values. Maybe they'd sell the items to a few eager buyers, maybe not. But they would influence other dealers seeing their inflated prices to buy those same items at book (retail) price, thinking they could make similar landslide profits. Naturally, that didn't happen and the majority of collectors resisted buying. Dealers sat with huge amounts of Laced Edge that "suddenly" quit selling. They keep asking me "why?" I spent two years studying the retail prices at which Laced Edge was actually selling before putting it in my book at those prices. When those prices are ignored because "so and so advertised this pattern at . . ." there's little I can say. COLLECTORS are wising up to advertising games. Dealers who wish to stay in business should also! Please know that the ADVERTISED price of a piece of glass is not necessarily the SELLING price!

Bowl, 4½" Fruit	12.00	Plate, 8" Salad	12.50
Bowl, 5"	15.00	Plate, 10" Dinner	25.00
Bowl, 5½"	16.00	Plate, 12" Luncheon (per	
Bowl, 7" Soup	17.50	catalogue description)	30.00
Bowl, 9", Vegetable	35.00	Platter, 13"	45.00
Bowl, 11" Divided Oval	35.00	Saucer	5.00
Bowl, 11" Oval	37.50	Sugar	17.50
Cup	16.00	Tidbit, 2/8" & 10" plates	50.00
Creamer	17.50	Tumbler, 9 oz.	25.00
Mayonnaise, 3 Pc.	9.00	Vase, 5½"	30.00
Plate, 6½" Bread & Butter	9.00		

LAKE COMO   HOCKING GLASS COMPANY, 1934-1937

Colors: White with blue scene.

In talking to those collectors seeking Lake Como, their conclusion, on a whole, is that there are very few platters and flat soups available at any price.

Occasionally, I run into a pair of shakers, but rarely do I find other pieces. Besides the limited availability, a major problem is that many pieces are very faded from use when you do find them.

Any number of people would collect this pattern if they could just find more of it. It sells very well in the shop when I can find it!

I still have been unable to locate the regular cup! If you have one, please let me know.

	White		White
Bowl, 6" Cereal	7.00	Plate, 9¼" Dinner	9.50
Bowl, 9¾" Vegetable	15.00	Platter, 11"	17.50
Bowl, Flat Soup	32.50	Salt & Pepper, Pr.	22.50
Creamer, Footed	10.00	Saucer	3.00
Cup, Regular	10.00	Saucer, St. Denis	3.50
Cup, St. Denis	7.50	Sugar, Footed	10.00
Plate, 7¼" Salad	5.00		

Please refer to Foreword for pricing information

LAUREL MCKEE GLASS COMPANY, 1930's

Colors: French ivory, jade green, white opal and poudre blue

Collecting Laurel has been fairly subdued lately except for the children's sets. There is still great demand for the blue at times; but little of it shows up, and eventually, all but the extremely patient surrender and start collecting something else.

Kitchenware collecting enthusiasts will immediately recognize these Laurel colors as being typical of McKee's cannisters and such. As you can see, they also made dinnerware items.

Note the 12 oz. iced tea on the left. The few I have seen all have the brownish edge as if they were supposed to be cut or polished lower. I have never understood this and have never received a satisfactory answer when I have inquired about it. If someone out there has an explanation, please write.

A few jadite 4½", 9 oz. tumblers have turned up as well as the jadite children's set shown. By the way, I always try to show each of the five different pieces rather than clutter the picture with the entire set. Of course, the Scotty Dog decal items are the most highly prized. However, you very seldom run into these any more.

Hardest to find pieces include tumblers, shakers, candlesticks and the three legged cosole bowl. The cheese dish bottom is simply the 7½" salad plate.

The blue plate shown below is a commemorative piece with Jeannette McKee's picture embossed on it and stating a week of celebration (Aug. 28-Sept.5) on the company achieving the fifty year mark (1888-1938). It was an unusual find!

	White Opal, Jade Green	French Ivory	Poudre Blue
Bowl, 5" Berry	3.50	4.50	7.50
Bowl, 6" Cereal	4.50	5.00	10.00
Bowl, 6", Three Legs	6.50	8.00	
Bowl, 8" Soup		13.50	
Bowl, 9" Large Berry	9.50	12.50	20.00
Bowl, 9¾" Oval Vegetable	12.00	15.00	22.50
Bowl, 10½", Three Legs	20.00	25.00	37.50
Bowl, 11"	16.50	27.50	30.00
Candlestick, 4" Pair	16.50	22.50	45.00
Cheese Dish and Cover	37.50	47.50	
Creamer, Short	6.50	7.50	
Creamer, Tall	7.50	8.50	15.00
Cup	4.00	5.00	11.00
Plate, 6" Sherbet	2.50	3.50	4.50
Plate, 7½" Salad	3.00	5.00	7.50
Plate, 9⅛" Dinner	4.50	5.00	9.50
Plate, 9⅛" Grill	6.50	7.50	10.00
Platter, 10¾" Oval	13.50	16.50	22.00
Salt and Pepper	45.00	35.00	
Saucer	2.00	2.50	4.00
Sherbet	6.50	9.50	
Sugar, Short	6.50	7.50	
Sugar, Tall	7.50	8.50	15.00
Tumbler, 4½", 9 oz. Flat	30.00	22.50	
Tumbler, 5", 12 oz. Flat		30.00	

CHILDREN'S LAUREL TEA SET

	Plain	Decorated Rims	Scotty Dog Decal	Green
Creamer	20.00	30.00	37.50	30.00
Cup	15.00	20.00	27.50	20.00
Plate	7.50	12.50	17.50	12.50
Saucer	5.50	7.50	12.50	7.50
Sugar	20.00	30.00	37.50	30.00
14 Piece Set	150.00	220.00	300.00	220.00

LINCOLN INN   FENTON GLASS COMPANY, Late 1920's

Colors: Red, cobalt, light blue, amethyst, black, green, pink, crystal, amber, jade (opaque).

The only color I see often in Lincoln Inn is crystal, and there are few collectors of crystal.

Why are the serving pieces of Lincoln Inn so hard to find? As compared with other Depression patterns, stemmed pieces are more easily obtained than regular luncheon pieces such as plates, cup and saucers. This could be a boon for people who enjoy collecting "something" but who have little interest in owning an entire set. No doubt the goblets could be blended with many types of tableware.

We were excited about discovering the amber Lincoln Inn pitcher before. Now, there are two blue pitchers to report and several crystal ones. It seems that a little more of this is turning up recently as more people learn to recognize the pattern. I hope to show you the blue pitcher next time.

Happily, red and cobalt items seem the easiest colors to find although red shakers are something of a nemesis.

As you can see from the tall sherbet, the red color tends to have an amberina (red/yellow) cast in some pieces, particularly stemware. With some glass collectors this is a "bonus" rather than a detriment. This color comes from reheating yellow glass to make it red. The yellow shows because of uneven heating of the glass. A perfect red is obtained if all of the piece stays at a constant temperature during reheating.

A pitcher was being marketed again by Fenton in a dark, iridized Carnival color, so be aware of that.

	Blue, Red	All Other Colors		Blue, Red	All Other Colors
Ash Tray	10.00	5.00	Nut Dish, Footed	12.50	6.50
Bon Bon, Handled Square	11.00	6.50	Pitcher, 7¼", 46 oz.	500.00	400.00
Bon Bon, Handled Oval	11.00	6.50	Plate, 6"	4.50	2.50
Bowl, 5" Fruit	6.00	4.00	Plate, 8"	6.50	4.00
Bowl, 6" Cereal	7.50	5.00	Plate, 9¼"	8.50	6.00
Bowl, 6" Crimped	8.50	5.50	Plate, 12"	14.50	8.50
Bowl, Handled Olive	8.50	5.50	Salt/Pepper, Pair	130.00	90.00
Bowl, Finger	10.00	6.50	Saucer	3.00	2.00
Bowl, 9", Shallow		10.00	Sherbet, 4½", Cone Shape		7.50
Bowl, 9¼" Footed	13.50	11.50	Sherbet, 4¾"	13.50	8.00
Bowl, 10½" Footed	25.00	20.00	Sugar	16.50	11.50
Candy Dish, Footed Oval	11.00	6.50	Tumbler, 4 oz. Flat Juice	11.50	6.50
Comport	8.50	5.50	Tumbler, 5 oz. Footed	12.50	8.00
Creamer	16.50	11.50	Tumbler, 7 oz. Footed	13.50	8.00
Cup	10.00	6.50	Tumbler, 9 oz. Footed	14.50	9.50
Goblet, Water	17.50	11.00	Tumbler, 12 oz. Footed	17.50	12.00
Goblet, Wine	15.00	10.00	Vase, 12" Footed	60.00	40.00

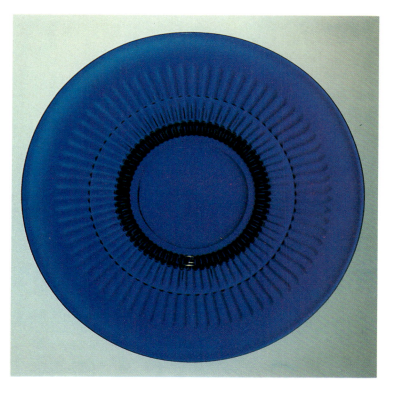

LORAIN, "BASKET", NO. 615   INDIANA GLASS COMPANY, 1929-1932

Colors: Green, yellow; some crystal.

Lorain is another regional collectible. In Indiana and surrounding territory, there are numerous collectors. Once you leave that area, there are few. People, being exposed to it more often because it is more plentiful there are hooked, and there is no rest until they have their own set.

Crystal Lorain is rarely seen although some snack sets (rectangular shaped with an off-center indent for a cup) have been found with flashed borders in primary colors of red, yellow, blue and green.

The luminescent yellow color of Lorain draws most collectors. Bowls, the 8″ deep berry and cereals, are very hard to find in both yellow and green. There are more collectors for yellow and that is why a price discrepancy exists. Everyone wishes they'd bought 8″ bowls at the first book price of $5.50! (People even wish they'd bought two first edition books, one to use and one to keep in mint condition to sell for the unbelievable price they're bringing!)

Prices for Lorain, as for some other patterns, have held during the past economic woes of the country. People with funds to spare have continued to buy. I see definite signs of a healthier economy just in my limited area of the business world.

The sherbet with "Lorain" design and a "Lace Edge" border in avocado green or white is of recent origin and Indiana must have made bushels of them!

	Crystal, Green	Yellow		Crystal, Green	Yellow
Bowl, 6″ Cereal	22.50	42.00	Plate, 10¼″ Dinner	27.50	40.00
Bowl, 7¼″ Salad	30.00	42.50	Platter, 11½″	17.50	27.50
Bowl, 8″ Deep Berry	62.50	100.00	Relish, 8″, 4 Part	13.50	22.50
Bowl, 9¾″ Oval Vegetable	27.50	37.50	Saucer	3.50	4.50
Creamer, Footed	10.00	16.00	Sherbet, Footed	13.50	22.50
Cup	8.50	11.50	Snack Tray, Crystal/Trim	12.00	
Plate, 5½″ Sherbet	4.00	6.00	Sugar, Footed	10.00	15.00
Plate, 7¾″ Salad	7.00	11.00	Tumbler, 4¾″, 9 oz. Footed	15.00	18.00
Plate, 8⅜″ Luncheon	12.50	20.00			

MADRID   FEDERAL GLASS COMPANY, 1932-1939; INDIANA GLASS COMPANY, 1980's

Colors: Green, pink, amber, crystal, "Madonna" blue.   *(See Reproduction Section)*

Madrid has been the subject of much letter writing and a lot of cussin' if my mail is any indication of what is happening. I will repeat the history below for newcomers to glass collecting, but first, let's get the pink out of the way. See pages 214 and 215 for what is now being made by Indiana in pink. Thankfully, it is a very light shade of pink and easy to spot.

Ostensibly, as their contribution to the Bicentennial celebration in 1976, Federal Glass Company redesigned moulds to make what they called "Recollection" glassware. Their "Recollection" was a new, sharper moulded MADRID pattern in AMBER glass with a tiny little '76 date marked in the design of each piece. We now think this was a last ditch effort to save their company by trying to cash in on the collectibles market. The amber color was a hair darker than the older Madrid and since the glass WAS marked, there was little reason for collectors to panic. They merely had to be more careful that they didn't buy new butter tops on old butter bottoms. (The new butter top's mould marks run through the North and South poles of the knob while the old mould marks formed an "equator" around the middle of the knob). You could get a twenty-piece starter set of "Recollection", 4 dinners, salads, cups, saucers and soups for $19.00. The butter and cover cost $6.00. Shortly thereafter, Federal Glass Company went out of business and "Recollection" butter dishes were selling at the local dish barns for $1.99 in early 1979. Even at that, the pieces were no bargain as an investment, of course. However, a few are now trying to recover their money by selling this as collectible glass from the Bicentennial. Unfortunately, Indiana Glass Company bought Federal's "Recollection" moulds, removed the date from them and is now selling crystal again. They've added some items, a footed cake stand and a goblet, but you need to be aware that these are newly manufactured. The new crystal is more sharply designed and has a "bluer" tint than the old; but for the time being, I'm taking crystal out of the listing prices so some newcomers to collecting don't get "taken" by the unscrupulous. This doesn't mean that old crystal Madrid is worthless by any stretch of the imagination. It's still old and reputable dealers know its worth. There has always been very little pink Madrid and the latest turn of events has not bothered older collectors.

The Madrid gravy boat and platter shown here came to Kentucky by way of Iowa which, for some reason, seems to be the state in which they're often found! The walnut lazy susan (pictured in the 5th edition) is often found in Kentucky, Virginia and West Virginia indicating that these items were regionally distributed. I know Madrid was given for premiums in my area in the '30's by the Kroger Company as well as the Jewel Tea Company. Notice the hot dish coasters with the indents. Probably cups were supposed to sit here making it a snack- type server. I see someone placed a sherbet there equally well when we photographed.

	Amber	Pink	Green	Blue		Amber	Pink	Green	Blue
Ash Tray, 6" Square	125.00		77.50		Pitcher, 8½", 80 oz. Ice Lip	50.00		177.50	
Bowl, 4¾" Cream Soup	9.00				Plate, 6" Sherbet	2.50	3.00	3.00	6.50
Bowl, 5" Sauce	5.00	5.50	5.00	7.50	Plate, 7½" Salad	8.00	8.00	7.50	12.50
Bowl, 7" Soup	9.50		10.00	12.50	Plate, 8⅞" Luncheon	5.50	6.00	7.50	12.50
Bowl, 8" Salad	11.50		15.00	22.50	Plate, 10½" Dinner	24.00		26.00	50.00
Bowl, 9⅜" Large Berry	14.50	17.50			Plate, 10½" Grill	8.00		13.50	
Bowl, 9½" Deep Salad	18.50				Plate, 10¼" Relish	8.50	8.50	9.50	
Bowl, 10" Oval Vegetable	12.50	12.00	13.50	20.00	Plate, 11¼" Round Cake	8.50	8.50	16.50	
*Bowl, 11" Low Console	11.50	8.00			Platter, 11½" Oval	10.00	9.00	12.50	17.50
Butter Dish and Cover	50.00		67.50		Salt/Pepper, 3½" Footed, pr.	57.50		77.50	110.00
Butter Dish Bottom	25.00		32.50		Salt/Pepper, 3½" Flat, pr.	35.00		55.00	
Butter Dish Top	25.00		35.00		Saucer	2.50	3.00	3.50	5.00
*Candlesticks, 2¼" Pair	15.00	13.50			Sherbet, Two Styles	6.50		7.50	9.50
Cookie Jar and Cover	32.50	25.00			Sugar	6.50		7.50	10.00
Creamer, Footed	6.00		8.00	11.50	Sugar Cover	24.50		25.00	72.50
Cup	5.00	6.00	6.50	10.00	Tumbler, 3⅞", 5 oz.	12.00		27.50	25.00
Gravy Boat and Platter	1000.00				Tumbler, 4¼", 9 oz.	11.00	11.00	17.50	17.50
Hot Dish Coaster	25.00		27.50		Tumbler, 5½", 12 oz. 2				
Hot Dish Coaster w/Indent	27.50		27.50		Styles	16.50		23.50	22.50
Jam Dish, 7"	16.00		13.50	22.00	Tumbler, 4", 5 oz. Footed	20.00		31.50	
Jello Mold, 2⅛" High	8.50				Tumbler, 5½", 10 oz. Footed	20.00		25.00	
**Pitcher, 5½", 36 oz. Juice	27.50				Wooden Lazy Susan, 7 Hot				
Pitcher, 8", 60 oz. Square	35.00	32.50	100.00	110.00	Dish Coasters	500.00			
Pitcher, 8½", 80 oz.	50.00		177.50						

*Iridescent priced slightly higher
**Crystal—$150.00

Please refer to Foreword for pricing information

MANHATTAN, "HORIZONTAL RIBBED"   ANCHOR HOCKING GLASS

COMPANY, 1938-1941

Colors: Crystal, pink; some green, ruby and iridized.

Yes! This pattern is getting to be a heavily collected pattern and it has stepped from the ranks of relative anonymity.

Dealers from Florida to Oregon have asked me what pattern was going to be on the cover of THIS book so they could stock up for the surge in collecting that followed the last two covers. As I write this, I am not completely sure. I thought Floral was set for the last book cover and it turned out to be Manhattan, so we will all be surprised. Blending of book color with glass color sometimes precedes author's recommendations.

Manhattan turned out to be a great cover choice two years ago because it was relatively cheap, readily available and made an attractive display. Today, it is not as cheap and harder to find, but it still sets a great table as many new collectors have found out.

Pictured here is the first iridized piece of Manhattan I've ever encountered along with the green tumbler previously shown. Are there pitchers in these colors? A ruby juice pitcher has turned up as well as several other pieces like the red plate shown.

That large relish tray, shown here with pink or ruby inserts is a big seller in our shop. Collectors tend to prefer the ruby inserts when they can be found.

That covered candy and small wine glass in the top picture are not actually a part of this pattern, but they blend nicely. The same is true of the double branched candlestick made by L.E. Smith shown in the bottom shot. These are what is known as "go-with" pieces. Personally, I find it refreshing that new collectors are willing to blend in look-alikes without getting bent out of shape over it. As long as we all know that these are not truly Manhattan, what difference does it make? Anchor Hocking made the small, squared candle pictured for this pattern.

Probably the hardest item to find in Manhattan is the small 42 ounce pitcher in pink. Please notice the pink cup! I saw two different pink dinner plates in my travels this year. So, we'll list these items again!

Notice that little sauce dish with the metal frame which originally held a spoon of some kind. You will often find bowls with various metal embellishments. The metal pieces were made by another company and were probably added for some special promotion.

	Crystal	Pink		Crystal	Pink
Ashtray, 4"	5.50		Relish Tray, 14", 5 Part	10.00	15.00
Bowl, 4½" Sauce	5.00	6.00	* Relish Tray Insert	3.50	4.50
Bowl, 5⅜" Berry			Pitcher, 42 oz.	14.50	25.00
With Handles	5.50	6.50	Pitcher, 80 oz. Tilted	20.00	32.50
Bowl, 7½" Large Berry	7.50	7.50	Plate, 6" Sherbet	2.50	12.50
Bowl, 8", Closed Handles	11.00	15.00	Plate, 8½" Salad	6.00	6.50
Bowl, 9" Salad	9.50	11.00	Plate, 10¼" Dinner	7.50	25.00
Bowl, 9½" Fruit	16.00	17.50	Plate, 14" Sandwich	9.50	10.00
Candlesticks, 4½"			Salt/Pepper, 2" Pr.		
(Double) Pr.	9.50		(Square)	13.50	27.50
Candy Dish, 3 Legs	5.00	6.50	Saucer	2.50	12.50
Candy Dish and Cover	20.00		Sherbet	5.00	6.00
Coaster, 3½"	4.00	3.00	Sugar, Oval	5.00	6.00
Comport, 5¾"	9.00	10.00	** Tumbler, 10 oz. Footed	9.00	10.00
Creamer, Oval	5.00	6.00	Vase, 8"	8.50	
Cup	9.00	25.00	Wine, 3½"	5.00	
Relish Tray, 14", 4 Part	10.00	12.00			

*Ruby—$3.50
**Green or iridized—$7.00

Please refer to Foreword for pricing information

MAYFAIR   FEDERAL GLASS COMPANY, 1934

Colors: Crystal, amber, green.

Mayfair still gets little attention although I did stir up a little action by advertising some transitional cream soups recently. You're looking at a really rare Depression glass pattern which still can be obtained reasonably. That isn't to say it is plentiful, and therein lies the reason the price has stayed down. People are discouraged from attempting to collect it. However, my wife met a lady in Texas who'd nearly completed her set in a two year time period. So, it still can be done! I've always thought it an extremely attractive pattern with those roses and arches. It looks like the perfect wedding gift!

The reason the pattern is so limited resides in the fact Hocking had patented the name ''Mayfair'' which caused Federal to redesign their Mayfair moulds into what became the Rosemary pattern. The green items pictured here (as well as one cup, cream soup and sugar in amber) represent what is called the ''transitional period'' or the glass made BETWEEN Mayfair and Rosemary. You'll notice that these pieces have arching in the bottom of each piece rather than the waffle design and there is no waffling between the top arches. If you turn to the picture of Rosemary, you'll see that the glass under the arches has been left perfectly plain. We traditionally include the TRANSITIONAL pieces with the Mayfair pattern because they more closely resemble them than they do Rosemary. Would you have noticed the difference had I not pointed it out to you? Strictly speaking, however, it must have waffling to be Mayfair. So far, cream soup dishes have only been found in the transitional mode.

There are no sherbets! Those are the sugar bowls without handles.

	Amber	Crystal	Green
Bowl, 5″ Sauce	4.00	3.00	5.00
Bowl, 5″ Cream Soup	13.50	9.00	12.50
Bowl, 6″ Cereal	12.00	6.00	13.50
Bowl, 10″ Oval Vegetable	12.50	9.00	13.50
Creamer, Footed	9.00	7.00	8.50
Cup	6.50	3.50	6.50
Plate, 6¾″ Salad	3.50	2.25	4.50
Plate, 9½″ Dinner	9.50	6.50	8.50
Plate, 9½″ Grill	9.00	7.00	7.50
Platter, 12″ Oval	12.50	9.00	13.50
Saucer	2.00	1.25	2.00
Sugar, Footed	9.00	7.00	8.50
Tumbler, 4½″, 9 oz.	13.50	6.50	15.00

MAYFAIR, "OPEN ROSE"   HOCKING GLASS COMPANY, 1931-1937

Colors: Ice blue, pink; some green, yellow, crystal. *(See Reproduction Section)*

There have been some new discoveries in Mayfair pattern since the last book. In pink, a frosted console bowl and a five-part relish were found in Ohio. There was also a batch of nine round cups found. In yellow, the third known sugar lid turned up. Now, does anyone have a sugar bowl for sale? A console bowl in green was found for $7.00 in North Carolina! This bowl has a chipped foot, but since it was the first one found in green, that can be forgiven!

There is an interesting story behind each piece mentioned above. Ask me about them at a show sometime, and I will explain. For example, that yellow sugar lid was found by one of Grannie Bear's customers in a "junk shop" for $3.15. It had previously been found under a log cabin in Eastern Kentucky. That is a brief idea of how rare glass is sometimes found today.

In the yellow and green Mayfair, you are looking at some of the most expensive and rare items in Depression glass! It was believed that you couldn't collect an entire set in these colors. Obviously, that was an erroneous assumption! (A yellow butter bottom has been found for the butter dish just since this was photographed with a yellow lid on a crystal bottom.) WARNING: the cookie jar (green and pink) and the whiskey (green, pink, blue, cobalt?) have been reproduced. See the Reproduction section at the back of this book for further discussion.

Some pieces of Mayfair were acid dipped or "satinized". They originally came with painted flowers which dishwashers have subsequently removed. Collectors pay little attention to these, and, therefore, these items bring about 30 percent less than prices listed for regular Mayfair.

In blue Mayfair, you have perhaps the most beloved color of any in Depression glass (it's always held first place in my mind), and in the pink Mayfair, you have the most universally owned pattern of any in Depression glass! Many people are now collecting it due to having inherited a piece or two in pink from a grandmother or aunt! It seems likely that half the population of the thirties had a piece of Mayfair in their possession. If you bought cookies at the store, you got a cookie jar; if you sent in a coupon from soap, you got a hat-shaped bowl. The local hardware stores sold it as well as the five and dime; movie houses gave away a piece each week if you bought a ticket for their show; gasoline stations gave pieces with the purchase of so many gallons of gas; ad infinitum! Mayfair enjoyed an extremely long run at the factory and the pattern was made into numerous items (which required expenditure for various moulds). All of this points to the fact that it was an extremely popular pattern back then, and I can tell you that it's an extremely popular pattern now!

Crystal shakers and juice pitchers sell for about half the prices listed for pink, and the crystal five-part relish sells in the $15.00 range. A new item reported but not yet confirmed is an ice bucket in Mayfair! I have to see that to believe it. Yellow and green prices have softened some because of a lack of new collectors.

	Pink*	Blue	Green	Yellow
Bowl, 5" Cream Soup	32.50			
Bowl, 5½" Cereal	14.50	30.00	50.00	50.00
Bowl, 7" Vegetable	15.00	32.50	87.50	87.50
Bowl, 9", 3⅛" High, 3 Leg Console	2,500.00		2,500.00	
Bowl, 9½" Oval Vegetable	16.00	37.50	77.50	77.50
Bowl, 10" Vegetable	14.00	40.00		87.50
Bowl, 10" Same Covered	65.00	75.00		250.00
Bowl, 11¾" Low Flat	32.00	45.00	20.00	90.00
Bowl, 12" Deep Scalloped Fruit	35.00	50.00	22.50	100.00
Butter Dish and Cover or 7" Covered Vegetable	40.00	200.00	900.00	900.00
Butter Bottom With Indent			250.00	250.00
Butter Dish Top	30.00	167.50	650.00	650.00
Cake Plate, 10" Footed	17.50	40.00	75.00	
Candy Dish and Cover	32.50	130.00	400.00	275.00
Celery Dish, 9" Divided			100.00	100.00

*Frosted or satin finish items slightly lower

Please refer to Foreword for pricing information

MAYFAIR, "OPEN ROSE" (Con't.)

	Pink*	Blue	Green	Yellow
Celery Dish, 10"	20.00	22.50	87.50	87.50
** Celery Dish, 10" Divided	100.00			
Cookie Jar and Lid	30.00	150.00	475.00	600.00
Creamer, Footed	14.50	47.50	150.00	150.00
Cup	12.50	35.00	125.00	125.00
Decanter and Stopper, 32 oz.	100.00			
Goblet, 3¾", 1 oz. Liqueur	350.00		350.00	
Goblet, 4", 2½ oz.	95.00			
Goblet, 4", 3½ oz. Cocktail	55.00		300.00	
Goblet, 4½", 3 oz. Wine	55.00		300.00	
Goblet, 5¼", 4½ oz. Claret	400.00		400.00	
Goblet, 5¾", 9 oz. Water	45.00		300.00	
Goblet, 7¼", 9 oz. Thin	105.00	100.00		
Pitcher, 6", 37 oz.	27.50	90.00	375.00	375.00
Pitcher, 8", 60 oz.	33.00	100.00	325.00	325.00
Pitcher, 8½", 80 oz.	60.00	127.50	400.00	400.00
Plate, 5¾" (Often Substituted as Saucer)	8.00	13.50	67.50	67.50
Plate, 6½" Round Sherbet	9.00			
Plate, 6½" Round, Off Center Indent	19.50	20.00	75.00	
Plate, 8½" Luncheon	15.50	25.00	57.50	57.50
Plate, 9½" Dinner	35.00	42.50	97.50	97.50
Plate, 9½" Grill	24.00	24.00	52.50	52.50
Plate, 11½" Handled Grill				80.00
Plate, 12" Cake w/Handles	25.00	40.00	25.00	
** Platter, 12" Oval, Open Handles	15.00	35.00	117.50	117.50
Platter, 12½" Oval, 8" Wide, Closed Handles			157.50	157.50
Relish, 8⅜", 4 part	17.50	32.50	97.50	97.50
Relish, 8⅜" Non-Partitioned	75.00		175.00	175.00
Salt and Pepper, Flat Pair	40.00	175.00	600.00	600.00
Salt and Pepper, Footed	2500.00			
Sandwich Server, Center Handle	27.50	45.00	20.00	87.50
Saucer (Cup Ring)	20.00		100.00	100.00
Saucer (See 5¾" Plate)				
Sherbet, 2¼" Flat	90.00	55.00		
Sherbet, 3" Footed	12.50			
Sherbet, 4¾" Footed	55.00	47.50	127.50	127.50
Sugar, Footed	15.00	45.00	150.00	150.00
Sugar Lid	975.00		900.00	900.00
Tumbler, 3½", 5 oz. Juice	30.00	72.50		
Tumbler, 4¼", 9 oz. Water	21.00	62.50		
Tumbler, 4¾", 11 oz. Water	100.00	85.00	157.50	157.50
Tumbler, 5¼", 13½ oz. Iced Tea	32.00	85.00		
Tumbler, 3¼", 3 oz. Footed Juice	52.50			
Tumbler, 5¼", 10 oz. Footed	25.00	67.50		157.50
Tumbler, 6½", 15 oz. Ftd. Iced Tea	27.50	80.00	177.50	
Vase (Sweet Pea)	105.00	65.00	150.00	
Whiskey, 2¼", 1½ oz.	45.00			

*Frosted or satin finish items slightly lower
**Divided Crystal—$12.50

Please refer to Foreword for pricing information

MISS AMERICA (DIAMOND PATTERN) HOCKING GLASS COMPANY,

1935-1937

Colors: Crystal, pink; some green, ice blue and red. *(See Reproduction Section)*

Miss America remains one of the most popular Depression glass patterns. There has been the usual cooling off of collectors buying the pitcher without ice lip and the water tumblers, since those items were reproduced. Other than that, there have been moderate price gains noted, especially in crystal. The pitcher with ice lip has been more in demand than ever!

Beginning collectors sometimes confuse Miss America with English Hobnail. See English Hobnail (p. 58) for an explanation of differences. If a piece does not conform to the listing below, then check English Hobnail. This list probably covers anything you will ever find in Miss America; but the longevity of English Hobnail makes almost anything in that pattern a possibility. Workers used to experiment with glass on their own time, or, I suspect, even on company time if they could.

The red Miss America shown in the bottom photo is rare and many collectors would settle for just one piece. The large bowl with an original sticker is a one-of-a-kind to date. I once corresponded with a relative of a factory worker who said that he had an eight-piece setting in red! I never got any proof such as a photograph, however.

Other experimental pieces in jadite have been found, and I doubt that the fired-on amethyst goblet shown will win any beauty contest. I would like to think that no complete set of that color exists. The ice blue is very similar in color to that of English Hobnail. I have a sherbet in a new style to show you in the next book, so stay tuned until then. Sorry. We found it too late to include it this time.

Other items reproduced in Miss America are shakers and the butter dish. There is a detailed explanation of the differences between old and new in the back of book (p. 216). Prices for Miss America butter dishes really suffered when the reproductions first came out. After so many years, collectors are no longer as worried about these as they once were, and the prices in pink are slowly beginning to recover.

The footed juice has finally jumped ahead of the wine in price. I guarantee (based upon what I have seen in my years in glassware) that there are at least ten wines for every juice. Most people are just happy to find two styles of goblets, letting the third one go, so there is less demand than if everyone wanted all three. Thus, the price doesn't properly reflect its relative rarity.

Candy jars in crystal are more plentiful than ever, and the supply of pink has been more than adequate for the demand in that color, also.

	Crystal	Pink	Green	Red
Bowl, 4½" Berry			7.00	
*Bowl, 6¼" Berry	6.00	11.00	10.00	
Bowl, 8" Curved in at Top	30.00	45.00		325.00
Bowl, 8¾" Straight Deep Fruit	22.50	37.50		
Bowl, 10" Oval Vegetable	10.00	15.00		
**Butter Dish and Cover	150.00	360.00		
Butter Dish Bottom	6.00	11.00		
Butter Dish Top	144.00	349.00		
Cake Plate, 12" Footed	16.50	27.50		
Candy Jar and Cover, 11½"	45.00	90.00		
Celery Dish, 10½" Oblong	7.50	15.00		
Coaster, 5¾"	11.00	16.50		
Comport, 5"	10.00	16.00		
Creamer, Footed	6.50	12.50		135.00
Cup	7.50	15.00	8.00	
Goblet, 3¾", 3 oz. Wine	15.00	45.00		175.00
Goblet, 4¾", 5 oz. Juice	18.00	55.00		175.00
Goblet, 5½", 10 oz. Water	17.50	33.50		160.00

	Crystal	Pink	Green	Red
Pitcher, 8", 65 oz.	40.00	72.50		
Pitcher, 8½", 65 oz. w/Ice Lip	57.50	90.00		
***Plate, 5¾" Sherbet	3.00	5.00	5.00	
Plate, 6¾"			6.00	
Plate, 8½" Salad	5.00	13.00	8.00	60.00
****Plate, 10¼" Dinner	9.50	16.00		
Plate, 10¼" Grill	7.50	12.50		
Platter, 12¼" Oval	10.00	16.00		
Relish, 8¾", 4 Part	7.50	13.50		
Relish, 11¾" Round Divided	12.50	125.00		
Salt and Pepper, Pr.	22.50	42.50	257.50	
Saucer	2.50	4.00		
***Sherbet	6.50	10.00		
Sugar	6.00	12.50		135.00
****Tumbler, 4", 5 oz. Juice	12.50	33.00		
Tumbler, 4½", 10 oz. Water	12.00	18.00	13.50	
Tumbler, 5¾", 14 oz. Iced Tea	20.00	40.00		

*Also has appeared in Cobalt Blue—$125.00
**Absolute mint price
***Also in Ice Blue—$35.00
****Also in Ice Blue—$80.00

Please refer to Foreword for pricing information

MODERNTONE, "SAILBOAT" MODERNTONE, & "LITTLE HOSTESS PARTY DISHES", HAZEL ATLAS GLASS CO., 1934-1942; Late 1940's-Early 1950's

Moderntone collectors are beginning to notice the later Platonite pastels more than in the past. These collectors are the new breed and are finding that starting some of the "established" sets in popular colors is prohibitive to the pocketbook. Therefore, they start with the less expensive patterns and colors which initiates the cycle again by pushing up the price on these patterns. Note the price jumps in Platonite. Notice the cobalt saucer and plate pictured with the SAILBOAT design. These pieces are beginning to attract the attention of some collectors. Only the saucer is decorated, the cup remains plain. After including this in the 6th Edition, I have included the whole line under "SHIPS" (p. 186). Cobalt blue glass has always had admirers, so people rushing to get sets of cobalt Moderntone are not necessarily Depression glass devotees. Supply of this color Moderntone is dwindling which is beginning to trigger rises in price. Watch out for pieces too badly scratched to command mint prices! The tumbler and small whiskey glass pictured were made in amethyst, cobalt, pink, green and crystal. These were not officially listed as Moderntone. Collectors have adopted these for this pattern. The butter dish has a rim of glass around which the metal lid fits, so, don't buy a cereal bowl with a lid resting atop it as a butter. The cheese dish needs to have that wooden insert to be labeled a cheese dish. The bottom to the cheese is a salad plate. Very few of these have been found to date. Notice that the cheese and butter lids differ. Thank Sherry McClain for the picture of amethyst Moderntone below. She wanted to make sure I listed all the tumblers this time! The children's sets are as much in demand as the adult patterns. There are quite a few collectors looking for the child's teapot, and even more hoping to find a lid for theirs.

	Cobalt	Amethyst	Platonite Fired On Colors		Cobalt	Amethyst	Platonite Fired On Colors
*Ash Tray, 7¾", Match Holder in Center	87.50			Plate, 5⅞" Sherbet	3.50	3.00	.75
Bowl, 4¾" Cream Soup	12.00	9.50		Plate, 6¾" Salad	6.50	4.50	1.50
Bowl, 5" Berry	13.50	6.50	1.25	Plate, 7¾" Luncheon	5.00	5.00	1.75
Bowl, 5" Cream Soup, Ruffled	15.00	11.50		Plate, 8⅞" Dinner	9.00	6.50	3.00
Bowl, 6½" Cereal	35.00	25.00	3.00	Plate, 10½" Sandwich	15.00	11.50	4.00
Bowl, 7½" Soup	40.00	35.00	4.00	Platter, 11" Oval	20.00	13.00	6.00
Bowl, 8¾" Large Berry	22.50	17.50	5.00	Platter, 12" Oval	30.00	20.00	7.50
Butter Dish with Metal Cover	57.50			Salt and Pepper, Pr.	27.50	27.50	12.50
Cheese Dish, 7" with Metal Lid	135.00			Saucer	2.00	2.00	.75
				Sherbet	7.50	6.50	3.00
Creamer	7.50	6.00	2.50	Sugar	7.50	6.50	2.50
Cup	7.50	6.00	1.50	Sugar Lid in Metal	20.00		
Cup (Handle-less or Custard	10.00	9.00		Tumbler, 5 oz.		12.50	
				Tumbler, 9 oz.	15.00	15.00	5.00
*Pink — $52.50				Tumbler, 12 oz.	45.00	35.00	
				Whiskey, 1½ oz.	13.00		

LITTLE HOSTESS PARTY SET

	Pastel	Dark		Pastel	Dark
Cup, 1¾"	2.50	3.25	Sugar, 1¾"	3.00	4.00
Saucer, 3⅞"	1.00	2.00	Teapot and Lid, 3½"		30.00
Plate, 5¼"	2.00	3.00	Set, 14 Pc.	30.00	
Creamer, 1¾"	3.00	4.00	Set, 16 Pc.		65.00

MOONDROPS NEW MARTINSVILLE GLASS COMPANY, 1932-1940

Colors: Amber, pink, green, cobalt, ice blue, red, amethyst, crystal, dark green, light green, jadite, smoke, black.

Notice the three footed powder jar in amber and the tab handled three footed piece in green. The latter could be a mint or jelly. Both are new pieces to the list. The spouted dark green item is possibly a gravy.

	Blue/Red	Other Colors		Blue/Red	Other Colors
Ash Tray	27.50	10.00	Goblet, 5⅛", Metal Stem Wine	12.00	8.50
Bowl, 5¼" Berry	6.00	4.00	Goblet, 5½", Metal Stem Wine	13.50	8.50
Bowl, 6¾" Soup	10.00	80.00	Goblet, 6¼", 9 oz. Water	17.50	13.50
Bowl, 7½" Pickle	12.00	9.50	Gravy Boat	75.00	55.00
Bowl, 8⅜" Footed, Concave Top	13.00	12.00	Mug, 5⅛", 12 oz.	25.00	15.00
Bowl, 8½" 3 Footed Divided Relish	12.50	9.50	Perfume Bottle, "Rocket"	45.00	25.00
Bowl, 9½" Three Legged Ruffled	17.50	12.50	Pitcher, 6⅞", 22 oz. Small	125.00	70.00
Bowl, 9¾" Oval Vegetable	22.50	17.50	Pitcher, 8⅛", 32 oz. Medium	137.50	97.50
Bowl, 9¾" Covered Casserole	67.50	45.00	Pitcher, 8", 50 oz. Large, with Lip	147.50	105.00
Bowl, 9¾" Two Handled Oval	32.50	25.00	Pitcher, 8⅛", 53 oz. Large, No Lip	145.00	110.00
Bowl, 11½" Boat Shaped Celery	20.00	17.50	Plate, 5⅞" Bread and Butter	3.50	3.00
Bowl, 12" Round 3 Footed Console	32.50	22.50	Plate, 6⅛" Sherbet	4.00	2.50
Bowl, 13" Console with "Wings"	57.00	30.00	Plate, 6" Round, Off-Center Sherbet Indent	5.00	4.00
Butter Dish and Cover	357.50	225.00	Plate, 7⅛" Salad	6.00	4.00
Butter Dish Bottom	57.50	35.00	Plate, 8½" Luncheon	9.00	5.00
Butter Dish Top	300.00	190.00	Plate, 9½" Dinner	12.50	8.50
Candles, 2" Ruffled Pair	22.50	17.50	Plate, 15" Round Sandwich	25.00	13.50
Candles, 4½" Sherbet Style Pr.	19.50	15.00	Plate, 15" Two Handled Sandwich	27.50	20.00
Candlesticks, 5" "Wings" Pr.	52.50	32.50	Platter, 12" Oval	17.50	12.50
Candlesticks, 5¼" Triple Light Pr.	65.00	35.00	Powder Jar, 3 Footed	75.00	65.00
Candlesticks, 8½" Metal Stem Pr.	25.00	20.00	Saucer	3.50	3.00
Candy Dish, 8" Ruffled	15.00	12.50	Sherbet, 2⅝"	10.00	6.50
Cocktail Shaker, with or without			Sherbet, 4½"	15.00	8.50
Handle, Metal Top	25.00	17.00	Sugar, 2¾"	13.50	8.50
Comport, 4"	12.50	7.50	Sugar, 4"	11.50	6.50
Comport, 11½"	27.50	17.50	Tumbler, 2¾", 2 oz. Shot	10.00	6.50
Creamer, 2¾" Miniature	14.00	9.00	Tumbler, 2¾", 2 oz. Handled Shot	12.50	7.50
Creamer, 3¾" Regular	12.00	7.50	Tumbler, 3¼", 3 oz. Footed Juice	11.50	7.50
Cup	9.00	7.50	Tumbler, 3⅝", 5 oz.	10.00	6.00
Decanter, 7¾" Small	50.00	32.50	Tumbler, 4⅜", 7 oz.	11.00	7.50
Decanter, 8½" Medium	57.50	32.50	Tumbler, 4⅜", 8 oz.	12.00	8.50
Decanter, 11¼" Large	67.50	37.50	Tumbler, 4⅞", 9 oz. Handled	13.50	9.50
Decanter, 10¼" "Rocket"	77.50	47.50	Tumbler, 4⅞", 9 oz.	13.50	10.00
Goblet, 2⅞", ¾ oz. Liquor	17.50	12.50	Tumbler, 5⅛", 12 oz.	17.50	11.00
Goblet, 4", 4 oz. Wine	15.00	9.50	Tray, 7½", For Mini Sugar/Creamer	22.50	15.00
Goblet, 4¾", "Rocket" Wine	25.00	17.50	Vase, 7¾" Flat, Ruffled Top	42.50	32.50
Goblet, 4¾", 5 oz.	12.50	8.00	Vase, 9¼" "Rocket" Style	77.50	55.00

MOONSTONE   ANCHOR HOCKING GLASS CORPORATION, 1941-1946

Colors: Crystal with opalescent hobnails, some green.

Did the Moonstone cover catch you by surpise? This pattern sells very well in my shop, and since the powers that be wanted to change the color of the cover, it seemed to work well. From past cover experiences with blue Mayfair and Manhattan, I suggest you grab all the Moonstone you can as the price may be going up!

There is some speculaltion that the four pieces with Moonstone labels refer to the opalized effect rather than the pattern. That seems likely! Note that the Lace Edge sherbet and the Bubble bowl are standard Hocking patterns but the other pieces are not.

The candy below is the only item I have encountered with that fired-on red coloration. I'm not sure whether it adds or detracts from the candy. It is just different!

The cologne bottle sold as Moonstone, as well as pitchers, shakers and stemmed water goblets, were made by Fenton Glass Company rather than by Anchor Hocking. Many collectors of Moonstone mix these two patterns to obtain items that were not made in Hocking's Moonstone. The listing below is for Anchor Hocking's glass only.

The picture with the odd pieces below is courtesy of Anchor Hocking, using glass out of their morgue.

	Opalescent Hobnail
Bowl, 5½″ Berry	8.50
Bowl, 5½″ Crimped Dessert	6.00
Bowl, 6½″ Crimped Handled	7.00
Bowl, 7¾″ Flat	8.00
Bowl, 7¾″ Divided Relish	7.50
Bowl, 9½″ Crimped	12.50
Bowl, Cloverleaf	8.50
Candleholder, Pr.	15.00
Candy Jar and Cover, 6″	17.50
Cigarette Jar and Cover	15.00
Creamer	6.00
Cup	6.00
Goblet, 10 oz.	15.00
Heart Bonbon, One Handle	7.50
Plate, 6¼″ Sherbet	2.50
Plate, 8″ Luncheon	8.50
Plate, 10″ Sandwich	15.00
Puff Box and Cover, 4¾″ Round	16.00
Saucer (Same as Sherbet Plate)	2.50
Sherbet, Footed	6.00
Sugar, Footed	6.00
Vase, 5½″ Bud	8.50

Please refer to Foreword for pricing information

MOROCCAN AMETHYST   HAZEL WARE, DIVISION OF CONTINENTAL CAN, 1960's

Color: Amethyst.

We received Moroccan Amethyst as a wedding gift in 1964. Cathy was a member of Sigma Kappa sorority whose color was violet. Naturally, someone started us out in life with violet tumblers. A few years later, I found iced tea tumblers at a garage sale and we used those until after Chad was born. A major design fallacy in this pattern is that the small bottom makes the tumbler extremely top heavy when it is filled with liquid. A small child creates disaster around these, and we retired them from use.

The name Moroccan Amethyst refers to the color and not a particular pattern. You will probably find additional pieces to this non-Depression era pattern. I feel a lot older than forty-one putting this pattern in my book on Depression glass. Yet, I have met any number of collectors for Moroccan Amethyst at shows.

	Amethyst
Ash Tray, 6⅞", Triangular	5.00
Bowl, 4¾", Fruit	3.00
Bowl, 5¾", Cereal	4.00
Candy w/Lid	15.00
Cocktail Shaker, 32 oz.	12.50
Cup	2.75
Plate, 7¼", Salad	1.75
Plate, 9⅜", Dinner	3.50
Plate, 12", Sandwich	5.00
Saucer	.75
Tumbler, Juice, 2½", 4 oz.	3.00
Tumbler, Old Fashion, 3¼", 8 oz.	5.00
Tumbler, Water, 4½", 11 oz.	4.50
Tumbler, Iced Tea, 16 oz.	7.50

MT. PLEASANT, "DOUBLE SHIELD"   L.E. SMITH GLASS COMPANY, 1920's-1934

Colors: Black amethyst, amethyst, cobalt blue, crystal, pink, green.

My thanks to the many readers who sent pictures of Mt. Pleasant and to those who wrote me about this pattern. Because of you, there are many additions to the Mt. Pleasant listing. When sending such information, it helps to send measurements along with the photos! The 8" blue, leaf dish pictured has caused concern for several years. Various collectors have said it accompanied sets that they bought. Now, several boxed sets have been found in the midwest with these leaves packed in them, so it appears the leaf dish was SOLD with the sets! This makes it a truly interesting piece of Mt. Pleasant. That square snack plate with a crystal cup was found the week before we photographed. It is the same cup found with many of the luncheon sets in black. These are definitely more photogenic than the black.

Not only was Mt. Pleasant given away as promotional items in western New York in the early 1930's, but at hardware stores in Kansas and Nebraska. Keep me informed of any more items not listed. I hope I have them all, but that may not be the case.

	Pink, Green	Black Amethyst, Amethyst, Cobalt		Pink Green	Black Amethyst Cobalt
Bon Bon, Rolled Up Handles, 7"	12.50	16.50	Cup	5.00	8.50
Bowl, 4" Opening, Rose	15.00	17.50	Leaf, 8"		10.00
Bowl, 4", Square Ftd. Fruit	10.00	15.00	Mayonnaise, 5½", 3 Ftd.	12.50	17.50
Bowl, 6", 2 Handled, Sq.	9.00	12.50	Mint, 6", Center Handle	10.00	15.00
Bowl, 7", 3 Ftd., Rolled Out Edge	12.50	16.50	Plate, 7", 2 Handled, Scalloped	6.50	10.00
Bowl, 8", Scalloped, 2 Handled	15.00	20.00	Plate, 8", Scalloped or Square	7.50	11.00
Bowl, 8", Square, 2 Handled	15.00	20.00	Plate, 8", 2 Handled	7.50	13.50
Bowl, 9", Scalloped, 1¾" Deep, Ftd.		25.00	Plate 8¼", Sq. w/Indent for Cup		12.00
Bowl, 9¼", Sq. Ftd. Fruit	15.00	22.50	Plate, 9", Grill		8.50
Bowl, 10", Scalloped Fruit		25.00	Plate, 10½", Cake, 2 Handled	13.50	20.00
Bowl, 10", 2 Handled, Turned Up Edge		22.50	Plate, 12", 2 Handled	15.00	25.00
Candlestick, Single, Pr.	15.00	20.00	Salt and Pepper, 2 Styles	20.00	32.50
Candlestick, Double, Pr.	20.00	30.00	Sandwich Server, Center Handled		27.50
Creamer	9.50	12.50	Sherbet	6.50	12.50
Cup (Waffle-Like Crystal)	3.50		Sugar	9.00	12.50
			Vase, 7¼"		17.50

Please refer to Foreword for pricing information

NEW CENTURY AND INCORRECTLY, "LYDIA RAY" HAZEL ATLAS

GLASS COMPANY, 1930-1935

Colors: Green, pink, amethyst, cobalt and some crystal.

I have had more reports of cobalt cups being found, but strangely enough, no saucers have surfaced with these cups.

That crystal "powder jar" can be made in most patterns if you want to have some fun. All you need is a sherbet and a sugar lid.

New collectors, Ovide has been incorrectly called New Century by another author. This can cause some confusion, but New Century is the name given this pattern by the factory.

	Green, Crystal	Pink, Cobalt Amethyst		Green, Crystal	Pink, Cobalt, Amethyst
Ash Tray/Coaster, 5⅜"	25.00		Plate, 7⅛" Breakfast	5.50	
Bowl, 4½" Berry	5.00		Plate, 8½" Salad	5.50	
Bowl, 4¾" Cream Soup	8.50		Plate, 10" Dinner	9.50	
Bowl, 8" Large Berry	10.00		Plate, 10" Grill	7.50	
Bowl, 9" Covered Casserole	42.50		Platter, 11" Oval	11.00	
Butter Dish and Cover	47.50		Salt and Pepper, Pr.	25.00	
Cup	4.50	12.50	Saucer	2.00	5.00
Creamer	5.50		Sherbet, 3"	5.50	
Decanter and Stopper	35.00		Sugar	5.00	
Goblet, 2½" oz. Wine	11.50		Sugar Cover	8.50	
Goblet, 3¼" oz. Cocktail	12.50		Tumbler, 3½", 5 oz.	7.50	6.50
Pitcher, 7¾", 60 oz. with			Tumbler, 4⅛", 9 oz.	7.50	6.50
or without Ice Lip	25.00	22.50	Tumbler, 5", 10 oz.	9.50	9.00
Pitcher, 8", 80 oz. with			Tumbler, 5¼", 12 oz.	15.00	10.00
or without Ice Lip	27.50	27.50	Tumbler, 4", 5 oz. Footed	8.50	
Plate, 6" Sherbet	2.00		Tumbler, 4⅞", 9 oz. Footed	12.50	
			Whiskey, 2½", 1½ oz.	7.50	

NEWPORT, "HAIRPIN" HAZEL ATLAS GLASS COMPANY, 1936-1940

Colors: Cobalt blue, amethyst, pink, "Platonite" white and fired-on colors.

Pink Newport does exist in more than the berry bowl as many readers have confirmed. I now have a sherbet and large berry bowl. The amazing thing is that a whole set was the gift for selling seeds from a catalogue in the 1930's. That must not have been a banner year for seeds since the pink is hard enough to find a piece at a time! Thanks to the reader who sent me a copy of that information. I will try to get more of these ads in my books as space permits. The major obstacle is that the printer has to have the original and not a copy.

Several collectors wrote to thank me for suggesting white Newport shakers to go with their collections of Petalware, so, I will repeat that idea.

Cereal bowls continue to be the "albatross" for Newport collectors; if you have yours, consider yourself fortunate.

	*Cobalt	Amethyst		*Cobalt	Amethyst
Bowl, 4¼" Berry	10.00	8.50	Plate, 11½" Sandwich	20.00	15.00
Bowl, 4¾" Cream soup	11.00	9.50	Platter, 11¾" Oval	25.00	20.00
Bowl, 5¼" Cereal	20.00	15.00	Salt and Pepper	35.00	32.50
Bowl, 8¼" Large Berry	27.50	25.00	Saucer	2.50	2.50
Cup	7.50	6.50	Sherbet	8.50	7.50
Creamer	9.50	8.00	Sugar	9.50	8.00
Plate, 6" Sherbet	3.50	3.00	Tumbler, 4½", 9 oz.	22.50	20.00
Plate, 8½" Luncheon	7.50	7.50			

*White 50% of Cobalt price.

Please refer to Foreword for pricing information

"NORA BIRD", PADEN CITY GLASS COMPANY, LINE 1300, 1929-30's

Colors: Pink, green.

Collectors have "named" this pattern. To Paden City it was a certain numbered etching on their popular #300 line blank. I've found it in pink and green, possibly it exists in their other colors of yellow and blue. This etching is distinguished by the bird being poised ready for flight. On the cup, saucer and candy holders, however, the bird is already in flight.

	Pink/Green
Candlestick, pr.	40.00
Candy dish w/cover, 6½", 3 pt.	40.00
Creamer, rnd. handle	20.00
Creamer, pointed handle	18.50
Cup	15.00
Ice tub, 6"	42.50
Mayonnaise and liner	45.00
Plate, 8"	15.00
Saucer	10.00
Sugar, rnd, handle	20.00
Sugar, pointed handle	18.50
Tumbler, 3"	20.00
Tumbler, 4"	25.00
Tumbler, 4¾", ftd.	30.00

NORMANDIE, "BOUQUET AND LATTICE" FEDERAL GLASS COMPANY

1933-1940

Colors: Iridescent, amber, pink, crystal

Finding pink Normandie is beginning to drive even the most patient collectors to drink! (They drink only water, of course, because they are saving their money for dinner plates, tumblers, shakers, pitcher and the almost non-existent sugar lid.) Pink could break your pocketbook should you be lucky enough to find these items. Finding them in the first place is the trick.

Amber collectors have fewer problems awaiting them since only the sugar lid and pitcher pose much of a threat to collector's sanity.

Iridescent collectors have it made except for finding salad plates. This color abounds, the only concern is sometimes convincing an owner that what he has is not "rare" Carnival glass.

	Amber	Pink	Iridescent		Amber	Pink	Iridescent
Bowl, 5" Berry	4.00	5.00	4.00	Platter, 11¾"	10.00	14.00	10.00
*Bowl, 6½" Cereal	7.50	9.50	6.50	Salt and Pepper, Pr.	35.00	50.00	
Bowl, 8½" Large Berry	10.00	13.00	9.50	Saucer	1.50	2.00	1.50
Bowl, 10" Oval Veg.	11.00	20.00	12.50	Sherbet	5.00	6.50	6.00
Creamer, Footed	6.00	8.50	6.50	Sugar	5.00	6.00	5.00
Cup	5.00	6.00	5.00	Sugar Lid	65.00	95.00	
Pitcher, 8", 80 oz.	47.50	75.00		Tumbler, 4", 5 oz.			
Plate, 6" Sherbet	2.00	2.00	2.00	Juice	12.00	30.00	
Plate, 8" Salad	6.00	7.50	40.00	Tumbler, 4¼", 9 oz.			
Plate, 9¼" Luncheon	5.00	8.50	7.50	Water	10.00	27.50	
Plate, 11" Dinner	15.00	50.00	12.00	Tumbler, 5", 12 oz.			
Plate, 11" Grill	8.50	10.50	9.00	Iced Tea	15.00	40.00	

*Mistaken by many as butter bottom.

NO. 610, "PYRAMID"   INDIANA GLASS COMPANY, 1926-1932

Colors: Green, pink, yellow, white, crystal and black in 1974-1975 for Tiara

The white bowl shown must be from Indiana's 1950's marketing splurge of white. Pitchers for this pattern are very difficult to find in all colors. The crystal one shown in the 6th Edition was found in Washington C.H., Ohio, for $8.00.

The prices quoted below are for mint condition glassware. The pattern chipped easily with all those protruding points, so check it carefully **before** you buy.

All yellow Pyramid is difficult to find. Footed iced teas in all colors are also hard to locate.

	Crystal, Pink	Green	Yellow
Bowl, 4¾" Berry	12.50	13.50	22.50
Bowl, 8½" Master Berry	17.50	20.00	40.00
Bowl, 9½" Oval	22.50	22.50	45.00
Bowl, 9½" Pickle	22.50	22.50	45.00
Creamer	16.50	16.50	25.00
Ice Tub	65.00	75.00	175.00
Ice Tub and Lid			550.00
Pitcher	150.00	185.00	395.00
Relish Tray, 4 Part Handled	30.00	37.50	50.00
Sugar	16.50	17.50	25.00
Tray for Creamer and Sugar	16.00	20.00	40.00
Tumbler, 8 oz. Footed	20.00	25.00	42.50
Tumbler, 11 oz. Footed	35.00	45.00	55.00

NO. 612. "HORSESHOE"   INDIANA GLASS COMPANY, 1930-1933

Colors: Green, yellow, pink, crystal.

"Horseshoe", as collectors have dubbed this Indiana pattern, has suffered the same fate of many other expensive Depression glass patterns. It has been priced so high that most beginning collectors can not afford to collect it. This has brought the old law of supply and demand into effect. The supply is growing as more people recognize Depression glass, but without new collectors for the pattern, the price on some harder-to-get items has dropped a little lately. In the long run, this may help collecting by reducing the price so new collectors will be tempted to start acquiring this desirable pattern.

Be aware that plates and platters come with and without the center motif. You can see both types in the picture.

Grill plates are difficult to find, but a lot of collectors do not like divided plates, so the price does not readily reflect how rare they are because they aren't in demand.

	Green	Yellow		Green	Yellow
Bowl, 4½" Berry	15.00	14.00	Plate, 8⅜" Salad	6.00	7.00
Bowl, 6½" Cereal	14.50	15.00	Plate, 9⅜" Luncheon	7.50	7.50
Bowl, 7½" Salad	12.50	15.00	Plate, 10⅜" Dinner	14.50	15.00
Bowl, 8½" Vegetable	16.00	22.50	Plate, 10⅜" grill	22.50	22.50
Bowl, 9½" Large Berry	22.50	25.00	Plate, 11" Sandwich	9.00	11.50
Bowl, 10½" Oval Vegetable	15.00	17.50	Platter, 10¾" Oval	14.50	15.00
Butter Dish and Cover	425.00		Relish, 3 Part Footed	20.00	35.00
Butter Dish Bottom	125.00		Saucer	3.00	3.50
Butter Dish Top	300.00		Sherbet	10.00	11.50
Candy in Metal Holder			Sugar, Open	10.00	10.50
Motif on Lid—82.50			Tumbler, 4¼", 9 oz.	55.00	
Also, Pink	125.00		Tumbler, 4¾", 12 oz.	70.00	
Creamer, Footed	11.50	12.50	Tumbler, 9 oz. Footed	14.00	15.00
Cup	7.00	7.50	Tumbler, 12 oz. Footed	70.00	72.50
Pitcher, 8½", 64 oz.	195.00	210.00			
Plate, 6" Sherbet	3.00	4.50			

Please refer to Foreword for pricing information

NO. 616, "VERNON"   INDIANA GLASS COMPANY, 1931-1932

Colors: Green, crystal, yellow.

"Vernon", as it is known to most collectors, has a problem being accepted due to its few number of pieces. Collect seven different pieces and you have all the ones you are going to find.

It really is an attractive pattern in green or yellow. We used to have the crystal tumblers for every day use, but after breaking a few, they were retired from circulation. It was them or my nerves.

Since there are new sugar and creamer collectors today, you will find some demand for these.

	Green	Crystal	Yellow
Creamer, Footed	20.00	9.00	17.50
Cup	12.00	5.00	11.00
Plate, 8" Luncheon	5.00	4.00	5.50
Plate, 11" Sandwich	17.50	10.00	16.00
Saucer	3.50	2.00	3.50
Sugar, Footed	19.50	8.00	17.50
Tumbler, 5" Footed	25.00	10.00	22.50

NO. 618, "PINEAPPLE & FLORAL"   INDIANA GLASS COMPANY, 1932-1937

Colors: Crystal, amber; some fired-on red, green; Late 60's; avocado.

Pink salad bowls are currently being made by Indiana in Pineapple & Floral. I have been seeing an abundance of these around the flea market priced at $3.00. If you check your local dish outlet, you will find these for less than a dollar.

I received numerous calls for the fired-on red when I advertised it; there are collectors of that color! Besides those red pieces shown, I have only seen a small tumbler. Note that the sugar and creamer are slightly different shades of red.

If this pattern has any drawback, it has to be the mould roughness along the mould seams on most of the pieces. Some of the tumblers I have owned would cause lip damage if not used carefully.

Most of the large cone-shaped vases are being found in black metal stands in funeral homes. I did see a white stand, but it may have been painted to hide rust or chipped paint.

	Crystal	Amber, Red		Crystal	Amber, Red
Ash Tray, 4½"	13.00	16.00	Plate, 11½" Indentation	20.00	
Bowl, 4¾" Berry	17.50	13.00	Plate, 11½" Sandwich	12.50	13.50
Bowl, 6" Cereal	17.50	15.00	Platter, 11" Closed Handles	10.00	11.50
Bowl, 7" Salad	2.50	8.50	Platter, Relish, 11½"		
Bowl, 10" Oval Vegetable	18.00	15.00	Divided	14.00	9.50
Comport, Diamond Shaped	1.50	6.50	Saucer	2.00	2.00
Creamer, Diamond Shaped	6.50	8.50	Sherbet, Footed	15.00	15.00
Cream Soup	17.50	17.50	Sugar, Diamond Shaped	6.50	8.50
Cup	6.50	6.00	Tumbler, 4¼", 8 oz.	20.00	25.00
Plate, 6" Sherbet	3.00	4.00	Tumbler, 5", 12 oz.	30.00	
Plate, 8⅜" Salad	5.00	6.00	Vase, Cone Shaped	25.00	
*Plate, 9⅜" Dinner	10.00	12.50	Vase Holder (17.50)		

*Green—$21.50

OLD CAFE   HOCKING GLASS COMPANY, 1936-1938; 1940

Colors: Pink, crystal, Royal Ruby

Old Cafe is a less expensive pattern to collect, and as such, it is being sought by several beginning Depression glass enthusiasts. Due to this, there are a few pieces that are in shorter supply than they have ever been, and the price is rising fast on these.

The dinner plate may be one of the things that attracts people to Old Cafe. Most smaller patterns do not have one. These are increasingly difficult to find as are the lamps. Still around for now are the tumblers, but they are being bought up fast!

The juice pitcher was never shown in old catalogues, but I am willing to accept it as Old Cafe (as many collectors have). However, I am having difficulty accepting the larger one as Old Cafe. The major reason is that it is found more frequently in green than pink, and green is not one of the colors found in this pattern. The pitcher was made by Hocking, but not for Old Cafe. If you want it as a "go-with" piece, fine.

Another "go-with" cookie jar is being collected with this set. It is ribbed like Old Cafe but has a cross hatched lid design. Made by Hocking as a numbered item, it will serve as a substitute for a cookie jar in this pattern.

Please note there are no Royal Ruby saucers for the cups. Ruby cups were sold on crystal saucers.

	Crystal, Pink	Royal Ruby		Crystal, Pink	Royal Ruby
Bowl, 3¾" Berry	2.00	4.00	Pitcher, 6", 36 oz.	47.50	
Bowl, 5", One or Two Handles	3.00		Pitcher, 80 oz.	67.50	
Bowl, 5½" Cereal	4.00	8.50	Plate, 6" Sherbet	1.50	
Bowl, 9", Closed Handles	7.50	11.50	Plate, 10" Dinner	15.50	
Candy Dish, 8" Low	5.00	10.00	Saucer	1.50	
Cup	3.00	6.00	Sherbet, Low Footed	4.50	
Lamp	12.50	20.00	Tumbler, 3" Juice	6.50	7.50
Olive Dish, 6" Oblong	4.00		Tumbler, 4" Water	6.00	
			Vase, 7¼"	8.50	13.50

OLD ENGLISH, "THREADING"   INDIANA GLASS COMPANY

Colors: Green, amber; some pink, crystal, forest green.

Old English has not jumped dramatically in price, but it has made some steady increases. Lack of plates, cups and saucers have kept more collectors from seeking this pattern. Art Deco advocates admire it more than others, and a few of the decorated crystal pitcher and tumbler sets have really caused a stir among them.

The chip and dip (cheese and cracker) set is shown with mismatched colors. When buying for pictures, you take what you can get. Pink seems to be the hardest color to find, but green is the color usually collected. There are few collectors for amber; other colors surface infrequently. The crystal egg cup sells for around $7.50 and has never been found in any other color to date.

The center handled server in Old English is the hardest single item to find.

The pitcher lid has the same cloverleaf knob as that shown on the sugar. These pitcher lids are similar in size to the candy lid, but they are notched to allow pouring.

	Pink, Green, Amber		Pink, Green, Amber
Bowl, 4" Flat	11.00	Pitcher and Cover	85.00
Bowl, 9" Footed Fruit	22.50	Plate, Indent for Compote	17.50
Bowl, 9½" Flat	22.50	Sandwich Server, Center Handle	37.50
Candlesticks, 4" Pr.	22.50	Sherbet, 2 Styles	14.50
Candy Dish & Cover, Flat	37.50	Sugar	11.00
Candy Jar with Lid	35.00	Sugar Cover	20.00
Candy Jar, 9¾", 2 Handles	25.00	Tumbler, 4½" Footed	12.50
Compote, 3½ Tall, 7" Across	12.50	Tumbler, 5½" Footed	20.00
Creamer	11.50	Vase, 5⅜", Fan Type, 7"	
Egg Cup (Crystal)	6.50	Across	32.50
Fruit Stand, 11" Footed	30.00	Vase, 12" Footed	35.00
Goblet, 5¾", 8 oz.	20.00		
Pitcher	50.00		

Please refer to Foreword for pricing information

"ORCHID"   PADEN CITY GLASS COMPANY, Early 1930's

Colors: Yellow, cobalt blue, green, amber, pink, red and black.

Orchid pattern is found as a console set more frequently than any other way, (that's a bowl and candlesticks for those who are just learning glassware terminology).

The designs of Orchid are etched on several blanks but most appear on Paden City's "crows foot" blanks (line #412). See the teardrop/"crow's foot" effect in the picture.

The square plate shown in cobalt blue is one of six that sat at a flea market for two years with an astronomical price on them. My wife tried to buy them several times and so did I. The price was so high that no one else ever bought them. Finally, the dealers had a half price sale. Since they are lightly scratched, it was still no great bargain. It was just that I had never seen any other plates to get one to photograph for you.

	Amber, Pink, Green, Yellow	Red, Black Cobalt Blue
Bowl, 4⅞" Square	10.00	20.00
Bowl, 8½", 2 handled	22.50	42.50
Bowl, 8¾" Square	20.00	40.00
Candlesticks, 5¾" Pair	30.00	47.50
Creamer	15.00	30.00
Comport, 6¼"	15.00	25.00
Ice Bucket, 6"	35.00	57.50
Mayonnaise, 3 Pc.	30.00	45.00
Plate, 8½", Square		25.00
Sandwich Server, Center Handled	25.00	45.00
Sugar	15.00	30.00
Vase, 10"	40.00	75.00

OVIDE, incorrectly dubbed "NEW CENTURY"   HAZEL ATLAS GLASS
COMPANY, 1930-1935

Colors: Green, black, white Platonite trimmed with fired-on colors.

Ovide has few collectors although those Art Deco designed items would sell well if more were available! The "flying ducks" (geese?) design was borrowed from the same collector who has the Art Deco set. I finally own a sugar and creamer in the Art Deco decoration, but I have never found other pieces for sale.

The sterling floral designs on black Ovide are eagerly picked up by some. The word "sterling" will be found incorporated in the floral design.

Some Ovide is being bought because it is reasonably inexpensive, but the plainer patterns have never had a history of being widely accepted by collectors.

	Black	Green	Decorated White		Black	Green	Decorated White
Bowl, 4¾" Berry			10.00	Plate, 8" Luncheon		1.50	9.00
Bowl, 5½" Cereal			12.50	Plate, 9" Dinner			10.00
Bowl, 8" Large Berry			25.00	Platter, 11"			15.00
Candy Dish and Cover	25.00	15.00	35.00	Salt and Pepper, Pr.	20.00	9.00	35.00
Cocktail, Footed Fruit	3.00	2.00		Saucer	2.00	1.25	4.00
Creamer	5.00	2.50	25.00	Sherbet	5.00	1.50	17.50
Cup	5.00	2.00	15.00	Sugar, Open	5.00	2.50	25.00
Plate, 6" Sherbet		1.00	5.00	Tumbler			25.00

Please refer to Foreword for pricing information

OYSTER AND PEARL   ANCHOR HOCKING GLASS CORPORATION, 1938-1940

Colors: Pink, crystal, Royal Ruby, white with fired-on pink or green.

Oyster and Pearl is a pattern that few collectors buy as a set. Mostly, this is bought as accessory items. The pattern is inexpensive except for the Royal Ruby. Actually, even the red is a bargain when you consider the size of the large bowl and plate.

For some reason the fired-on colors have been ignored. Personally, I can not find much to say about them in a positive vein because I am not overly fond of them myself.

People who buy their friends old glass instead of new find the oblong relish a great gift item. It sells for less than most anything you can find new. It's useful; and it has the advantage of being nearly antique!

Note the difference in the one handled bowls. Unfortunately, the red does not come with the spout, making it heart shaped. That would be a great seller for Valentine's Day.

	Crystal, Pink	Royal Ruby	White With Fired On Green Or Pink
Bowl, 5¼" Heart Shaped One Handled	5.00		5.00
Bowl, 6½" Deep handled	8.00	15.00	
Bowl, 10½" Deep Fruit	16.00	30.00	11.00
Candleholder, 3½" Pr.	15.00	30.00	12.50
Plate, 13½" Sandwich	10.00	27.50	
Relish Dish, 10¼" Oblong	6.00		

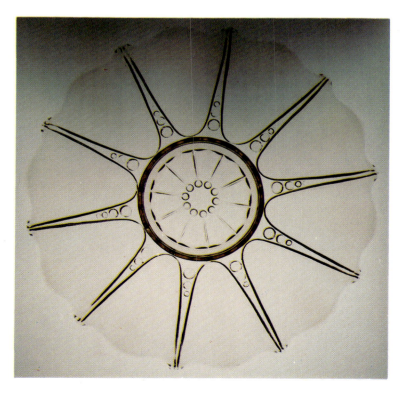

"PARROT", SYLVAN   FEDERAL GLASS COMPANY, 1931-1932

Colors: Green, amber; some crystal and blue.

After showing you the blue Parrot in the 6th Edition, I hoped to receive a few letters from readers telling me that they had seen a whole set, but . . . no such luck. As long as I have been researching glassware, I have been told over and over by factory employees that the factory never made only one of an item. They always made several dozen at least, so I am astounded at how many one-of-a-kind items are known today.

The newest discovery in Parrot is another style hot plate. The first style is like those of Madrid with points around the edge (pictured p.113). The new style, below, is like the Georgian, round without points. Two separate moulds on such a rare piece is hard to imagine.

Federal named this pattern Sylvan (a woods dweller), and, of course, that's apt. However, it's universally called "Parrot" by collectors, and thus, it's listed here by its "nickname" since few could locate it by its real name.

Prices for "Parrot", like other Depression glass patterns, have increased only slightly, but steadily during the past economic crisis. This is probably due less to economics than to the limited supply available at the present time. Only sherbets and the green oval vegetable bowl and platter seem to be abundant.

A "find" of 37 green pitchers in an old hardware store years ago was diminished by two in handling. That is one reason why so few pitchers have been found; there's some fragility factor at work in the design. These "Parrot" pitchers are like an endangered species and should be treated accordingly! To date, no amber pitcher has turned up.

The pointed ridges on the cups, sherbets, sugar lids, et cetera, should be carefully checked for damage. They tend to flake and chip. Again, don't pay MINT Prices for DAMAGED or noticeably REPAIRED glassware! Sugar lids, in particular, fit the latter category. I have no quarrel with repairing glass, it salvages much that would otherwise be lost to us. However, repaired glass should always be so marked, and you should exercise caution as to who repairs your glass. Some so called repairmen are grinders and butchers. Ask to see examples of their work and then decide. Are edges rounded and smoothed to near mint condition, or are they left flattened and sharp? Are chips and flakes ground away leaving dips in the surface, or is the entire edge reworked to insure uniformity? Does their equipment leave minute "scars" and "hairline" cracks, or is the resultant work indeed as "smooth as glass"?

	Green	Amber		Green	Amber
Bowl, 5" Berry	12.50	10.00	Sherbet, 4¼" High	150.00	
Bowl, 7" Soup	25.00	25.00	Sugar	20.00	19.50
Bowl, 8" Large Berry	50.00	60.00	Sugar Cover	85.00	277.50
Bowl, 10" Oval Vegetable	35.00	45.00	Tumbler, 4¼", 10 oz.	80.00	80.00
Butter Dish and Cover	227.50	557.50	Tumbler, 5½", 12 oz.	100.00	100.00
Butter Dish Bottom	27.50	200.00	Tumbler, 5¾" Footed		
Butter Dish Top	200.00	257.50	Heavy	90.00	95.00
Creamer, Footed	20.00	22.50	Tumbler, 5½", 10 oz.		
Cup	22.50	22.50	Thin (Madrid Mold)		90.00
Hot Plate, 5", 2 Styles	400.00				
Pitcher, 8½", 80 oz.	750.00				
Plate, 5¾" Sherbet	15.00	10.00			
Plate, 7½" Salad	15.00				
Plate, 9" Dinner	27.50	25.00			
Plate, 10½" Round Grill	17.50				
Plate, 10½" Square Grill		16.00			
Plate, 10¼" Square	45.00	45.00			
Platter, 11¼" Oblong	25.00	45.00			
Salt and Pepper, Pr.	177.50				
Saucer	8.50	8.50			
*Sherbet, Footed Cone	15.00	13.50			

*Blue $75.00

PATRICIAN, "SPOKE"   FEDERAL GLASS COMPANY, 1933-1937

Colors: Pink, green, amber ("Golden Glow"), yellow.

Federal's "Golden Glow" Patrician is still the most popular color with today's collector, and except for a few pieces, it is still relatively easy to find! The dinner plates remain among the least expensive in Depression glass! In many patterns, now, dinner plates are becoming scarce! Some collectors are even turning to grill plates in order to have plates to use with their sets.

For some reason, the supply of sherbets exceeds the demand, and the price of the saucer is now equal to that of the cup.

Patrician has a pitcher and cookie jar shaped like a hexagon which has always intrigued collectors and non-collectors alike. Pitchers with applied handles (shown in crystal) are seen less frequently than those with molded handles. Neither type is frequently found. They both have a 75 ounce capacity, but the moulded handle type stands only 8" high, whereas the applied handle pitcher stands 8¼" tall.

Check all sugar lids for damage and repair.

	Amber, Crystal	Pink	Green		Amber, Crystal	Pink	Green
Bowl, 4¾" Cream Soup	10.00	15.00	15.00	Plate, 7½" Salad	9.50	12.50	9.50
Bowl, 5" Berry	6.50	9.50	7.50	Plate, 9" Luncheon	7.00	6.50	6.50
Bowl, 6" Cereal	15.00	17.50	17.50	Plate, 10½" Dinner	5.00	14.00	25.00
Bowl, 8½" Large Berry	30.00	17.50	17.50	Plate, 10½" Grill	7.50	9.50	9.50
Bowl, 10" Oval				Platter, 11½" Oval	10.00	10.00	12.50
Vegetable	17.50	15.00	15.00	Salt and Pepper, Pr.	40.00	65.00	45.00
Butter Dish and Cover	60.00	190.00	89.50	Saucer	5.00	5.00	5.00
Butter Dish Bottom	45.00	145.00	50.00	Sherbet	7.50	8.00	8.00
Butter Dish Top	22.50	45.00	39.50	Sugar	5.00	7.00	7.00
Cookie Jar and Cover	55.00		275.00	Sugar Cover	30.00	40.00	40.00
Creamer, Footed	6.00	8.50	9.50	Tumbler, 4", 5 oz.	20.00	20.00	20.00
Cup	5.00	7.50	8.00	Tumbler, 4½", 9 oz.	18.00	18.50	18.50
Jam Dish	15.00	20.00	25.00	Tumbler, 5½", 14 oz.	25.00	22.00	25.00
Pitcher, 8", 75 oz.	75.00	75.00	80.00	Tumbler, 5¼", 8 oz.			
Pitcher, 8¼", 75 oz.	77.50	75.00	80.00	Footed	28.00		37.50
Plate, 6" Sherbet	6.50	4.50	4.50				

"PATRICK"   LANCASTER GLASS COMPANY, Early 1930's

Colors: Yellow, pink.

For reasons I can not understand, collectors have largely ignored this brother pattern to "Jubilee". How the pattern ever got the name "Patrick" is beyond me.

Patrick is characterized by a three flowered bouquet in the center of the design which is accompanied by flowers at either side attached to gracefully sprangled fronds. Although there are seemingly more pieces to be found in "Patrick" than in "Jubilee", it could use a better publicity agent to inform collectors of that.

Since serving pieces in both patterns are so hard to find, many collectors are turning to the plainer yellow pieces of Depression glass to use with their sets.

	Yellow/ Pink		Yellow/ Pink
Bowl, 9", Handled Fruit	20.00	Mayonnaise, 3 Pc.	27.50
Bowl, 11", Console	22.50	Plate, 7" Sherbet	5.00
Candlesticks, Pr.	30.00	Plate, 7½" Salad	6.00
Candy Dish, 3 Ftd.	32.50	Plate, 8" Luncheon	6.50
Cheese & Cracker Set	30.00	Saucer	2.00
Creamer	10.50	Sherbet, 4¾"	12.50
Cup	8.00	Sugar	10.00
Goblet, 4" Cocktail	15.00	Tray, 11", 2 Handled	17.50
Goblet, 4¾", 6 oz. Juice	15.00	Tray, 11", Ctr. Handled	22.50
Goblet, 6", 10 oz. Water	22.00		

Please refer to Foreword for pricing information

"PEACOCK REVERSE", LINE 412   PADEN CITY, 1930's

Colors: Cobalt blue, red, yellow, black.

"Peacock Reverse" tumblers are found on Paden City's Penny Line # 991. The rest of the pattern can be found on Line #412 which is commonly called "Crow's Foot" by collectors. I have seen a number of "Crow's Foot" pieces since the last book, however, I've seen only a very few pieces of "Peacock Reverse". Except for a divided candy dish in yellow discovered at a Louisville flea market, every piece has been in red or black.

Please let me know what you find! I am sure that we have only scratched the surface of discoveries in this pattern.

	All Colors		All Colors
Bowl, 4⅞" Square	20.00	Plate, 5¾" Sherbet	17.50
Bowl, 8¾" Square	50.00	Plate, 8½" Luncheon	25.00
Bowl, 8¾" Square with Handles	57.50	Saucer	10.00
Candlesticks, 5¾" Sq. Base, Pr.	72.50	Sherbet, 4⅝" Tall, 3⅜" Diameter	32.50
Candy Dish, 6½" Squared	57.50	Sherbet, 4⅞" Tall, 3⅝ Diameter	32.50
Creamer, 2¾" Flat	47.50	Sugar, 2¾" Flat	47.50
Cup	27.50	Tumbler, 4", 10 oz. Flat	42.50
		Vase, 10"	67.50

"PEACOCK & WILD ROSE"   PADEN CITY GLASS CO., LINE 1300, 1930's

Colors: Pink, green, cobalt blue, black, red.

Peacock and Wild Rose is a pattern that grows on you. Most often you will see the 10" vase as it is the most commonly found piece. My surprise was in finding these in black which I had never seen before.

This was a popular line for Paden City. It's probable there are other new pieces to be found with this particular etching. Thank you for reporting any new pieces you find.

	All Colors
Bowl, 8½", Flat	22.50
Bowl, 8½", Fruit, Oval, Ftd.	32.50
Bowl, 8¾", Ftd.	25.00
Bowl, 9½", Ctr. Hand.	30.00
Bowl, 9½", Ftd.	27.50
Bowl, 10½", Ctr. Hand.	32.50
Bowl, 10½", Ftd.	37.50
Bowl, 10½", Fruit	35.00
Bowl, 11", Console	30.00
Bowl, 14", Console	37.50
Candlestick, 5"	18.00
Candy Dish w/Cover, 7"	57.50
Comport, 6¼"	20.00
Ice Bucket, 6"	45.00
Ice Tub, 4¾"	40.00
Plate, Cake, Low Ft.	27.50
Relish, 3 pt.	20.00
Vase, 10"	57.50

PETALWARE   MACBETH-EVANS GLASS COMPANY, 1930-1940

Colors: Monax, cremax, pink, crystal, cobalt and fired-on red, blue, green and yellow.

Petalware sells very well in decorated monax, but the plain and pink are slow to move from dealers' shelves. Now would be a good time to buy in quantity if you can find it that way. I look for there to be more awareness of this pattern in the future.

The red edged pieces of Petalware in the top photograph were marketed as "Florette" and are perhaps the most desirable of all Petalware dishes to own! You generally find a piece here and there rather than bunches of items at one time. Notice how attractive the fired-on red sherbet is when grouped with these red trimmed pieces. Seeing it alone at a market isn't nearly so stimulating or interesting.

In the bottom photograph, you see the cobalt mustard dish (sans its metal lid) which my wife uses to individually serve fruit, custard, or sherbet at home. Also, notice the gold trimmed cremax pieces which more collectors admire than they do the perfectly plain cremax color. There, too, are representatives of pink Petalware which is a good buy at today's prices.

The red "ribbon" decorator plates were sold with eight different fruits--among them a "Florence Cherry" which appealed to me for obvious reasons!

No shakers are found for Petalware, however, many collectors blend Newport shakers in Monax with their sets.

Many lamp shades are to be found with Petalware design from small individual types to large Chinese coolie hat shapes. These are more interesting than collectible today, due to a dearth of the type lamps these fit. The small shades are generally priced $8.00-$10.00, and the larger ones around $15.00. I'm certain some Petalware collector out there has a unique use for these. Let me hear about it so I can pass the information to other collectors.

I'm often asked for an idea of a pattern to collect that is attractive, inexpensive and easily found. Here it is! Monax Petalware fits the criteria to a tee. Not only that, but it can be "dressed up" simply with a bright tablecloth, centerpiece flowers and food! It's like nothing you find in the stores today and friends and guests will love it!

	Pink, Crystal	Plain	CREMAX, MONAX Fired-On Decorations
Bowl, 4½" Cream Soup	4.00	5.50	8.50
Bowl, 5¾" Cereal	3.00	4.50	6.50
Bowl, 7" Soup		6.50	12.00
*Bowl, 9" Large Berry	7.50	12.50	15.00
Cup	2.25	4.50	6.00
**Creamer, Footed	2.50	4.50	8.00
Lamp Shade (many Sizes) $8.00 to $15.00			
Mustard with Metal Cover in cobalt Blue Only $6.00			
Pitcher, 80 oz. (Crystal Decorated Bands)	20.00		
Plate, 6" Sherbet	1.50	2.00	4.00

	Pink, Crystal	Plain	CREMAX, MONAX Fired-On Decorations
Plate, 8" Salad	1.75	3.00	6.00
Plate, 9" Dinner	2.50	3.50	7.50
Plate, 11" Salver	3.50	5.00	12.00
Plate, 12" Salver		6.50	15.00
Platter, 13" Oval	5.00	7.50	15.00
Saucer	1.00	1.50	2.50
Sherbet, 4" Low Footed		12.50	
**Sherbet, 4½" Low Footed	3.00	4.50	7.50
**Sugar, Footed	2.50	4.50	7.50
Tidbit Servers or Lazy Susans, Several Styles 12.00 to 17.50			
***Tumblers (Crystal Decorated Bands) 2.50 to 7.50			

*Also in cobalt at 37.50
**Also in cobalt at 20.00
***Several Sizes

Please refer to Foreword for pricing information

"PRETZEL", NO. 622,   INDIANA GLASS COMPANY, 1930's-1970's

Colors: Crystal, teal.

This is another of Indiana's numbered patterns that has been nicknamed so long that now it's "Pretzel" and nothing else. A pitcher and three sizes of tumblers are listed in Indiana's catalogues, and compliments of Byron Canine, you can see these for the first time. Note also the teal cup which I had never seen.

There are many pieces found with fruits embossed in the bottom, and you will find both plain and stippled designs inside the loops making up the pattern.

Another new piece is the square snack tray with indent for cup.

The plentiful leaf-shaped olive dish, the 8½", 2 handled pickle and the 10¼" celery tray have all been made in recent years.

Besides the pitcher and tumblers, the sherbet cups and 9⅜" berry bowl are the hardest pieces to locate.

	Crystal
Bowl, 7½" Soup	5.00
Bowl, 9⅜" Berry	10.00
Celery, 10¼" Tray	2.50
Creamer	4.50
Cup	3.50
Olive, 7" Leaf Shape	1.50
Pickle, 8½", 2 Hdld.	2.00
Pitcher, 39 oz.	50.00
Plate, 6"	1.50
Plate 7¼" Square, Indent	6.00
Plate, 7¼" Square, Indent 3-Part	6.00
Plate, 8⅜" Salad	3.00
Plate, 9⅜" Dinner	4.00
Plate, 11½" Sandwich	7.00
Saucer	1.00
Sherbet, Flat	3.00
Sugar	3.50
Tumbler, 5 oz., 3½"	5.00
Tumbler, 9 oz., 4½"	8.00
Tumbler, 12 oz., 5½"	10.00

PRIMO, "PANELLED ASTER",   U.S. GLASS COMPANY, Early 1930's

Colors: Green, yellow.

Primo comes in green and yellow, but there are black and pink coaster/ash trays just like the ones under the tumblers in the picture. These coasters do not have the pattern impressed on them, so they have been used for patterns other than Primo.

This small line of glassware has some unique shapes!

My wife is positive she's seen a center-handled server in it; I'm awaiting a picture as proof.

A lot of mould roughness is found on most pieces.

	Yellow/Green		Yellow/Green
Bowl, 4½"	6.50	Plate, 10" Dinner	10.00
Bowl, 7¾"	12.50	Plate, 10" Grill	7.50
Cake Plate, 10", 3 Ftd.	13.50	Saucer	1.50
Coaster/Ash Tray	6.00	Sherbet	6.50
Creamer	7.50	Sugar	7.50
Cup	6.50	Tumbler, 5¾", 9 oz.	10.00
Plate, 7½"	5.00		

Please refer to Foreword for pricing information

PRINCESS   HOCKING GLASS COMPANY, 1931-1935.

Colors: Green, topaz and apricot yellow, pink, blue.

A new find in Princess is an 8½", three-footed bowl in pink! It was found in Texas!

There are two distinct shades of yellow Princess. Topaz yellow is a very pretty, light shade, whereas apricot is more amber than yellow. Both are collectible, but there is more demand for the topaz. Amber pieces are considered to be more novel than rare.

Satinized pieces, represented in the picture by the pink sugar and creamer, are virtually ignored by collectors. These items bring 20 to 30 percent less when they sell.

I never do a show that someone doesn't walk up and ask what the name of this pattern is because their grandmother or someone "had" a piece of it. The next question is, "Is this what's called Depression glass?" It still astounds me that there are MULTITUDES of people in this country who haven't the faintest idea what Depression glass is or that it has any value!

Also shown is the rarely seen blue cookie jar, cup and saucer. I talked with a dealer who turned down a set of the blue at a Texas show because he knew it came from Mexico and was leary of it. That brings us to the fact that there is quite a bit of "odd" glass coming from below the border, namely the Florentine sherbet from a Madrid shaped mould, the blue Florentine pitcher, and a crystal bowl similar to No. 612. As I see it, there are two thoughts on this. Either it's reproduction, or it was made by the various companies for a specific market there. Quite a bit of Depression glass is found in Canada and I'm getting letter after letter from England from people who are discovering it there and are wanting books for more information. People find it in Scotland, the Virgin Islands, Hawaii and Alaska. So, it seems likely that there were markets for the glass in these areas. Perhaps there was a specific market for blue Princess below our borders. I would like to think so since it is so good looking!

The 4½" berry bowl is becoming hard to find in all colors. Some dealers call the non-divided relish a "soup" bowl.

The 5½" spice shakers, which closely match Princess, were sold with "Dove" black pepper rather than by Hocking as Princess pattern as far as I can tell. Collectors call these "Dove".

	Green	Pink	Yellow Amber		Green	Pink	Yellow Amber
Ash Tray, 4½"	50.00	57.50	67.50	Plate, 11½" Grill, Closed			
Bowl, 4½" Berry	16.50	10.00	27.50	Handles	7.50	5.00	6.00
Bowl, 5" Cereal or Oatmeal	18.50	13.50	22.50	Plate, 11½" Handled			
Bowl, 9" Octagonal Salad	22.50	16.50	65.00	Sandwich	9.50	7.50	8.50
Bowl, 9½" Hat Shaped	25.00	14.50	85.00	Platter, 12" Closed Handles	12.50	11.00	30.00
Bowl, 10" Oval Vegetable	16.00	15.00	37.50	Relish, 7½" Divided	17.50	12.50	47.50
Butter Dish and Cover	55.00	70.00	450.00	Relish, 7½" Plain	60.00		100.00
Butter Dish Bottom	20.00	20.00	200.00	Salt and Pepper, 4½" Pair	37.50	30.00	40.00
Butter Dish Top	35.00	45.00	250.00	Spice Shakers, 5½" Pair	30.00		
Cake Stand, 10"	14.50	12.00		*** Saucer (Same as Sherbet			
Candy Dish and Cover	35.00	37.50		Plate)	3.50	3.00	3.00
Coaster	22.50	52.50	67.50	Sherbet, Footed	13.50	11.00	25.00
* Cookie Jar and Cover	35.00	40.00		Sugar	8.50	6.50	9.50
Creamer, Oval	9.00	8.50	9.50	Sugar Cover	12.50	11.50	12.50
** Cup	8.00	6.50	7.50	Tumbler, 3", 5 oz. Juice	20.00	16.00	18.00
Pitcher, 6", 37 oz.	35.00	25.00	500.00	Tumbler, 4", 9 oz. Water	20.00	14.00	18.00
Pitcher, 7⅜", 24 oz. Footed	400.00	400.00		Tumbler, 5¼", 13 oz. Iced			
Pitcher, 8", 60 oz.	32.50	32.00	55.00	Tea	25.00	16.50	20.00
*** Plate, 5½" Sherbet	5.00	3.50	4.50	Tumbler, 4¾", 9 oz. Sq. Ftd.	50.00	42.50	
Plate, 8" Salad	8.50	6.50	7.50	Tumbler, 5¼", 10 oz. Footed	20.00	15.00	15.00
Plate, 9" Dinner	17.50	11.00	11.00	Tumbler, 6½", 12½ oz.			
** Plate, 9" Grill	9.50	6.50	6.50	Footed	55.00	35.00	75.00
				Vase, 8"	22.00	17.50	

*Blue—$500.00

**Blue—$75.00

***Blue—$45.00

Please refer to Foreword for pricing information

QUEEN MARY (PRISMATIC LINE), "VERTICAL RIBBED"   HOCKING

GLASS COMPANY, 1936-1949

Colors: Pink, crystal; some Ruby Red.

Queen Mary pink dinner plates and footed tumblers are the key to completing a set of this pattern. There are no reports of pink shakers, but don't give up yet! At a Texas show, one lady was delighted to find Queen Mary dinner plates that she claimed to have been seeking for over two years! Perhaps that should tell us something!

Beginning collectors should know that there are two sizes of cups to be found in this "Prismatic Line" as Hocking called it. The smaller cup is the easiest to locate, and it fits on a saucer with a cup ring. The larger cup fits on Hocking's typical saucer/sherbet plate, one plate serving a dual purpose. During the Royal Ruby promotion of the early '40's, some pieces of Queen Mary were made in red. I've seen the candlestick and large bowl. In the early '50's, a 3½" round ash tray was made in Forest Green and Royal Ruby.

	Pink	Crystal		Pink	Crystal
Ash Tray, 2" x 3¾" Oval	3.50	2.00	Comport, 5¾"	5.00	4.50
*Ash Tray, 3½" Round		2.00	Creamer, Oval	4.50	4.00
Bowl, 4" One Handle Or None	3.00	2.00	Cup (2 sizes)	5.00	4.50
Bowls, 5" Berry, 6" Cereal	3.50	2.50	Plate, 6" and 6⅝"	2.50	2.50
Bowl, 5½", Two Handles	4.00	3.00	Plate, 8½" Salad	4.00	3.50
Bowl, 7" Small	5.00	4.00	Plate, 9¾" Dinner	20.00	7.00
Bowl, 8¾" Large Berry	7.50	6.00	Plate, 12" Relish, 3 Sections	8.50	6.00
Butter Dish or Preserve and			Plate, 12" Sandwich	6.50	5.50
Cover	75.00	20.00	Plate, 14" Serving Tray	8.00	7.50
Butter Dish Bottom	10.00	4.00	Relish Tray, 12", 3 Part	8.50	8.50
Butter Dish Top	65.00	16.00	Relish Tray, 14", 4 Part	8.50	8.50
Candy Dish and Cover	20.00	12.00	Salt and Pepper, pr.		12.50
**Candlesticks, 4½" Double			Saucer	1.50	1.50
Branch, Pr.		12.00	Sherbet, Footed	4.00	3.50
Celery or Pickle Dish, 5" x 10"	4.50	3.50	Sugar, Oval	4.50	4.00
Cigarette Jar, 2" x 3" Oval	5.50	3.50	Tumbler, 3½", 5 oz. Juice	6.00	2.50
Coaster, 3½"	2.50	2.00	Tumbler, 4", 9 oz. Water	5.50	4.00
Coaster/Ash Tray, 4¼"			Tumbler, 5", 10 oz. Footed	16.50	12.00
Square	4.50	4.50			

*Ruby Red—$5.00; Forest Green—$3.00   **Ruby Red—$27.50

"RAINDROPS", OPTIC DESIGN   FEDERAL GLASS COMPANY, 1929-1933

Colors: Green, crystal.

"Raindrops" humps are ROUNDED little hills occuring on the inside of pieces or undersides of plates. This pattern is often confused with "Thumbprint"/Pear Optic pattern which has ELONGATED impressions which are slightly "scooped out" in the center like "thumbprints".

I've now looked eight years for a mate to this shaker. Yes, "Raindrops" shakers are that rare. However, since there are relatively few collectors for this pattern, the price for such a rare Depression glass item remains low! (One collector did tell me he had one in his collection, but it was not for sale. That collector called me and tried to buy mine, and he **really** wants it!)

I've owned three "Raindrops" sugar lids in all the years I've dealt with Depression glass. It's one of the rarest lids to be found in this glass. However, due to few collectors for this pattern, these rare lids won't command anywhere near the prices accorded a Monax American Sweetheart or Mayfair sugar lid. DEMAND, not necessarily RARITY, determines price in Depression glass. I borrowed a 7½" berry bowl to photograph but it was left out of the picture since it was packed with the Art Deco Ovide and I forgot it was there. Sorry!

	Green		Green
Bowl, 4½" Fruit	2.00	Sherbet	4.50
Bowl, 6" Cereal	3.00	Sugar	3.50
Bowl, 7½" Berry	12.00	Sugar Cover	22.00
Cup	3.00	Tumbler, 3", 4 oz.	3.00
Creamer	4.50	Tumbler, 2⅛", 2 oz.	3.00
Plate, 6" Sherbet	1.00	Tumbler, 3⅞", 5 oz.	5.00
Plate, 8" Luncheon	2.00	Tumbler, 4⅛", 9½ oz.	7.50
Salt and Pepper, Pr.	100.00	Tumbler, 5", 10 oz.	7.50
Saucer	1.00	Whiskey, 1⅞", 1 oz.	3.50

Please refer to Foreword for pricing information

RADIANCE   NEW MARTINSVILLE, 1936-1939

Colors: Red, cobalt and ice blue, amber, crystal, emerald green.

Most Radiance is found in that lovely red color. Indeed, if you work at it, a set can be gathered in red. I've run into pieces in lofty antique shows and in little, out of the way, jumbled shops. This was your better glassware of the Depression era, not the kind found among the groceries or hidden in huge bags of flour. That probably accounts for its scarcity today.

Item collectors love this pattern. It has various butter dishes and pitchers to be on the lookout for when traveling. Further, the items have an appealing shape.

Cobalt blue is considered a rare find. The pitcher, tumbler and decanter are pictured here. The little handled decanter shown, as well as the five-piece condiment set in red, are considered to be choice items. A lady in Tennessee discovered she had the decanter in Radiance when I had one on display at a show. Hers was a gift from her father. She had kept it because she liked the color and because he gave it to her, not because she knew it to be valuable! She had hers in reach of the grandchildren until she discovered its worth!

Crystal items command about half the prices listed below unless they're decorated with gold or silver like those pictured. Decorated items sell for a bit more.

Punch bowl ladles are very elusive. I've now seen six bowls in various colors in my travels. Only one had the glass ladle. It was that lovely ice blue color, too, complete with liner plate and cups--and a whopping price! Punch bowls in this pattern are a pumpkin shape (without the humps or Halloween lid)!

	Red	Ice Blue, Amber		Red	Ice Blue, Amber
Bowl, 5″, nut, 2 hand	10.00	6.50	Creamer	10.00	7.00
Bowl, 6″, bonbon	9.50	6.00	Cruet, indiv.	30.00	22.50
Bowl, 6″, bonbon, ftd.	10.00	6.50	Cup	8.50	
Bowl, 6″, bonbon w/cover	20.00	14.00	Cup, punch	7.00	4.00
Bowl, 7″m relish, 2 pt.	12.50	7.50	Decanter w/stopper, hand.	85.00	52.50
Bowl, 7″, pickle	9.50	6.50	Ladle for punch bowl	75.00	40.00
Bowl, 8″, relish, 3 pt.	15.00	9.00	Lamp, 12″	70.00	37.50
Bowl, 10″, celery	12.50	7.50	Mayonnaise, 3 pc., set	25.00	12.00
Bowl, 10″, crimped	17.50	11.50	Pitcher, 64 oz. (cobalt		
Bowl, 10″, flared	20.00	10.00	$225.00)	152.50	107.50
Bowl, 12″, crimped	23.50	13.50	Plate, 8″, luncheon	7.00	5.00
Bowl, 12″, flared	22.50	12.50	Plate, 14″, punch bowl liner	30.00	16.50
Bowl, punch	77.50	37.50	Salt & pepper, pr.	32.50	22.50
Butter dish	317.50	147.50	Saucer	3.00	2.50
Candlestick, 8″	15.00	9.00	Sugar	11.00	7.00
Candlestick, 2-lite	19.00	11.00	Tray, oval	20.00	15.00
Cheese/cracker, (11″ plate) set	30.00	15.00	Tumbler, 9 oz. (cobalt $25.00)	15.00	9.00
Comport, 5″	12.00	8.50	Vase, 10″, flared	32.50	21.50
Comport, 6″	13.00	8.00	Vase, 12″, crimped	47.50	37.50
Condiment set, 4 pc. w/tray	125.00	87.50			

"RIBBON" HAZEL ATLAS GLASS COMPANY, Early 1930's

Colors: Green; some black, crystal, pink.

"Ribbon" collecting has awakened and I don't mean saving those on the Christmas packages to use again next year. I'm encountering more pieces of "Ribbon" in my travels which encourages my belief that a set of this is not such an impossibility as was once believed. Too, I see more people buying it than ever before. You used to find only a piece or two at a time, now there are usually three or four pieces grouped together. You will notice large price increases on some of these items. The demand for tumblers, creamer and sugar, and the candy has surprised even me!

You will notice the similarity of shapes to Hazel Atlas's Cloverleaf and Ovide patterns. The company seems to have gotten a lot of mileage out of their moulds which was sensible since moulds were costly but could be reworked for a different design.

Pink and black shakers are in demand by item collectors only. Shakers are the only items noted so far in pink.

	Green	Black		Green	Black
Bowl, 4″ Berry	3.00		Salt and Pepper, Pr.	16.00	27.50
Bowl, 8″ Large Berry	10.00	13.00	Saucer	1.50	
Candy Dish and Cover	25.00		Sherbet, Footed	4.00	
Creamer, Footed	7.50	9.00	Sugar, Footed	7.50	9.00
Cup	2.50		Tumbler, 5½″, 10 oz.	7.00	
Plate, 6¼″ Sherbet	1.25		Tumbler, 6½″, 13 oz.	15.00	
Plate, 8″ Luncheon	2.00	8.00			

RING, "BANDED RINGS" HOCKING GLASS COMPANY, 1927-1933

Colors: Crystal, crystal w/pink, red, blue, orange, yellow, black, silver, etc. rings; green, some pink, "Mayfair" blue, red.

Banded Ring was advertised as "New Fiesta" and suitably festooned with colorful sombreros and gaily skirted dancing girls outfitted in like colors of orange, yellow and green! There are various bands of colors. Don't even TRY to get them all to match. Go for an over-all appearance of color. If you try to get the colored bands to match on all your pieces, you may end up needing psychiatric help.

Ring shakers are difficult to locate. At one time it was a common practice to rob Ring shakers of their tops to put them on the more prestigious Mayfair shakers. No more! Ring collectors want their shakers intact, and suddenly, dealers are finding they aren't so plentiful!

Unusual colors of red and "Mayfair" blue Ring have only been found in luncheon plates, cups and tumblers. Let me hear from you if you find other items, please.

	Crystal	Crystal Decor., Green		Crystal	Crystal Decor., Green
Bowl, 5″ Berry	2.00	3.00	Sandwich Server, Center		
Bowl, 7″ Soup	7.50	9.50	Handle	10.00	17.50
Bowl, 8″ Large Berry	4.00	6.00	Saucer	1.00	1.50
Butter Tub or Ice			Sherbet, Low (for 6½″		
Bucket	8.50	15.00	Plate)	4.00	8.00
Cocktail Shaker	7.50	15.00	Sherbet, 4¾″ Footed	4.00	7.00
**Cup	2.50	3.50	Sugar, Footed	3.00	4.00
Creamer, Footed	3.50	4.50	Tumbler, 3½″, 5 oz.	2.50	3.50
Decanter and Stopper	14.50	25.00	Tumbler, 4¼″, 9 oz.	3.50	4.50
Goblet, 7″ to 8″ (Varies)			Tumbler, 5⅛″, 12 oz.	4.00	4.50
9 oz.	4.50	10.00	Tumbler, 3½″ Footed		
Ice Tub	8.50	12.00	Cocktail	4.00	4.50
Pitcher, 8″, 60 oz.	8.50	15.00	Tumbler, 5½″ Footed		
*Pitcher, 8½″, 80 oz.	10.50	17.50	Water	3.50	4.50
Plate, 6¼″ Sherbet	1.25	2.50	Tumbler, 6½″, Footed		
Plate, 6½″, Off Center			Iced Tea	5.00	8.50
Ring	1.50	4.50	Vase, 8″	12.50	27.50
**Plate, 8″ Luncheon	1.50	2.50	Whiskey, 2″, 1½ oz.	3.50	5.00
***Salt and Pepper, Pr., 3″	12.50	22.50			

*Also found in Pink. Priced as Green.
**Red—17.50. Blue—25.00
***Green—52.50.

Please refer to Foreword for pricing information

ROCK CRYSTAL, "EARLY AMERICAN ROCK CRYSTAL"

MCKEE GLASS COMPANY, 1920's and 1930's in colors

Colors: Four shades of green, aquamarine, vaseline, yellow, amber, pink and satin frosted pink, red slag, dark red, red, amberina red, crystal, frosted crystal, crystal with goofus decoration, crystal with gold decoration, amethyst, milk glass blue frosted or "Jap" blue and cobalt.

Rock crystal sets a beautiful table in either red or crystal. A major drawback is not serving anything which will have your guests scratching the surface of those now expensive dinner plates. You also ignore the question, "How much is this red goblet worth?", as it is held over a dinner plate.

Just so you'd know it could be done, we put a set together in red! Actually, it was found mostly intact as you see it here, having belonged to a former employee. Notice the varying shades of red, from the amberina plate at the back (small center) to the very dark covered pitcher and candy dish bottom. Notice, also, that the pieces come with scalloped or plain edges. Many collectors refer to the small centered plates as "serving" plates and to the larger centered plates as dinner plates.

I realize that my listings here are not entirely complete in regard to actual pieces made. There are numerous bowls, for instance, with varying edges, heights and diameters. I chose to give a representative sample that could be easily read rather than the reams of information that would have been more than you'd have wanted to know or pay for in extra book cost!

We were recently able to replace the small footed fruit bowl in crystal that belonged to my wife and which was smashed at a photography session. It is seldom a piece is damaged in one of those horrendous three days of setting up thousands of pieces of glass to be photographed. I hope you fully appreciate the money, time, effort and skill each of these color photographs represent, not just on my part, but on the part of friends who lend glass or help during sessions and the employees who spend hours on their knees trying to arrange the pieces so that the camera can "see" them advantageously.

	Crystal	All Other Colors	Red
*Bon Bon, 7½" S.E.	12.50	20.00	37.50
Bowl, 4" S.E.	7.50	10.00	20.00
Bowl, 4½" S.E.	8.00	10.00	22.50
Bowl, 5" S.E.	9.50	12.50	25.00
**Bowl, 5" Finger Bowl with 7" Plate, P.E.			
Bowl, 7" Pickle or Spoon Tray	15.00	22.00	37.50
Bowl, 7" Salad S.E.	15.00	22.50	35.00
Bowl, 8" Salad S.E.	15.00	22.00	40.00
Bowl, 9" Salad S.E.	17.50	23.00	45.00
Bowl, 10½" Salad S.E.	18.50	25.00	50.00
Bowl, 11½" Two Part Relish	20.00	27.00	40.00
Bowl, 12" Oblong Celery	20.00	27.00	42.50
***Bowl, 12½" Footed Center Bowl	35.00	70.00	195.00
Bowl, 13" Roll Tray	25.00	40.00	
Bowl, 14" Six Part Relish	22.50	37.50	
Butter Dish and Cover	225.00		
Butter Dish Bottom	125.00		
Butter Dish Top	100.00		
****Candelabra, Two Lite Pr.	32.50	60.00	150.00
Candelabra, Three Lite Pr.	35.00	65.00	175.00
Candlestick, 5½" Low Pr.	27.50	45.00	75.00
Candlestick, 8½" Tall Pr.	57.50	75.00	150.00
Candy and Cover, Round	25.00	45.00	125.00
Cake Stand, 11", 2¾" High, Footed	19.50	35.00	75.00

*S.E. McKee Designation for scalloped edge
**P.E. McKee designation for plain edge

***Red Slag—$300.00. Cobalt—$137.50
****Cobalt—$75.00

Please refer to Foreword for pricing information

ROCK CRYSTAL, "EARLY AMERICAN ROCK CRYSTAL" (Con't.)

	Crystal	All Other Colors	Red
Comport, 7"	27.50	37.50	52.50
Creamer, Flat S.E.	20.00		
Creamer, 9 oz. Footed	15.00	25.00	45.00
Cruet and Stopper, 6 oz. Oil	47.50		
Cup, 7 oz.	11.00	20.00	40.00
Goblet, 7½" oz., 8 oz. Low Footed	13.50	22.50	45.00
Goblet, 11 oz. Low Footed Iced Tea	15.00	22.00	55.00
Jelly, 5" Footed S.E.	13.50	20.00	35.00
Lamp, Electric	60.00	145.00	300.00
Parfait, 3½" oz. Low Footed	8.50		
Pitcher, Quart S.E.	77.50	150.00	
Pitcher, ½ Gal., 7½" High	95.00	165.00	
Pitcher, 9" Large Covered	125.00	200.00	400.00
Pitcher, Fancy Tankard	137.50	325.00	550.00
Plate, 6" Bread and Butter S.E.	4.50	6.50	11.00
Plate, 7½" P.E. & S.E.	6.50	9.00	15.00
Plate, 8½" P.E. & S.E.	7.50	9.50	25.00
Plate, 9" S.E.	12.50	17.50	35.00
Plate, 10½" S.E.	13.50	18.50	37.50
Plate, 11½" S.E.	14.50	20.00	40.00
Plate, 10½" Dinner S.E. (Large Center Design)	40.00	50.00	85.00
Punch Bowl and Stand, 14"	265.00		
Salt and Pepper (2 styles)	60.00	90.00	
Salt Dip	20.00		
Sandwich Server, Center Handled	20.00	35.00	85.00
Saucer	4.50	6.50	10.00
Sherbet or Egg, 3½ oz. Footed	10.00	20.00	45.00
Spooner	27.50		
Stemware, 1 oz. Footed Cordial	13.50	35.00	50.00
Stemware, 2 oz. Wine	14.00	23.00	40.00
Stemware, 3 oz. Wine	15.00	25.00	40.00
Stemware, 3½ oz. Footed Cocktail	12.00	17.50	35.00
Stemware, 6 oz. Footed Champagne	12.50	17.50	30.00
Stemware, 8 oz. Large Footed Goblet	13.50	22.50	45.00
Sundae, 6 oz. Low Footed	9.50	15.00	30.00
Sugar, 10 oz. Open	11.00	18.00	30.00
Sugar, Lid	25.00	35.00	50.00
Syrup with Lid	75.00		
Tumbler, 2½" oz. Whiskey	.50	15.00	35.00
Tumbler, 5 oz. Juice	12.00	18.00	35.00
Tumbler, 5 oz. Old Fashioned	12.00	18.00	35.00
Tumbler, 9 oz. Concave or Straight	15.00	22.00	37.50
Tumbler, 12 oz. Concave or Straight	20.00	25.00	50.00
Vase, Cornucopia	45.00	65.00	
Vase, 11" Footed	32.50	55.00	150.00

ROSE CAMEO   BELMONT TUMBLER COMPANY, 1931

Colors: Green

I still have not been able to confirm my suspicions that Hazel Atlas made this. Since shards of Rose Cameo have turned up in "digs" at the old factory site, it seems likely that company may have made this even though the patent was registered to the Belmont Tumbler Company.

Amazingly, a few collectors have adopted this small pattern, and the prices for some pieces have increased since they are in short supply.

Tumblers are the most frequently seen items. There are two styles, one having a slightly flared edge. It is pictured.

The hard-to-find straight-sided bowl is turned on edge behind the tumbler. Notice the bottom surface is much wider than on the other bowls shown.

This pattern is still confused with Cameo. Rose Cameo has a rose inside the cameo rather than the little dancing girl, hence the name "Rose" Cameo.

	Green		Green
Bowl, 4½" Berry	4.00	Plate, 7" Salad	5.00
Bowl, 5" Cereal	7.50	Sherbet	4.50
Bowl, 6" Straight Sides	10.00	Tumbler, 5" Footed (2 Styles)	10.00

ROSEMARY, "DUTCH ROSE"   FEDERAL GLASS COMPANY, 1935-1937

Colors: Amber, green, pink; some iridized.

Rosemary collectors all ask the same question: "Where do I find cereal bowls?" So far I have been asked this question in states from Florida to Oregon and Texas to California. Unfortunately, I haven't had any bowls for a few years. Keep searching. There are bound to be a few out there!

Amber is the most plentiful color in this pattern, but pink and green are most in demand.

Rosemary pattern resulted from Federal's having to change their Mayfair pattern after learning that Hocking had beaten them to the patent office with the name "Mayfair". You will notice that Rosemary has perfectly plain glass at the base of its pieces save for the center Rose motif. It has neither the "arches" of the "transitional" Mayfair pieces nor the "arches and waffling" of the traditional Mayfair pieces.

The pink footed item with the creamer is the sugar bowl. In this pattern, the sugar has no handles. It's not a tumbler nor a sherbet. It's the sugar bowl! One lady told me she had eight, using them as sherbets!

The scarcity of tumblers and cereal bowls is reflected in their price increase.

Few iridized salad plates are to be found today.

	Amber	Green	Pink		Amber	Green	Pink
Bowl, 5" Berry	4.00	4.50	5.00	Plate, Dinner	5.50	10.00	10.00
Bowl, 5" Cream Soup	7.50	13.50	12.50	Plate, Grill	6.00	10.00	8.00
Bowl, 6" Cereal	10.00	12.50	10.00	Platter, 12" Oval	9.50	14.50	12.50
Bowl, 10" Oval Vegetable	8.50	15.00	12.00	Saucer	2.00	3.50	2.00
Creamer, Footed	6.50	9.50	9.00	Sugar, Footed	6.50	9.50	9.00
Cup	4.00	7.00	4.50	Tumbler, 4¼", 9 oz.	15.00	20.00	25.00
Plate, 6¾" Salad	4.00	6.00	3.50				

Please refer to Foreword for pricing information

ROULETTE, "MANY WINDOWS" HOCKING GLASS COMPANY, 1935-1939

Colors: Green; some pink and crystal

As a dealer, I have found the best way to learn about a pattern is to buy a complete set and see how it sells. Having bought a twelve place setting, I have found that sherbets, cups, saucers and luncheon plates are plentiful and most collectors already have them. I learned that I could have sold all the other items ten times over! There are numerous collectors out there searching for Roulette! Actually, it's a very attractive pattern when you get a set of it together at one time.

New collectors, please notice that the rouletting occurs toward the upper third of the pitcher. There is a pitcher with a cubed design at the bottom that is sometimes mistaken for Roulette. There is also a cobalt pitcher with an embossed design (rather than impressed) which is much like Roulette. Neither are Roulette, however!

Pink Roulette has appeared only in pitcher and tumbler sets so far. Do notice the one·crystal whiskey glass pictured. That wee glass may indicate a pitcher. Watch for it since one has never been found.

The old fashioned tumbler shown in right foreground in pink is the most difficult of the tumblers to find.

	Pink, Crystal	Green
Bowl, 9″ Fruit	8.50	9.00
Cup	3.50	3.50
Pitcher, 8″, 64 oz.	22.50	25.00
Plate, 6″ Sherbet	2.00	2.00
Plate, 8½″ Luncheon	4.00	4.00
Plate, 12″ Sandwich	7.50	7.50
Saucer	1.00	1.00
Sherbet	3.00	4.00
Tumbler, 3¼″, 5 oz. Juice	4.50	9.00
Tumbler, 3¼″, 7½″ oz. Old Fashioned	6.00	15.00
Tumbler, 4⅛″, 9 oz. Water	10.00	12.00
Tumbler, 5⅛″, 12 oz. Iced Tea	10.00	15.00
Tumbler, 5½″, 10 oz. Footed	9.50	15.00
Whiskey, 2½″, 1½ oz.	6.50	8.00

Please refer to Foreword for pricing information

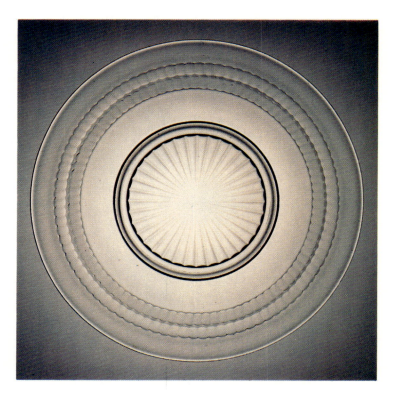

"ROUND ROBIN"   MANUFACTURER UNKNOWN, Probably Early 1930's

Colors: Green: some iridized and crystal.

Crystal "Round Robin" has been reported. That stands to reason as there has to be crystal before it can be iridized. Evidently, some crystal got out before iridizing, or perhaps it was issued that way.

Sherbets and the domino tray are elusive pieces of Round Robin. For those who wonder about the name of the tray, it comes from using sugar cubes around the inside ring which held the creamer.

Actually, I ran into a four place setting in Ohio and found six sherbets in southern Kentucky in order to fill in the pieces I have been missing in my earlier edition pictures.

This pattern is interesting in that it has footed cups and the domino drip tray, rather "fancy" pieces for such a small pattern.

	Green	Iridescent		Green	Iridescent
Bowl, 4" Berry	3.50	4.00	Plate, 8" Luncheon	2.50	3.00
Cup, Footed	3.00	4.00	Plate, 12" Sandwich	3.50	4.50
Creamer, Footed	4.50	5.50	Saucer	1.00	1.00
Domino Tray	20.00		Sherbet	3.50	4.00
Plate, 6" Sherbet	1.50	1.50	Sugar	4.50	5.00

ROXANA   HAZEL ATLAS GLASS COMPANY, 1932

Colors: Yellow, crystal; some white

Roxana continues to be the only pattern with a saucer and no cup.

This is one of the patterns you'll have to ask for by name at shows. Most dealers won't have it with them, but they may have pieces at home or in their shops.

The 6" cereal bowl is pictured here on the stand at the left. Unfortunately, the camera doesn't allow for depth and it looks more like a plate than a bowl.

Notice the sherbet pictured. If you find other pieces in this pattern, I'd appreciate hearing from you. To date, these are all that are known.

This would be a fun little pattern to search out and use at breakfast with cereal or for brunch with fruit and salad!

	Yellow	White		Yellow
Bowl, 4½" x 2⅜"	5.00	10.00	Plate, 6" Sherbet	2.50
Bowl, 5" Berry	3.50		Saucer	2.00
Bowl, 6" Cereal	5.50		Sherbet, Footed	3.50
			Tumbler, 4", 9 oz.	8.50

ROYAL LACE   HAZEL ATLAS GLASS COMPANY, 1934-1941

Colors: Cobalt blue, crystal, green, pink; some amethyst.

There is always confusion regarding the three style 10″ bowls in Royal Lace. In order to facilitate knowing the difference between the **expensive** rolled edge and the **common** straight edged bowl, I have provided a pattern shot of the rolled edge bowl. The straight edge is shown in blue in the bottom picture on the right. I hope that clears up any confusion and will save a few letters explaining the differences. Think of a French bread ''rolled'' around the edge of the bowl. Royal Lace is one of those Depression glass patterns that sells itself. Everyone seems to like it! Even crystal is in demand, something that can be said for few other pattern save, perhaps, Miss America and Manhattan. You or your progenitor could have bought a 44-piece set in 1934 for $2.99! Even so, these dishes would have been totally out of the question for many families then.

In spite of what the picture would indicate, pitchers are not that easily found, particularly the bulbous type. Yet, even the 48 ounce straight side, (yes, 48 ounce, not 54 ounce as stated in old catalogue listings), is rapidly disappearing from the market. Blue Royal Lace is a favorite color with collectors and it seems plentiful enough. Many collectors favor the green, but most of that has disappeared into collections of people who started their collecting a dozen years ago when Depression glass first came into vogue. The odd-looking piece in the center of the photo is the toddy set. It should have a ladle with a cherry red knob like the one on the metal top. The cookie jar is the insert. It's found in amethyst and cobalt with eight roly-poly cups which are usually plain, but which can be found bearing the tiny ''Ships'' motif.

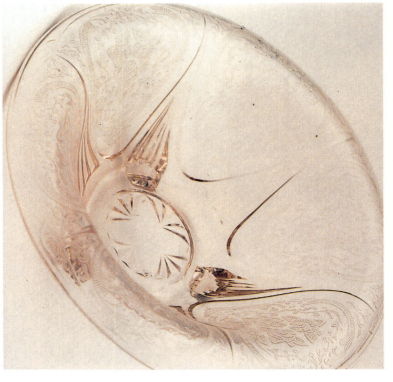

	Crystal	Pink	Green	Blue	Amethyst
Bowl, 4¾″ Cream Soup	7.50	11.50	22.50	22.50	
Bowl, 5″ Berry	6.00	12.00	17.50	27.50	
Bowl, 10″ Round Berry	10.00	12.50	20.00	35.00	
Bowl, 10″, 3 Leg Straight Edge	12.50	18.50	30.00	42.50	
Bowl, 10″, 3 Leg Rolled Edge	75.00	25.00	60.00	185.00	
Bowl, 10″, 3 Leg Ruffled Edge	17.50	19.50	45.00	175.00	
Bowl, 11″ Oval Vegetable	12.50	15.00	19.50	35.00	
Butter Dish and Cover	52.50	95.00	225.00	335.00	
Butter Dish Bottom	37.50	60.00	150.00	225.00	
Butter Dish Top	25.00	35.00	75.00	132.50	
Candlestick, Straight Edge Pair	18.50	25.00	42.50	65.00	
Candlestick, Rolled Edge Pair	37.50	35.00	50.00	95.00	
Candlestick, Ruffled Edge Pair	22.50	35.00	50.00	95.00	
Cookie Jar and Cover	25.00	37.50	52.50	200.00	
Cream, Footed	8.00	11.00	17.50	25.00	
Cup	5.00	9.50	14.00	22.50	
Pitcher, 48 oz., Straight Sides	30.00	40.00	80.00	70.00	
Pitcher, 8″, 68 oz.	40.00	39.50	75.00	117.50	
Pitcher, 8″, 86 oz.	42.50	55.00	95.00	127.50	
Pitcher, 8½″, 96 oz.	45.00	62.50	120.00	157.50	
Plate, 6″ Sherbet	2.50	3.50	6.00	8.50	
Plate, 8½″ Luncheon	4.00	6.50	9.50	22.50	
Plate, 10″ Dinner	7.50	11.50	17.50	27.50	
Plate, 9⅞″ Grill	5.50	8.50	15.00	22.50	
Platter, 13″ Oval	12.00	15.00	25.00	35.00	
Salt and Pepper, Pr.	32.50	40.00	100.00	185.00	
Saucer	2.50	3.50	5.00	6.50	
Sherbet, Footed	7.00	9.00	17.50	25.00	
Sherbet in Metal Holder	3.50			17.50	27.50
Sugar	7.00	7.50	15.00	20.00	
Sugar Lid	13.00	22.50	27.50	95.00	
Tumbler, 3½″, 5 oz.	7.50	12.50	20.00	27.50	
Tumbler, 4⅛″, 9 oz.	8.50	10.00	18.00	25.00	
Tumbler, 4⅞″, 10 oz.	12.50	20.00	30.00	50.00	
Tumbler, 5⅜″, 12 oz.	12.50	20.00	25.00	40.00	
Toddy or Cider Set: Includes Cookie Jar Metal Lid, Metal Tray, 8 Roly-Poly Cups and Ladle				100.00	120.00

Please refer to Foreword for pricing information

ROYAL RUBY   ANCHOR HOCKING GLASS COMPANY, 1938-1960's; 1977

Colors: Ruby Red

The term "Royal Ruby" refers to the red glassware made by the Anchor Hocking Company only. Many people erroneously group any red glass under that term. Anchor Hocking initially started promoting Royal Ruby in 1938 and continued the promotion through the early 1940's.

A newly discovered playing card holder is shown in the center of the photograph. The lid is Royal Ruby (sticker attached to lid) and the base is a divided crystal holder. I have now seen two of these and I believe it is quite rare. Only time will tell in this case, but the price quoted below is an actual selling price and not a "hoped-for" price.

The squared red items were a 1950's issue, made at the same time as the Forest Green items of like shape. See Fire-King dinnerware (p.60-61) for additional colors in the square shape. Presently, there is not as much demand for the red as for the green; but in talking with collectors, the squared items appear to be in shorter supply than the older round ones. Many dealers tell me people buy this specifically for their Christmas tables. Perhaps we could promote the red for Valentine's Day, also.

That 5¼" bowl located in front of the card holder was sold in a set of seven as popcorn set, one larger 10" bowl included.

The 13¾" salad plate with the 11½" salad bowl has become one of the most sought after items in Royal Ruby; and the oval vegetable bowl is becoming one of the hardest to find in all Depression glass! They're missing from most collections at the moment!

The price for the ball stemmed goblet has remained about the same; the supply has always kept slightly ahead of the demand.

In 1977 Anchor Hocking re-introduced 4½" and 8" bowls in red Bubble; 7, 9, 12 and 16 ounce plain tumblers; an ivy ball vase; a punch cup and a square ash tray. All these items supposedly carry the anchor trademark of the company and, in general, were lighter in weight and color than the older glassware.

Not all footed sugars take the slotted lid; and some lids simply will not properly fit the sugar; so buying pieces separately presents a problem.

That tumbler (with the metal lid) on the left has "Old Reliable Tea Bags" packaged inside. This tumbler also carried Anchor Hocking's "Royal Ruby" sticker.

The piece you see at the bottom of the page is a ball vase containing a citronnella candle which was lit to scare away mosquitoes as you sat on the patio. This probably explains why there are so many of these vases to be found today, and many of these are being found in the Southern states! Whether the product had any affect on mosquitoes, I don't know.

	Red		Red
Ash Tray, 4½" Square	2.50	Plate, 9" or 9¼" Dinner	7.50
Bowl, 4¼" Berry	4.00	Plate, 13¾"	15.00
Bowl, 5¼"	6.50	Punch Bowl and Stand	32.50
Bowl, 7½" Soup	9.50	Punch Cup	2.00
Bowl, 8" Oval Vegetable	17.50	Saucer (Round or Square)	1.50
Bowl, 8½" Large Berry	12.50	Sherbet, Footed	6.50
Bowl, 10" Deep	15.00	Sugar, Flat	6.00
Bowl, 11½" Salad	20.00	Sugar, Footed	5.00
Card Holder	30.00	Sugar Lid	7.50
Creamer, Flat	6.00	Tumbler, 2½" oz. Footed Wine	8.50
Creamer, Footed	7.50	Tumbler, 3½" oz. Cocktail	6.50
Cup (Round or Square)	3.50	Tumbler, 5 oz. Juice, 2 Styles	5.00
Goblet, Ball Stem	6.50	Tumbler, 9 oz. Water	5.00
Lamp	20.00	Tumbler, 10 oz. Water	5.00
Pitcher, 22 oz. Tilted or Upright	20.00	Tumbler, 13 oz. Iced Tea	8.50
Pitcher, 3 qt. Tilted	25.00	Vase, 4" Ball Shaped	4.50
Pitcher, 3 qt. Upright	30.00	Vase, 6½" Bulbous, Tall	7.50
Plate, 6½" Sherbet	2.00	Vases, Several Styles (Small)	5.00
Plate, 7" Salad	3.50	Vases, Several Styles (Large)	10.00
Plate, 7¾" Luncheon	4.00		

Please refer to Foreword for pricing information

"S" PATTERN, "STIPPLED ROSE BAND"   MACBETH-EVANS GLASS
COMPANY, 1930-1933

Colors: Crystal; crystal w/trims of silver, blue, green, amber; pink; some amber, green, fired-on red, Monax, and light yellow.

"S" Pattern is a delicate, lovely little pattern that has been virtually ignored by collectors except for its pitchers, tumblers and cake plates. That's really a shame because it has a simple charm and delicacy that I find appealing. I think collectors would also, if they'd stop to really consider this pattern! The silver rimmed pieces are elegant looking in a complete table setting! This is another pattern I can heartily recommend to people with limited funds to spend, but who want a pretty pattern to collect. It would be especially suitable for young people. I've recently met a beautiful fifteen-year-old girl who was buying "S" Pattern with her allowance . . . as an investment, so she'd really have something in the future. I was impressed with her maturity of thought.

The pink and green pitchers in the back are rarely seen. Tumblers have now been found to match both. (You can see the green pictured). A boxed set of six pink tumblers turned up; oddly enough, three were silk screened with the "S" Pattern, and three were perfectly plain! The normally found "S" Pattern pitcher has the fat shape of the American Sweetheart pitcher.

There are two sizes of cake plates to be found in "S" Pattern. Unlike it's sister Dogwood pattern, the harder-to-find one is the 13" rather than the 11". That amber cake plate pictured is one of two that I've ever seen.

Two distinct shades of yellow occur in "S" Pattern, a very light, pretty yellow and a more honey amber color, like the cake plate. There seems to be more amber available than the lighter color, subsequently, there are more collectors for the amber.

	Crystal	Yellow, Amber, Crystal With Trims
*Bowl, 5½" Cereal	2.50	3.50
Bowl, 8½" Large Berry	6.50	12.50
*Creamer, Thick or Thin	4.00	5.50
*Cup, Thick or Thin	2.50	3.50
Pitcher, 80 oz. (Like "Dogwood") (Green or Pink 500.00)	35.00	67.50
Pitcher, 80 oz. (Like "American Sweetheart")	45.00	67.50
Plate, 6" Sherbet (Monax 14.00)	1.50	2.00
**Plate, 8" Luncheon	2.00	2.50
Plate, 9¼" Dinner	3.50	4.50
Plate, Grill	2.50	4.50
Plate, 11" Heavy Cake	30.00	32.50
***Plate, 13" Heavy Cake	47.50	57.50
*Saucer	1.00	1.50
Sherbet, Low Footed	3.50	4.50
*Sugar, Thick and Thin	4.00	5.50
Tumbler, 3½", 5 oz.	2.50	4.50
Tumbler, 4", 9 oz. (Green or Pink 57.50)	3.50	5.50
Tumbler, 4¼", 10 oz.	3.50	6.00
Tumbler, 5", 12 oz.	4.50	6.50

*Fired-on red items will run approximately twice price of amber
**Deep Red—$40.00
***Amber—$77.50

SANDWICH, HOCKING GLASS COMPANY, 1939-1964; 1977

Colors:

Crystal - 1950's-1960's	Pink - 1939-1940	Forest Green - 1950's-1960's
Amber - 1960's	Royal Ruby - 1939-1940	White (opaque) - 1950's

It is amazing what you discover in going through old catalogues that you haven't looked at in years. I found answers to several perplexing problems for Sandwich collectors. One was why the punch bowl bases are found so infrequently. The 9¼" bowl was sold in other ways than just a punch bowl. It was also sold as a salad set with the 12" plate. Not only that, but a smaller punch set, consisting of a bowl and six cups, was marketed. I noticed that one of my later catalogues listed the cereal bowl at 6½". That is the correct size listing instead of the 6" seen in an earlier catalog. I thank a collector for bringing the matter to my attention.

Thankfully, the Sandwich pattern most collected is that of Anchor Hocking. (When you turn the page, you'll understand that statement a little better). Crystal is the color most sought with Forest Green presently running a close second. Some investment-minded collectors noted the shortage of all items in green (save for the five pieces which were packaged in Mother's Oats and sold all over the nation) and set out to latch onto those items. That caused quite a flurry of activity in green Sandwich for a time. The five commonly found items in green Sandwich include: the 5 oz. juice, 9 oz. water, 4⅞" berry bowl and the custard cup and liner. That same liner in CRYSTAL, however, is an elusive piece of glass and highly prized when found. Speaking of the custard cup, do you notice anything unusual about the green one in front? Someone rolled the edge at the factory making it 2" high and 4" wide as opposed to the more normal 2¼" high and 3⅜" wide. A collector in Ashland, Ky. found this.

I explained the scarcity of the pitchers in Forest Green in the 3rd and 4th editions. The larger pitcher has turned out to be even more scarce than the juice, however, a small hoard of them which turned up in a warehouse basement recently took care of present demands.

No lid has been found for the green cookie jar. It was promoted as a vase. There is an opaque white punch bowl set (stand, bowl, 12 cups) which is presently selling for $30.00-$35.00 It sold in my area in the mid '60's for $1.79 with an oil change and lubrication at Ashland Oil stations. Anchor Hocking got briefly into the re-issue business by again making a Sandwich cookie jar. The newer version is larger than the old, so there's no reason to mistake the two. The newer one has a height of 10¼", a 5½" opening and a 20" circumference at its largest part. The old Sandwich cookie jar is only 9¼" tall, has a mouth of 4⅞" and is only 19" in circumference. Notice the pattern shot of a never-before-seen 9 ounce footed AMBER tumbler!

On the subject of re-issues, since my sentiments haven't changed at all, I would like to repeat the following from the 6th edition: It's only my opinion, of course, but I feel companies only hurt themselves with re-issues. They sacrifice their integrity or the "trust" factor they have with the collecting public which numbers in the millions; and they sabotage all that free prideful publicity the collectors give them when bragging to friends about their collections made by thus and so glass company during such and such years. That's got to be PRICELESS material (feed-back) to that company since it's BOUND to make persons hearing that "testimony" sit up and take notice of any other glassware that company advertises or is historically associated with. Really, it's beyond me to understand the reasoning behind re-issues. If they absolutely HAVE to use old molds, they should always make pieces in untried colors. That way, the pieces MIGHT become collectible and thus would be marketable to larger numbers of people. Trying for old colors, besides showing no imagination, just destroys everybody's taste for any of it! What's being accomplished? A large scale destruction of an invaluable reputation for making fine collectible, valuable glassware, a reputation which was being built free of charge! Where's the sense ("cents") in that? Excuse me, ladies, but a former boss called that logic "pinching pennies to blow hell out of dollars".

	Crystal	Desert Gold	Ruby Red	Forest Green	Pink		Crystal	Desert Gold	Forest Green
Bowl, 4⅞" Berry	3.00	2.50	9.00	1.50	2.50	Pitcher, 6" Juice	40.00		90.00
Bowl, 5¼"			14.00			Pitcher, ½ gal. Ice Lip	40.00		155.00
Bowl, 6½" Cereal	12.50	6.00				Plate, 7" Dessert	6.50	2.50	
Bowl, 6½" Smooth						Plate, 8"	2.00		
or Scalloped	5.00	6.00	17.50	22.50		Plate, 9" Dinner	10.00	5.00	35.00
Bowl, 7" Salad	6.50			35.00		Plate, 9" Indent			
Bowl, 8" Smooth						For Punch Cup	3.00		
or Scalloped	6.50		27.50	40.00	10.00	Plate, 12" Sandwich	7.50	8.50	
Bowl, 8¼" Oval	5.00					Punch Bowl	15.00		
Bowl, 9¼" Salad	15.00					Punch Bowl Stand	15.00		
Butter Dish, Low	32.50					Punch Cup	2.00		
Butter Dish Bottom	17.50					Saucer	1.00	3.00	4.50
Butter Dish Top	15.00					Sherbet, Footed	6.00		
Cookie Jar and						Sugar and Cover	12.50		*15.00
Cover	30.00	27.50		*16.00		Tumbler, 3 oz. Juice	6.00		
Creamer	4.00			15.00		Tumbler, 5 oz. Juice	5.00		2.00
Cup, Tea or Coffee	1.50	3.50		12.50		Tumbler, 9 oz. Water	6.50		2.50
Custard Cup	3.50			1.50		Tumbler, 9 oz. Footed	15.00	30.00	
Custard Cup Liner	7.50			1.50					

*No Cover

Please refer to Foreword for pricing information

SANDWICH, INDIANA GLASS COMPANY, 1920's-1980's

Colors:

Crystal Late 1920's-Today	Pink Late 1920's-Early 1930's	Teal Blue 1950's
Amber Late 1920's-1970's	Red 1933-1970's	Lt. Green 1930's

THIS GLASSWARE IS FAST BECOMING VIRTUALLY UNCOLLECTIBLE. READ ON!

If you haven't already read it, please read the last paragraph on the preceding page. I didn't have room on this page for all my opinions. The big "news" is that Indiana has made for Tiara a butter dish which is extremely close to the old teal color made in the 1950's. It's available as a hostess gift item for selling a certain amount of Tiara glass. Because of the new Sandwich being made today by Indiana, I'm dropping crystal from my listing. It's become a collector's pariah! The list is too long to examine each piece to tell the difference between old and new. In many cases, there is little difference since the same moulds are being used. Hopefully, somebody at Indiana will wise up and stop making the old colors as I was told they would do after the "pink Avocado" fiasco in 1974. Instead of trying to entice collectors to new wares, they are stuck on trying to destroy the market for the old glassware which has been collectible for years but which may never be again. Perhaps you could start collecting Hocking Sandwich if you like the pattern. They remade a cookie jar, but they carefully made it different from the old which showed their awareness of collectors in the field! For those of you who have collected the crystal Indiana Sandwich or the teal butter dish and have a sizable investment involved, I can only say that time will tell as to the future collectiblity of this pattern. At present, it doesn't look too promising. The really maddening thing is that all this "new" Sandwich is being touted to prospective buyer as glass that's going to be worth a great deal in the future based on its past history--and the company is steadily destroying those very properties they're using to sell the new glass! Supreme irony!

I can vouch for six items in red Sandwich dating from 1933, i.e. cups, saucers, luncheon plates, water goblets, creamers and sugars. However, in 1969, Tiara Home Products produced red pitchers, 9 oz. goblets, cups, saucers, wines, wine decanters, 13" serving trays, creamers, sugars and salad and dinner plates. Now, if your dishes glow yellow under a black light or if you KNOW that your Aunt Sophie held her red dishes in her lap while fording the swollen stream in a buggy, then I'd say your red Sandwich pieces are old. Other than that, I know of no way to tell if they are or aren't. NO, I won't even say that old red glass glows under black light. I know SOME of it does because of a certain type ore they used then. However, I've seen some newer glass glow, but Tiara's 1969 red Sandwich glass does not. Presently, the only two colors remotely worth having are pink and green, and who knows but what the company will make those tomorrow!

	Pink, Green	Teal Blue	Red		Pink, Green	Teal Blue	Red
Ash Tray Set (Club, Spade, Heart, Diamond Shapes)				Goblet, 9 oz.	15.00		35.00
$2.50 each crystal	15.00			Pitcher, 68 oz.	80.00		
Bowl, 4¼" Berry	3.00			Plate, 6" Sherbet	2.50	4.50	
Bowl, 6"	3.50			Plate, 7" Bread and Butter	3.50		
Bowl, 6" 6 Sides		7.50		Plate, 8" Oval, Indent for Sherbet	5.00	7.50	
Bowl, 8¼"	10.00			Plate, 8⅜" Luncheon	4.50		12.50
Bowl, 9" Console	15.00			Plate, 10½" Dinner	12.50		
Bowl, 10" Console	18.00			Plate, 13" Sandwich	12.50		
*Butter Dish and Cover, Domed	157.50	150.00		Sandwich Server, Center Handle	27.50		
Butter Dish Bottom	47.50	40.00		Saucer	2.50	3.50	6.00
Butter Dish Top	110.00	110.00		Sherbet, 3¼"	5.00	6.00	
Candlesticks, 3½" Pr.	15.00			Sugar, Large Open	8.50		35.00
Candlesticks, 7" Pr.	37.50			Tumbler, 3 oz. Footed Cocktail	15.00		
Creamer	6.50		35.00	Tumbler, 8 oz. Footed Water	12.50		
Creamer and Sugar on Diamond Shaped Tray		27.50		Tumbler, 12 oz. Footed Iced Tea	22.50		
Cruet, 6½ oz. and Stopper		127.50		Wine, 3", 4 oz.	17.50		
Cup	4.50	4.50	20.00				
Decanter and Stopper	77.50						

*Beware new Teal

Please refer to Foreword for pricing information

SHARON, "CABBAGE ROSE" FEDERAL GLASS COMPANY, 1935-1939

Colors: Pink, green, amber; some crystal. *(See Reproduction Section)*

Due to its popularity, this pattern has been hassled by reproductions of the shakers, sugar with lid and creamer as well as those older reproductions of the butter and cheese dish. However, new is easily told from old! See the section on reproductions. Sharon prices for pink have decreased while prices for amber and green have remained steady or even shown some increases! No amber has been re-made, and in green, only the butter and cheese dishes were copied. There never was a green cheese dish originally.

You're looking at one of the most durable patterns in Depression glass. You'll find pieces scratched from years of usage, but you seldom find one chipped. I was told salesmen used to put a plate on the floor and stand on it to prove its durability! It was manufactured at a time when items were made to last rather than programmed for deterioration. There's always been a pricing difference between green pitchers with and without the ice lip. That same distinction is now being noticed in pink and amber pitchers. Pitchers without ice lips are more desirable to collectors because they seem to be more scarce.

Both the cheese and butter dishes are pictured in pink. You'll notice the cheese dish bottom has a ledge of glass OUTSIDE the rim of the top. Otherwise, the bottom is the same as a regular salad plate. (The cheese dish is pictured on the left of the butter). The butter bottom, which was made from a 1½" deep jam dish, has a tiny ledge of glass on the INSIDE of that butter top lid. It's a very shallow ledge. If you tried to scoot the original butter across the table by the knob, you'd scoot the top off the bottom. The tops are the same on the butter and cheese dishes. New collectors confuse the 2" high soup bowl with the 1½" high jam dish. Jam dishes are just like the butter bottoms only they don't have the ridge of glass for a butter top to rest against. Carry your pocket measuring tapes! Three items have been found in crystal Sharon: a 7½" salad plate, footed tumblers (both pictured in the 5th edition) and a few thousand cake plates. These cake plates are hard to sell to collectors, but present day cake decorating enthusiasts like them! You may find these with an aluminum top.

	Amber	Pink	Green
Bowl, 5″ Berry	6.00	6.00	7.50
Bowl, 5″ Cream Soup	16.50	27.50	32.50
Bowl, 6″ Cereal	10.00	13.00	12.50
Bowl, 7½″ Flat Soup, 2″ Deep	22.50	25.00	
Bowl, 8½″ Large Berry	4.50	15.00	20.00
Bowl, 9½″ Oval Vegetable	10.00	15.00	15.00
Bowl, 10½″ Fruit	15.00	20.00	22.50
Butter Dish and Cover	40.00	35.00	67.50
Butter Dish Bottom	20.00	17.50	30.00
Butter Dish Top	20.00	17.50	37.50
*Cake Plate, 11½″ Footed	16.00	22.00	45.00
Candy Jar and Cover	35.00	32.00	110.00
Cheese Dish and Cover	145.00	535.00	
Creamer, Footed	9.50	10.00	13.50
Cup	8.00	7.50	10.00
Jam Dish, 7½″	25.00	95.00	32.50
Pitcher, 80 oz. with Ice Lip	97.50	95.00	295.00
Pitcher, 80 oz. without Ice Lip	95.00	90.00	300.00
Plate, 6″ Bread and Butter	3.00	3.00	4.50
**Plate, 7½″ Salad	10.00	15.00	13.50
Plate, 9½″ Dinner	9.50	10.00	12.00
Platter, 12½″ Oval	11.50	13.00	16.00
Salt and Pepper, Pr.	32.50	30.00	55.00
Saucer	4.00	5.50	5.50
Sherbet, Footed	8.50	9.00	20.00
Sugar	6.50	7.50	10.00
Sugar Lid	16.50	17.50	25.00
Tumbler, 4⅛″, 9 oz. Thick	21.00	20.00	42.50
Tumbler, 4⅛″, 9 oz. Thin	19.00	18.00	40.00
Tumbler, 5¼″, 12 oz. Thin	22.50	32.50	70.00
Tumbler, 5¼″, 12 oz. Thick	35.00	50.00	65.00
**Tumbler, 6½″, 15 oz. Footed	55.00	31.50	

*Crystal—$5.00
**Crystal—$13.50

Please refer to Foreword for pricing information

"SHIPS" or "SAILBOAT" also known as "SPORTSMAN SERIES"

HAZEL ATLAS GLASS COMPANY, Late 1930's

Colors: Cobalt blue w/white and red decorations.

"Ships" has been called by several names and I tend to favor "Sailboats", but more collectors seem to use "Ships". The sailboat motif is the most commonly found decoration, but you can find a multitude of others including skiers, angel fish, windmills, dogs, polo players and other style boats. The items with red and white decorations along with the shot glass are the most difficult to find. Most of the designs seem to appear only as cocktail shakers and tumblers. I have only seen pitchers with the "Ships" and angel fish decorations, Have you others?

Moderntone with "Ships" decorations is the most collected form and the only dinnerware available with this decoration. You will find saucers, 5⅞" sherbet and 9" dinner plates. The cups that go with the saucers are plain.

In this book I will list all the pieces we have found in our two year search. There are probably others. Not pictured is a 12" blue, round metal tray with a white sailing ship which was found as a cocktail set holding the cocktail stirrer and eight glasses. The prices for items with BOTH white and red decorations will sell about 20-25% more than the prices listed.

	Blue/white		Blue/white
Cup (plain)	7.50	Tumbler, shot glass	30.00
Cocktail Mixer w/Stirrer	17.50	Tumbler, 5 oz., 3¾", Juice	7.50
Cocktail Shaker	20.00	Tumbler, 6 oz., Roly Poly	7.50
Ice Bowl	22.50	Tumbler, 8 oz., 3⅜", Old Fashion	10.00
Pitcher w/o Lip, 82 oz.	32.50	Tumbler, 9 oz., 3¾", Straight Water	10.00
Pitcher w/Lip, 86 oz.	35.00	Tumbler, 9 oz., 4⅝", Water	8.00
Plate, 5⅞", Sherbet	10.00	Tumbler, 10½ oz., 4⅞", Iced Tea	10.00
Plate, 9", Dinner	16.50	Tumbler, 12 oz., Iced Tea	12.50
Saucer	9.50		

SIERRA, "PINWHEEL"   JEANNETTE GLASS COMPANY, 1931-1933

Colors: Green, pink.

Sierra is "famous" in Depression glass circles for its combination "Adam--Sierra" butter dish. One is pictured in pink (p.9). Looking closely, you can see the saw-toothed Sierra pattern moulded on the inside of the butter top while the Adam pattern motif is clearly imprinted on the outside of the top! Many collectors still lack this gem!

It took me several years to find an oval vegetable bowl in green which is shown next to the platter. Besides that bowl, the pitcher and tumblers are the next pieces remaining elusive in today's market.

This is a surprisingly attractive pattern when you get bunches of pieces together and it's still relatively inexpensive. Sierra is the Spanish word for "saw" and because of it's "saw-toothed" design, you'll have to check every little serration for chips.

Notice that cups must have the saw-like (uneven) edges before the rim of clear glass. Some people put any paneled cup atop a Sierra saucer. No, there are no serrated edges on the cups. It would make drinking from them rather difficult.

	Pink	Green		Pink	Green
Bowl, 5½" Cereal	6.00	7.00	Platter, 11" Oval	12.50	15.00
Bowl, 8½" Large Berry	10.00	14.50	Salt and Pepper, Pr.	27.50	30.00
Bowl, 9¼" Oval Vegetable	23.50	40.00	Saucer	3.50	4.00
Butter Dish and Cover	45.00	47.50	Serving Tray, 10¼", 2 Handles	8.50	9.50
Creamer	8.50	12.50	Sugar	12.50	12.50
Cup	6.00	8.50	Sugar Cover	8.00	8.00
Pitcher, 6½", 32 oz.	40.00	65.00	Tumbler, 4½", 9 oz. Footed	25.00	40.00
Plate, 9" Dinner	9.50	12.50			

Please refer to Foreword for pricing information

SPIRAL, HOCKING GLASS COMPANY, 1928-1930

Colors: Green, pink.

There is one piece of Twisted Optic shown here. Can you spot it? It is the center-handled server right in front. If you will refer to Twisted Optic, you will see the same thing. It is easier to compare these in the same picture, so I hope you can see the difference clearly. In the last book, this happened by mistake. Several collectors told me it helped them. So, we did it deliberately for this photograph.

Generally speaking, Hocking's spirals go to the left or with the clock and Imperial's Twisted Optic spirals go the right or counterclockwise. However, Imperial's candy jar appears to go left--unless you turn it upside down; and Spiral's center-handled server goes right--unless you look through the bottom. That Spiral server is pictured, by the way, with Twisted Optic.

Learn to ask for this pattern at shows if you collect it. Most dealers leave Spiral at their shop. In fact, so many companies made "spiraling" patterns, most dealers tend to lump them all under that heading. Looking on the bright side, that broadens your range of choice!

The flat sugar and creamer were an early issue. The footed variety came last.

	Crystal, Iridescent	Pink Green		Crystal, Iridescent	Pink Green
Bowl, 4" Berry	4.50	6.50	Pickle Dish, 8¼" Oval	7.00	9.00
Bowl, 6¼", 2" Deep	20.00	35.00	** Pitcher, 7¾"	140.00	130.00
Bowl, 6½" Deep Salad	7.50	10.00	Plate, 6" Sherbet	3.50	5.00
Bowl, 7½" Deep Berry	9.50	13.50	Plate, 7½" Salad	6.50	8.50
* Butter Dish and Cover	97.50	125.00	Sherbet	5.50	6.50
Butter Dish Bottom	47.50	52.50	Sugar, Small Open	10.00	12.50
Butter Dish Top	50.00	72.50	Sugar Large	10.00	13.50
Comport, 5¾"	8.50	12.50	Sugar Cover	15.00	25.00
Creamer, Small	8.50	11.00	*** Tumbler, 3⅝", 9 oz.	13.50	20.00
Creamer, 4⅝" Large	12.50	17.50			
Olive Dish, 5" One Handled	6.50	9.00			

STARLIGHT HAZEL ATLAS GLASS COMPANY, 1938-1940

Colors: Crystal, pink; some white, cobalt.

There's another bowl to look for in Starlight. It is 12" wide, but only 2¾" tall. The bowl normally found is 11⅜" wide and 3⅝" high.

If you want a challenge, try collecting Starlight sherbet dishes. I've had collector after collector ask me if I'd seen any other than the one pictured! Yes! In fact, I found seven not long ago, but I passed them on to an eager collector.

Cobalt bowls are the only items to turn up so far in that color, and the items pictured in white are all that are known thus far.

Salt and pepper shakers are reaching the "endangered species" level.

	Crystal, White	Pink		Crystal, White	Pink
Bowl, 5½" Cereal	3.00	3.50	Plate, 9" Dinner	3.50	6.00
* Bowl, 8½", Closed Handles	3.00	8.50	Plate, 13" Sandwich	5.00	7.50
Bowl, 11½" Salad	11.50	17.50	Relish Dish	9.50	4.50
Bowl, 12", 2¾" Deep	15.00		Salt and Pepper, Pr.	15.00	
Plate, 6" Bread and Butter	2.00	3.00	Saucer	1.00	2.00
Creamer, Oval	3.00		Sherbet	7.00	
Cup	2.50	3.50	Sugar, Oval	3.00	
Plate, 8½" Luncheon	2.50	3.50			

*Cobalt—$20.00

STRAWBERRY and "CHERRYBERRY"   U.S. GLASS COMPANY, Early 1930's

Colors: Pink, green, crystal; some iridized.

The lack of new "item" collectors has caused those harder-to-find pieces with the "cherryberry" motif to be selling in the same price range of Strawberry. This trend probably will not last indefinitely.

Iridized pieces, especially with good color, are rare!

Only the tops of the butter carry a design. The bottom is the same plain rayed bottom as Aunt Polly, Floral and Diamond and U.S. Swirl.

The large sugar has no handle and is often found lidless and mistaken for a spooner.

Strawberry items are pictured on the right of the photo, "Cherryberry" is shown on the left.

	Crystal, Iridescent	Pink Green		Crystal, Iridescent	Pink Green
Bowl, 4" Berry	4.50	6.50	Olive Dish, 5" One Handled	6.50	9.00
Bowl, 6¼", 2" Deep	20.00	35.00	Pickle Dish, 8¼" Oval	7.00	9.00
Bowl, 6½" Deep Salad	7.50	10.00	** Pitcher, 7¾"	140.00	130.00
Bowl, 7½" Deep Berry	9.50	13.50	Plate, 6" Sherbet	3.50	5.00
* Butter Dish and Cover	97.50	125.00	Plate, 7½" Salad	6.50	8.50
Butter Dish Bottom	47.50	52.50	Sherbet	5.50	6.50
Butter Dish Top	50.00	72.50	Sugar, Small Open	10.00	12.50
Comport, 5¾"	8.50	12.50	Sugar Large	10.00	13.50
Creamer, Small	8.50	11.00	Sugar Cover	15.00	25.00
Creamer, 4⅝" Large	12.50	17.50	*** Tumbler, 3⅝", 9 oz.	13.50	20.00

SUNFLOWER   JEANNETTE GLASS COMPANY, 1930's

Colors: Pink, green, some delphite; some opaques

The delphite creamer has not found a sugar to accompany it as yet. Nor did I find a mustard colored sugar to go with that creamer, but I did find a slightly damaged cup. Of course, the odd colored creamer came with the mustard colored sugar over ten years ago. Surely, this awful color wasn't an entire luncheon set!

I finally was able to get a rare Sunflower trivet to photograph along side the PLENTIFUL cake plate.

I first saw this pink trivet at a show in Michigan in 1976. While at Seattle's Green River Depression Glass Show in February, 1985, I walked up to a display and picked up this Sunflower trivet. The owner sold it to me and asked if I remembered trying to buy it in 1976. It seems she had moved from Michigan and this was the first time since that 1976 show that she had ever displayed the trivet! It makes you think it was meant to be!

Green is more in demand but both colors sell well except for the ever present cake plate, and even that is selling in my shop occasionally.

	Pink	Green		Pink	Green
* Ash Tray, 5", Center Design Only	7.00	7.00	Saucer	3.00	3.00
Cake Plate, 10", 3 Legs	9.00	9.00	Sugar (Opaque $85.00)	9.00	10.00
** Creamer (Opaque $85.00)	9.50	10.50	Tumbler, 4¾", 8 oz. Footed	13.50	18..00
Cup	8.00	9.00	Trivet, 7", 3 Legs, Turned Up Edge	150.00	165.00
Plate, 9" Dinner	9.00	10.00			

*Found in ultramarine—$20.00
**Delphite—$65.00

SWANKY SWIGS 1930's-1950's

Swanky Swigs originally came with a Kraft Cheese product. In fact, the last one pictured still has the "Old English Sharp" cheese in it! The product was priced at 27 cents and the glass was packed in 1954 paper. I'm only scratching the surface on these. If you want to delve deeper, there are interesting articles on them in the Depression Daze newspaper, an ad for which is in the back of this book. You can still find these at bargain prices at yard sales! Pick a design you particularly like and perk up your serving of breakfast juices! The daffodils and cornflowers are favorites of customers in my shop.

Top Picture

Top Row	Band No. 1	Red & Black	3⅜	1.50- 2.50
		Red & Blue	3⅜"	2.00- 3.00
		Blue	3⅜"	2.50- 3.50
	Band No. 2	Red & Black	4¾"	3.00- 4.00
		Red & Black	3⅜"	2.00- 3.00
	Band No. 3	Blue & White	3⅜"	2.00- 3.00
	Circle & Dot:	Blue	4¾"	5.00- 7.50
		Blue	3½"	4.00- 5.00
		Red, Green	3½"	2.50- 3.50
		Black	3½"	4.00- 5.00
		Red	4¾"	5.00- 7.50
	Dot	Black	4¾"	6.00- 8.00
		Blue	3½"	4.00- 5.00
2nd Row	Star:	Blue	4¾"	4.00- 5.00
		Blue, Red, Green, Black	3½"	2.50- 3.50
		Cobalt w/White Stars	4¾"	12.00-14.00
	Centennials:	W. Va. Cobalt	4¾"	14.00-16.00
		Texas Cobalt	4¾"	14.00-16.00
		Texas Blue, Black, Green	3½"	7.50- 9.00
	Checkerboard	Blue, Red	3½"	15.00-17.50
3rd Row	Checkerboard	Green	3⅛"	20.00-22.50
	Sailboat	Blue	4½"	10.00-15.00
		Blue	3½"	8.00-10.00
		Red, Green	4½"	10.00-12.50
		Green, Lt. Green	3½"	8.00-10.00
	Tulip No. 1	Blue, Red	4½"	5.00- 6.00
		Blue, Red	3½"	2.50- 3.50
4th Row	Tulip No.1	Green	4½"	5.00- 6.00
		Green, Black	3½"	2.50- 3.50
		Green w/Label	3½"	4.00- 5.00
	Tulip No.2	Red, Green, Black	3½"	15.00-17.50
	Carnival	Blue, Red	3½"	2.00- 3.00
		Green, Yellow	3½"	4.00- 6.00
	Tulip No. 3	Dk. Blue, Lt. Blue	3¾"	1.00- 2.00

Second Picture

1st Row	Tulip No.3	Red, Yellow	3¾"	1.00- 2.00
	Posey: Tulip	Red	4½"	10.00-12.00
		Red	3½"	2.00- 3.00
		Red	3¼"	6.00- 8.00
	Posey: Violet, Jonquil, Cornflower No.1		4½"	10.00-12.00
	Posey: Violet, Jonquil, Cornflower No.1		3½"	2.00- 3.00
	Cornflower No.2	Lt. Blue, Dk. Blue	3½"	1.50- 2.50
2nd Row	Cornflower No.2	Red, Yellow	3½"	1.50- 2.50
	Forget-Me-Not	Dk. Blue, Blue, Red, Yellow	3½"	1.00- 2.00
		Yellow w/Label	3½"	3.00- 4.00
	Daisy	Red & White; Red, White, & Green	3¾"	1.00- 1.50
	Bustling Betsy	Blue	3¾"	1.00- 2.00
		Blue	3¼"	4.00- 5.00
		Green, Orange	3¾"	1.00- 2.00
3rd Row	Bustling Betsy	Yellow, Red, Brown	3¾"	1.00- 2.00
	Antique Pattern:			
	Clock & Coal Scuttle	Brown	3¾"	1.00- 2.00
	Lamp & Kettle	Blue	3¾"	1.00- 2.00
	Coffee Grinder & Plate	Green	3¾"	1.00- 2.00
	Spinning Wheel & Bellows	Red	3¾"	1.00- 2.00
	Coffee Pot & Trivet	Black	3¾"	1.00- 2.00
	Churn & Cradle	Orange	3¾"	1.50- 2.50
4th Row	Kiddie Cup:			
	Squirrel & Deer	Brown	3¾"	1.00- 2.00
	Bear & Pig	Blue	3¾"	1.00- 2.00
	Cat & Rabbit	Green	3¾"	1.00- 2.00
	Bird & Elephant	Red	3¾"	1.00- 2.00
	Bird & Elephant w/Label		3¾"	3.00- 4.00
	Duck & Horse	Black	3¾"	1.00- 2.00
	Dog & Rooster	Orange	3¾"	1.50- 2.00
	Dog & Rooster w/Cheese			8.00-10.00

Kay Spread

KRAFT
PIMENTO
KRAFT
Olive
Pimento
KRAFT
Old
English

SWIRL, "PETAL SWIRL"   JEANNETTE GLASS COMPANY, 1937-1938

Colors: Ultra-marine, pink, delphite; some amber, ice blue.

Swirl has followed a peculiar pattern. Some prices have increased slightly while others have decreased. I am guessing that the adjustment in prices is from collectors finally determining that some items are scarce, and some pieces thought to be rare really are not. The butter dish and the candy jar are two pieces in the latter category.

Since the ultra-marine Swirl pitcher was featured here as a pattern shot, two others have also been discovered! A picture is worth a thousand words . . . and that particular pitcher is worth quite a bit more!

There aren't as many collectors for pink Swirl as for the ultra-marine color. Therefore, ultra-marine prices often outshine those for pink. However, potential collectors should know that ultra-marine comes in both a green and a blue tint. Matching hues is oft times difficult! The greener pieces seem in shorter supply, but they are also in less demand.

Plates come with both round and fluted edges. Collectors generally prefer the fluted edges.

Coasters will have the concentric rings shown in the center of the ultra-marine plates. Sometimes collectors overlook these. Coasters were also used as an advertisement for General Tires and come encircled with small rubber tires! Tire surrounded coasters would certainly set a novel table.

Flat iced tea tumblers are hard to find in both colors.

Collectors of Swirl dinnerware have been delighted by the Jennyware kitchen items made by this same company. See my Kitchenware book for pictures.

There are few collectors of delphite, but as you can see there are quite a few pieces to be found. Perhaps these would make a more suitable breakfast set.

	Pink	Ultra-marine	Delphite		Pink	Ultra-marine	Delphite
Ash Tray, 5⅜"	5.00	7.50		Pitcher, 48 oz. Footed		850.00	
Bowl, 5¼" Cereal	5.00	7.50	8.50	Plate, 6½" Sherbet	2.00	3.50	3.00
Bowl, 9" Salad	9.50	15.00	16.00	Plate, 7¼"	4.50	7.50	
Bowl, 10" Footed,				Plate, 8" Salad	5.00	9.50	4.50
Closed Handles		20.00		Plate, 9¼" Dinner	6.00	10.00	5.50
Bowl, 10½" Footed				Plate, 10½"			10.00
Console	12.50	17.50		Plate, 12½" Sandwich	7.50	13.50	
Butter Dish	120.00	175.00		Platter, 12" Oval			20.00
Butter Dish Bottom	20.00	30.00		Salt and Pepper, Pr.		25.00	
Butter Dish Top	100.00	145.00		Saucer	1.50	2.00	2.00
Candleholders, Double				Sherbet, Low Footed	5.50	9.50	
Branch Pr.	20.00	20.00		Soup, Tab Handles			
Candleholders, Single				(Lug)	12.50	14.50	
Branch Pr.			77.50	Sugar, Footed	6.50	9.50	7.50
Candy Dish, Open, 3				Tumbler, 4", 9 oz.	7.50	15.00	
Legs	6.00	8.50		Tumbler, 4⅝", 9 oz.	10.00		
Candy Dish with Cover	52.50	67.50		Tumbler, 4¾", 12 oz.	15.00	40.00	
Coaster, 1" x 3¼"	5.50	6.50		Tumbler, 9 oz. Footed	12.50	18.00	
Creamer, Footed	6.50	9.50	7.50	Vase, 6½" Footed	11.50	15.00	
Cup	4.00	7.50	5.00	Vase, 8½" Footed		17.50	

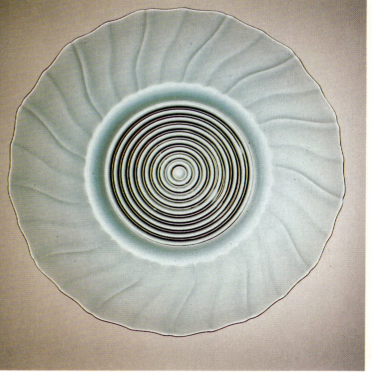

TEA ROOM, INDIANA GLASS COMPANY, 1926-1931

Colors: Pink, green, amber, some crystal

Tea Room collectors have enough problems finding all the sugar and creamers without compounding that problem, but another set has appeared in pink! The creamer is 3¼" tall and the sugar is 3" tall but has a lid. I have had them for over a year, unfortunately, they were left at the shop when we went to photograph. Between the two photos, you can see all the ruffled vases and the ruffled sundae. The ruffled 11" vase seems to be the most difficult to find although the ruffled sundaes are not exactly easy. Center handled sandwich servers are beginning to show up more often now, and some at ridiculous prices! The price below is not a "hoped-for" price but an actual selling price. There is a difference!

I've yet to see a complete green mustard.

According to old catalogues, the flat sugar came with a slotted or a plain lid. The one with a slotted lid is being called a marmalade by collectors. Whatever you call it, there are few to be found.

As the name implies, Tea Room was intended to be used in the "tea rooms" and "ice cream" parlors of the day. That's why you find so many soda fountain type items in this pattern. Plates, cups and saucers, however, in mint condition are very few and far between. People who seek this pattern are fanatic in their admiration for it; others can't abide the sight of it. There seems to be no middle ground of acceptability. Prices for Tea Room still tend to be regional. In the 32 shows and 37,000 miles of travel this past year, highest prices for the pattern were found in Indiana, where it was originally made; New York, where its Art Deco style is admired; Florida, where some avid collectors reside; and in Texas--everything has ALWAYS been BIGGER in TEXAS! Having examined many pieces found in their original packing, it is my firm belief that many of these items came from the original moulds with tiny nicks and cracks in them. Nevertheless, pricing here is for mint glassware. Nicks and chips should lower the prices on pieces. As with Pyramid, you'll have to examine all the little ridges for damage and determine how much imperfection you're prepared to live with for the price being asked. A new wrinkle to watch for with the unscrupulous is clear fingernail polish filling in nicks. Take your bi-focals if necessary!

	Green	Pink		Green	Pink
Bowl, Finger	25.00	20.00	* Saucer	12.50	12.00
Bowl, 7½" Banana Split	50.00	40.00	Sherbet, Low Footed	16.00	13.50
Bowl, 8½" Celery	25.00	20.00	Sherbet, Low Flared Edge	25.00	20.00
Bowl, 8¾" Deep Salad	65.00	45.00	Sherbet, Tall Footed	30.00	27.50
Bowl, 9½" Oval Vegetable	45.00	40.00	Sugar w/lid 3"		25.00
Candlestick, Low Pr.	30.00	25.00	Sugar, 4"	12.50	10.00
Creamer, 3¼"		15.00	Sugar, 4½" Footed		
Creamer, 4"	12.50	10.00	(Amber $45.00)	14.00	12.00
Creamer, 4½" Footed			Sugar, Rectangular	12.50	10.00
(Amber $45.00)	13.50	12.00	Sugar, Flat with Cover	90.00	80.00
Creamer, Rectangular	12.50	10.00	Sundae, Footed, Ruffled Top	75.00	60.00
Creamer & Sugar on Tray, 3½"	52.50	50.00	Tray, Center Handled	85.00	75.00
*Cup	25.00	20.00	Tray, Rectangular Sugar &		
Goblet, 9 oz.	52.50	42.50	Creamer	35.00	30.00
Ice Bucket	40.00	35.00	Tumbler, 8½ oz., Flat	52.50	40.00
Lamp, 9" Electric	32.50	30.00	Tumbler, 6 oz. Footed	20.00	15.00
Marmalade, Notched Lid	100.00	90.00	Tumbler, 9 oz. Footed		
Mustard, Covered	85.00	75.00	(Amber $45.00)	20.00	16.50
Parfait	37.50	32.50	Tumbler, 11 oz. Footed	30.00	25.00
**Pitcher, 64 oz. (Amber $300.00)	100.00	95.00	Tumbler, 12 oz. Footed	35.00	30.00
Plate, 6½" Sherbet	15.00	12.00	Vase 6" Ruffled Edge	75.00	60.00
Plate, 8¼", Luncheon	20.00	20.00	Vase, 9" Ruffled Edge	75.00	60.00
Plate, 10½", Two Handled	35.00	30.00	Vase 9" Straight	50.00	40.00
Relish, Divided	16.00	12.50	Vase 11" Ruffled Edge	125.00	110.00
Salt and Pepper, Pr.	37.50	37.50	Vase 11" Straight	65.00	60.00

*Prices for absolute mint pieces
**Crystal—$175.00

Please refer to Foreword for pricing information

THISTLE   MACBETH-EVANS, 1929-1930

Colors: Pink, green; some yellow, crystal.

Pink Thistle is more in demand than the green, possibly because luncheon items (cups, saucers, plates) are easier to find in pink than in green. Serving pieces are hard to find! That large 10¼″ bowl in pink is even harder to lay hands on than its Dogwood counterpart, and it probably won't be cheap when you find it!

You will, of course, notice that the shapes in this pattern strongly resemble Dogwood. The same basic moulds were used for both patterns. However, we're still hoping for pitchers, tumblers, sugars and creamers in Thistle. Dogwood pattern has such lovely ones. I hasten to add that there are perfectly plain pink and green pitchers of the Dogwood SHAPE that would work beautifully with the Thistle pattern. Be advised that it will take time to collect this pattern.

I still get letters regarding a heavy pink butter dish with a thistle design on it. This piece is a new version of an older Pattern glass butter dish. It is not Depression glass, nor does it belong to this pattern although you could use it with these dishes if you so desire. It's much heavier glass and a different color pink which, to my mind, argues against its blending well with this delicate Thistle pattern.

	Pink	Green		Pink	Green
Bowl, 5½″ Cereal	12.00	15.00	Plate, 10¼″ Grill	12.50	12.50
Bowl, 10¼″ Large Fruit	175.00	110.00	Plate, 13″ Heavy Cake	70.00	85.00
Cup, Thin	14.00	17.50	Saucer	7.50	7.50
Plate, 8″ Luncheon	8.00	12.50			

"THUMBPRINT", PEAR OPTIC   FEDERAL GLASS COMPANY, 1929-1930

Color: Green.

Thanks to photographer, Raymond Mills, you can see a set of "Thumbprint" owned by Imogene McKinney. She took me to task at the Houston show because I never had anything "good" to say about "Thumbprint". This is a picture of her collection for all to see, and I'll have to admit it looks good. I can't honestly claim that this is a great selling pattern in Depression glass, but if you enjoy challenges, this may be the pattern for you!

I will not say for certain that all items shown here are made by Federal, but as you can see they blend well together. You will note I have added a few new pieces to the listing this time.

This pattern is often confused with Raindrops pattern. The differences are explained there.

	Green		Green
Bowl, 4¾″ Berry	2.00	Salt and Pepper, Pr.	17.50
Bowl, 5″ Cereal	2.50	Saucer	1.00
Bowl, 8″ Large Berry	6.00	Sherbet	4.00
Creamer, Footed	8.50	Sugar, Footed	8.50
Cup	2.50	Tumbler, 4″, 5 oz.	3.50
Plate, 6″ Sherbet	1.25	Tumbler, 5″, 10 oz.	4.00
Plate, 8″ Luncheon	2.00	Tumbler, 5½″, 12 oz.	4.00
Plate, 9¼″ Dinner	4.50	Whiskey, 2¼″, 1 oz.	3.00

Please refer to Foreword for pricing information

TWISTED OPTIC   Imperial Glass Company, 1927-1930

Colors: Pink, green, amber; some blue, canary yellow.

There is one piece of Spiral shown here. Can you find it? If you have already read Spiral, it will be easy. If not, it is the center handled server. I have found, by accident, that it is easier to compare both patterns (which are often confused) by placing pieces of each in the same picture. The blue sherbet that turned up on an off center sherbet plate is shown here. The plates measures 7½ x 9″ and was found here in Kentucky. These same pieces have been spotted in the bright canary yellow color. I'm beginning to see an increased stir of acitivity in Twisted Optic; so don't sweep this under the rug quite yet! Twisted Optic's center handled server has a Y shaped handle. There's a space in the middle for gripping it. The spirals go left, also, which is generally the wrong direction for this pattern. You have to look at this piece from the bottom for the spirals to go in the proper direction. No wonder collectors confuse this with Spiral.

	*All Colors		All Colors
Bowl, 4¾″ Cream Soup	5.50	Plate, 8″ Luncheon	2.00
Bowl, 5″ Cereal	2.00	Preserve (Same as candy but	
Bowl, 7″ Salad or Soup	5.50	with Slot in Lid)	17.50
Candlesticks, 3″ Pr.	10.00	Sandwich Server, Center Handle	12.50
Candy Jar and Cover	15.00	Sandwich Server, Two Handled	5.50
Creamer	4.50	Saucer	1.00
Cup	2.50	Sherbet	4.00
Pitcher, 64 oz.	17.50	Sugar	4.50
Plate, 6″ Sherbet	1.50	Tumbler, 4½″, 9 oz.	4.50
Plate, 7″ Salad	2.00	Tumbler, 5¼″, 12 oz.	6.50
Plate, 7½″ x 9″ Oval with Indent	3.50		

*Blue, Canary Yellow 50% more

U.S. SWIRL   U.S. GLASS COMPANY Late 1920's

Colors: Pink, green.

Until now, the only claim to fame for this pattern was that the shaker tops could be stripped off for use on Aunt Polly's shakers; those tops are usually corroded and replacements are impossible to find. Notice that these pieces follow the same basic shapes of Aunt Polly, Strawberry or Floral and Diamond. I have dubbed the pattern "U.S. Swirl" to distinguish it from our Swirl pattern from Jeannette. I have been seeing this pattern for years, and it will give you something new to search for in your travels. The butter dish bottom is plain like U.S. Glass Company butter bottoms. It will be harder now to buy the butter bottom to use on Strawberry or another pattern.

	Green	Pink
Bowl, 4⅜″, Berry	4.50	5.00
Bowl, 5½″, One Handle	8.50	9.00
Bowl, 7⅞″, Large Berry	11.00	12.00
Bowl, 8¼″, Oval	12.50	13.50
Butter and Cover	52.50	67.50
Butter Bottom	42.50	52.50
Butter Top	10.00	15.00
Candy w/Cover, Two Handled	20.00	22.50
Creamer	10.00	11.00
Pitcher, 8″, 48 oz.	22.50	25.00
Plate, 6⅛″, Sherbet	1.50	1.75
Plate, 7⅞″, Salad	4.50	5.00
Salt and Pepper, Pair	27.50	30.00
Sherbet, 3¼″	3.50	4.00
Sugar w/Lid	15.00	16.50
Tumbler, 4⅝″, 12 oz.	8.50	9.00
Vase, 6½″	12.50	13.50

"VICTORY"   DIAMOND GLASS-WARE COMPANY, 1929-1932

Colors: Amber, green; some cobalt blue; black

Believe it or not there really is a set of cobalt blue! I was particularly impressed with the gravy boat and platter. Prices for the blue and the black are beginning to soar! Only Madrid and Florentine No. 2 have gravy boats and the prices are soaring on these.

Most pieces found in this pattern seem to come from the Ohio-Pennsylvania area.

The most desirable pieces to own besides the gravy boat and platter, are the goblets, soup and cereal bowls. All of these are rarely seen.

Most flat pieces have ground bottoms rather than moulded ones, further attesting to the fact that this was among the better glasswares of that day and probably why there is so little of it found today! More expensive glass of that time is rarer today than that which was less expensive. That makes sense, doesn't it?

	Amber, Pink, Green	Black, Blue		Amber, Pink, Green	Black, Blue
Bon Bon, 7"	9.00	15.00	Gravy Boat and Platter	100.00	175.00
Bowl, 6½" Cereal	7.50	15.00	Mayonnaise Set: 3½" Tall, 5½"		
Bowl, 8½" Flat Soup	10.00	20.00	Across, 8½" Indented Plate		
Bowl, 9" Oval Vegetable	25.00	40.00	w/Ladle	35.00	55.00
Bowl, 11" Rolled Edge	20.00	35.00	Plate, 6" Bread and Butter	3.00	6.00
Bowl, 12" Console	27.50		Plate, 7" Salad	5.50	8.00
Bowl, 12½" Flat Edge	22.50	40.00	Plate, 8" Luncheon	5.00	10.00
Candlesticks, 3" Pr.	25.00	50.00	Plate, 9" Dinner	12.50	17.50
Cheese & Cracker Set, 12" Indented Plate & Compote	25.00		Platter, 12"	17.50	35.00
Comport, 6" Tall, 6¾" Diameter	10.00		Sandwich Server, Center Handle	20.00	45.00
Creamer	10.00	22.50	Saucer	2.00	5.00
Cup	6.00	12.00	Sherbet, Footed	10.00	15.00
Goblet, 5", 7 oz.	17.50		Sugar	10.00	22.50

VITROCK, "FLOWER RIM"   HOCKING GLASS COMPANY, 1934-1937

Colors: White and white w/fired-on colors, usually red or green.

Vitrock, "Flower Rim", pattern is often mistaken for Indiana's white Custard line. An obvious difference is the SHAPE. Flowers predominate Vitrock where leaves seem to dominate Indiana's Custard design.

Actually, Hocking sold a whole raft of this white Vitrock ware, particularly kitchenware items. (See *Kitchen Glassware of the Depression Years* for further information on this). Notice the odd shaping of the sugar and creamer. That cream soup bowl on the right side is a very hard item to find and the platter seems to be even harder!

	White		White
Bowl, 4" Berry	3.00	Plate, 7¼" Salad	1.50
Bowl, 5½" Cream Soup	7.50	Plate, 8¾" Luncheon	2.00
Bowl, 6" Fruit	3.00	Plate, 9" Soup	5.00
Bowl, 7½" Cereal	2.50	Plate, 10" Dinner	3.50
Bowl, 9½" Vegetable	6.00	Platter, 11½"	15.00
Creamer, Oval	3.00	Saucer	1.00
Cup	2.00	Sugar, Oval	3.00

Please refer to Foreword for pricing information

WATERFORD, "WAFFLE", HOCKING GLASS COMPANY, 1938-1944

Colors: Crystal, pink; some yellow, white; 1950's, Forest Green.

Novel items to watch for in Waterford include some pieces styled like Miss America. They include a crystal creamer and sugar, a pink water goblet complete with three rings encircling the top, and a 3½", 5 oz. juice tumbler in pink. These items are pictured for the first time. Thank you, Ralph Leslie!

A 13½" relish tray was made in Forest Green in the early '50's. The tray sells for about $5.00 by itself. Usually, the inserts are missing. I get many letters about this piece.

I mentioned letters that I receive. I am happy to answer letters regarding pattens in this book provided you include a self addressed, STAMPED envelope. I receive around 400 letters a month and when my postage meter hit $275.00 for unstamped letters, I ceased to feel guilty about not answering them. I got to thinking that if an answer wasn't worth an extra 22 cents, why should I waste my time and money? Try to be as brief as possible. Twenty page letters listing the contents of a china cabinet are not fun to wade through after a week long trip to and from a show! I really enjoy most letters, especially the ones from children and people just getting into glass! They're so enthusiastic! One young entrepreneur wrote of how he'd bought a 15 cent piece at a yard sale, sold it for a profit, gotten interested enough to really study my book and now had an extra $200 in his college fund from his efforts at buying and selling Depression glass! Those kinds of letters are a real treat to get and enjoy! Thanks!

	Crystal	Pink		Crystal	Pink
Ash Tray, 4"	2.50		Plate, 6" Sherbet	1.50	3.50
Bowl, 4¾" Berry	3.50	6.50	Plate, 7⅛" Salad	2.00	3.50
Bowl, 5½" Cereal	6.50	12.00	Plate, 9⅝" Dinner	5.00	10.00
Bowl, 8¼" Large Berry	6.00	12.00	Plate, 10¼" Handled Cake	5.00	9.50
Butter Dish and Cover	20.00	165.00	Plate, 13¾" Sandwich	5.00	20.00
Butter Dish Bottom	5.00	27.50	Relish, 13¾", 5 Part	12.50	
Butter Dish Top	15.00	145.00	Salt and Pepper, 2 Types	7.50	
Coaster, 4"	1.50	4.00	Saucer	1.00	3.50
Creamer, Oval	2.50	7.50	Sherbet, Footed	2.50	6.50
Creamer (Miss America Style)	15.00		Sugar	2.50	6.50
Cup	3.50	9.50	Sugar Cover, Oval	2.50	10.00
Goblets, 5¼", 5⅝"	9.50		Sugar (Miss America Style)	15.00	
Goblets, 5½" (Miss America Style)	22.50	50.00	Tumbler, 3½", 5 oz. Juice		
Lamp, 4" Spherical Base	22.50		(Miss America Style)		30.00
Pitcher, 42 oz. Tilted Juice	17.50		Tumbler, 4⅞", 10 oz. Footed	8.50	12.00
Pitcher, 80 oz. Tilted Ice Lip	22.50	75.00			

Please refer to Foreword for pricing information

WINDSOR, "WINDSOR DIAMOND", JEANNETTE GLASS COMPANY,

1936-1946

Colors: Pink, green, crystal; some delphite, amberina red, ice blue.

Windsor in ice blue prompted letters wanting to purchase those two pieces shown! Pretty, isn't it!

Plates, cups and saucers have also shown up to match the amberina red pitcher and tumbler!

There are two styles of butter covers shown in crystal.

Difficult to find in pink are candlesticks and the 4½", 16 oz. juice pitcher. Neither of these items have been found in green. I did hear of a lady in California who seemed to have candlesticks in her otherwise complete setting of green. Upon her death, a dealer purchased her set of Windsor. When he washed the candlesticks, however, some sort of green dye she had used washed off the candlesticks revealing crystal ones. She'd made her own green ones!

Berry bowls come with both rounded and pointed edges; pointed edged ones are harder to find.

The original comport did not have a beaded edge. That beaded edged one turning up in crystal (with various sprayed on colors) is of recent vintage. The comport also, originally, served as a base for the rather unique punch bowl which was pictured in the 4th edition. The comport was inverted and used as a base upon which the large bowl rested. They were made to fit into one another in this fashion and sold with twelve cups. That explains why there are so many cups without saucers in crystal!

	Crystal	Pink	Green		Crystal	Pink	Green
* Ash Tray, 5¾"	11.50	27.50	37.50	Pitcher, 5", 20 oz.	5.00		
Bowl, 4¾" Berry	2.50	5.00	6.00	Pitcher, 6¾", 52 oz. (Red			
Bowl, 5" Pointed Edge		7.50		$300.00)	11.00	18.50	35.00
Bowl, 5" Cream Soup	4.50	12.50	13.50	Plate, 6" Sherbet	1.50	2.50	3.50
Bowl, 5⅛", 5⅜" Cereals	3.50	10.00	11.50	Plate, 7" Salad	3.00	9.50	10.00
Bowl, 7⅛", Three Legs	4.00	14.00		** Plate, 9" Dinner	3.50	9.50	9.50
Bowl, 8" Pointed Edge		17.50		Plate, 10¼" Handled Sandwich	4.00	9.00	10.00
Bowl, 8", 2 Handled	4.50	10.00	12.50	Plate, 13⅝" Chop	7.50	20.00	20.00
Bowl, 8½" Large Berry	4.50	10.00	11.00	Plate, 15½" Serving	6.00		
Bowl, 9½" Oval Vegetable	5.00	10.00	12.50	Platter, 11½" Oval	4.50	9.50	10.00
Bowl, 10½" Salad	5.00			Relish Platter, 11½" Divided	5.50		
Bowl, 10½" Pointed Edge		75.00		Salt and Pepper, Pr.	12.50	27.50	37.50
Bowl, 12½" Fruit Console	10.00	55.00		Saucer	1.50	2.50	3.00
Bowl, 7" x 11¾" Boat Shape	11.00	18.00	20.00	Sherbet, Footed	2.50	6.00	7.00
Butter Dish	22.50	37.50	67.50	Sugar and Cover	4.50	15.00	17.50
Cake Plate, 10¾" Footed	5.00	11.50	12.50	Sugar and Cover (Like "Holiday")	4.00		
Cake Plate, 13½" Thick	5.00	11.50	12.50	Tray, 4" Square	2.50	4.50	6.50
Candlesticks, 3" Pr.	12.50	50.00		Tray, 4⅛" x 9"	3.00	6.50	7.50
Candy Jar and Cover	8.50	20.00		Tray, 8½" x 9¾", w/Handles	5.00	18.50	19.50
Coaster, 3¼"	2.50	5.00		Tray, 8½" x 9¾", No Handles		55.00	
Comport	3.00	7.50		Tumbler, 3¼", 5 oz.	4.00	9.50	15.00
** Creamer	3.00	7.50	7.50	** Tumbler, 4", 9 oz.	4.50	9.00	12.00
Creamer (Shaped as "Holiday")	3.00			Tumbler, 5", 12 oz.	5.50	15.00	22.00
Cup	2.50	6.00	7.00	Tumbler, 4" Footed	4.00		
Pitcher, 4½", 16 oz.	17.50	85.00		Tumbler, 7¼" Footed	8.00		

*Delphite—$40.00   **Blue—$45.00   **Red—$50.00

Reproductions

NEW "ADAM"   PRIVATELY PRODUCED OUT OF KOREA THROUGH ST. LOUIS

IMPORTING COMPANY

The new Adam butter is being offered at $6.50 wholesale. Identification of the new is easy.
Top: Notice the veins in the leaves.
New: Large leaf veins do not join or touch in center of leaf.
Old: Large leaf veins all touch or join center vein on the old.
A further note in the original Adam butter dish the veins of all the leaves at the center of the design are very clear cut and precisely moulded, whereas in the new these center leaf veins are very indistinct - and almost invisible in one leaf of the center design.
Bottom: Place butter dish bottom upside down for observation.
New: Four (4) "Arrowhead-like" points line up in northwest, northeast, southeast, and southwest directions of compass.
Old: Four (4) "Arrowhead-like" points line up in north, east, south and west directions of compass.
There are very bad mold lines and very glossy light pink color on those butter dishes I have examined but these could be improved.

NEW "AVOCADO"   INDIANA GLASS COMPANY Tiara Exclusives Line, 1974 . . .

Colors: Pink, frosted pink, yellow, blue, red amethyst, green?

In 1979 a green Avocado pitcher was supposedly run. It was supposed to be darker than the original green and was to be limited to a hostess gift item. I was supposed to get one for photographing purposes. However, I've never seen said pitcher. Did they make it?

The pink they made was described under the pattern. It tends to be more orange than the original color. The other colors shown pose little threat as these colors were not made originally.

I understand that Tiara sales counselors tell potential clientelle that their newly made glass is collectible because it is made from old molds. I don't share this view. I feel it's like saying that since you were married in your grandmother's wedding dress, you will have the same happy marriage for the fifty-seven years she did. All you can truly say is that you were married in her dress. I think all you can say about the new Avocado is that it was made from the old molds. TIME, SCARCITY and PEOPLE'S WHIM determine collectibility in so far as I'm able to determine it. It's taken nearly fifty years or more for people to turn to collecting Depression Glass--and that's done, in part, because EVERYONE "remembers" it; they had some in their home at one time or another; it has universal appeal. Who is to say what will be collectible in the next hundred years. If we all knew, we could all get rich!

If you like the new Tiara products, then by all means buy them; but don't do so DEPENDING upon their being collectible just because they are made in the image of the old! You have an equal chance, I feel, of going to Las Vegas and DEPENDING upon getting rich at the Black Jack table.

Reproductions (Con't.)

NEW "CAMEO"

Colors: Green (shakers); yellow, green, pink (child's dishes).

Although the photographer I left this shaker with opted to shoot the side without the dancing girl, I trust you can still see how very weak the pattern is on this reproduction of Cameo shaker. Also, you can see how very much glass remains in the bottom of the shaker; and, of course, the new tops all make this very easy to spot at the market. These were to be bought wholesale at around $6.00; but did not sell well.

The children's dishes pose no problem to collectors since they were never made originally. The sugar and creamer are a shade over 1½ inches tall and the butter dish is just 3¾ inches from handle to handle. I'm told miniature cake plate, cups, saucers and plates are planned at a future date. This type of production I have no quarrel with as they aren't planned to "dupe" anyone.

NEW "CHERRY BLOSSOM"

Colors: Pink, green, blue, delphite, cobalt, red, iridized colors.

Several different people have gotten into the act of making reproduction Cherry Blossom. We've even enjoyed some reproductions of reproductions! All the items pictured on the next pages are extremely easy to spot as reproductions (colors never made!) once you know what to look for with the possible exception of the 13" divided platter pictured at the back. It's too heavy, weighing 2¾ pounds and has a thick, ⅜" of glass in the bottom; but the design isn't too bad! The edges of the leaves aren't smooth; but neither are they serrated like old leaves.

I could write a book on the differences between old and new scalloped bottom, AOP Cherry pitchers. The easiest way to tell the difference is to turn the pitcher over. My old Cherry pitcher has nine cherries on the bottom. The new one only has seven. Further, the branch crossing the bottom of my old Cherry pitchers LOOKS like a branch. It's knobby and gnarled and has several leaves and cherry stems directly attached to it. The new pitcher just has a bald strip of glass halving the bottom of the pitcher. Further, the old cherry pitchers have a plain glass background for the cherries and leaves in the bottom of the pitcher. In the new pitchers, there's a rough, filled in, straw-like background. You see no plain glass. (My new Cherry pitcher just cracked sitting in a box by my typing stand -- another tendency which I understand is common to the new)!

As for the new tumblers, the easiest way to tell old from new is to look at the ring dividing the patterned portion of the glass from the plain glass lip. The old tumblers have three indented rings dividing the pattern from the plain glass rim. The new has only one. (Turn back and look at the red cherry tumbler pictured with Cherry Blossom pattern). Further, as in the pitcher, the arching encircling the cherry blossoms on the new tumblers is very sharply ridged. On the old tumblers, that arching is so smooth you can barely feel it. Again, the pattern at the bottom of the new tumblers is brief and practically nonexistent in the center curve of the glass bottom. This was sharply defined on most of the old tumblers. You can see how far toward the edge the pattern came on the red cherry tumbler pictured with the pattern. The pattern, what there is, on the new tumblers mostly hugs the center of the foot.

Now for a quick run down of the various items.

2 handled tray - old: 1⅞ lbs; ³⁄₁₆" glass in bottom; leaves and cherries east/west from north/south handles; leaves have real spine and serrated edges; cherry stems end in triangle of glass. **new:** 2⅛ lbs; ¼" glass in bottom; leaves and cherries north/south with the handles; canal type leaves (but uneven edges); cherry stem ends before cup shaped line.

cake plate - new: color too light pink, leaves have too many parallel veins which give them a "feathery" look; arches at plate edge don't line up with lines on inside of the rim to which the feet are attached.

8½" bowl - new: crude leaves with smooth edges; veins in parallel lines.

cereal bowl - new: wrong shape, looks like 8½" bowl, small 2" center. **old:** large center, 2½" inside ring, nearly 3½" if you count the outer rim before the sides turn up.

plate - new: center shown close up; smooth edged leaves, fish spine type center leaf portion; weighs 1 pound plus; feels thicker at edge with mold offset lines clearly visible. (See next page). **old:** center leaves look like real leaves with spines, veins, and serrated edges; weights ¾ pound; clean edges; no mold offset.

cup new: area in bottom left free of design; canal leaves; smooth, thick top to cup handle (old has triangle grasp point).

saucer - new: off set mold line edge; canal leaf center.

Reproductions (Con't.)

NEW CHERRY BLOSSOM (Con't.)

First of all, notice the cup bottom and the close up of the center design on the reproduction plate. Once you learn to recognize these "fake" leaves, you'll be able to spot 95 percent of the reproduction Cherry Blossom. These new leaves look like orderly docking stations at the local marina with a straight canal going down the center. Old Cherry Blossom dishes have real looking leaves, complete with main stem, delicate veins branching from that stem, and serrated edges. Notice the smooth edges of the reproduction leaves.

The Cherry child's dishes were first made in 1973.

First to appear was a child's cherry cup with a slightly lop-sided handle and having the cherries hanging upside down when the cup was held in the right hand. (This defiance of gravity was due to the inversion of the design when the mold, taken from an original cup, was inverted to create the outside of the "new" cup). After I reported this error, it was quickly corrected by re-inverting the inverted mold. These later cups were thus improved in design but slightly off color. The saucers tended to have slightly off center designs, too. Next came the "child's butter dish" which was never made by Jeannette. It was essentially the child's cup without a handle turned upside down over the saucer and having a little glob of glass added as a knob for lifting purposes. You could get this item in pink, green light blue, cobalt, gray-green, and iridescent carnival colors. A blue one in pictured on the preceding page.

Pictured are the colors made so far in the butter dishes and shakers begun in 1977. Some shakers were dated '77 on the bottom and were marketed at the ridiculous price of $27.95, a whopping profit margin! Shortly afterward, the non dated variety appeared. How can you tell new shakers from old--should you get the one in a million chance to do so?

First, look at the tops. New tops COULD indicate new shakers. Next, notice the protruding ledges beneath the tops. They are squared off juts rather than the nicely rounded scallops on the old (which are pictured under Cherry Blossom pattern). The design on the newer shakers is often weak in spots. Finally, notice how far up inside the shakers the solid glass (next to the foot) remains. The newer shakers have almost half again as much glass in that area. They appear to be ¼ full of glass before you ever add the salt!

Butter dishes are naturally more deceptive in pink and green since that blue was not an original color. The major flaw in the new butter is that there is ONE band encircling the bottom edge of the butter top; there are TWO bands very close together along the skirt of the old top. Using your tactile sense, the new top has a sharply defined design up inside; the old was glazed and is smooth to touch. The knob on the new is more sharply defined than the smoothly formed knob on the old butter top.

NEW "MADRID" CALLED "RECOLLECTION"   Currently being made.

I hope you have already read about Recollection Madrid on page 112. The current rage of Indiana Glass is to make Madrid in pink and crystal. The pink is being sold through all kinds of outlets ranging from better department stores to discount catalogs. In the past few months we have received several ads stating that this is genuine Depression glass made from old moulds. None of this is made from old glass moulds unless you consider 1976 old. Most of the pieces are from moulds that were never made originally.

Look at the top picture! None of these items were ever made in the old pattern Madrid. The new grill plate has one division splitting the plate in half, but the old had three sections. A goblet or vase was never made. The vase is sold with a candle making it a "hurricane lamp". The heavy tumbler was placed on top of a candlestick to make this vase/hurricane lamp. That candlestick gets a workout. It was attached to a plate to make a pedestaled cake stand and to a butter dish to make a preserve stand. That's a clever idea, actually.

The shakers are short and heavy and you can see both original styles pictured on page 113. The latest item I have seen is a heavy 11 oz. flat tumbler being sold in a set of four or six called "On the Rocks" for $7.99. The biggest giveaway to this newer glass is the pale, washed out color. (It really looks washed out in the bottom photograph here. This is a little over done, but all the new is almost that bad.)

The bottom picture shows items that were originally made. The only concern in these pieces are the cups, saucers and oval vegetable bowl. These three pieces were made in pink in the 1930's. None of the others shown were ever made in the 1930's in pink, so realize that when you see the butter dish, dinner plate, soup bowl, or sugar and creamer. These are new items! Once you have learned what this washed out pink looks like by seeing these items out for sale, the color will let know when you see other pieces. My suggestion is to avoid pink Madrid except for the pitcher and tumblers.

The most difficult piece for new collectors to tell new from old is the candlestick. The new ones all have raised ridges inside to hold the candle more firmly. All old ones do not have these ridges. You may even find new candlesticks in black.

A special thanks to John and Trannie Davis for providing the "Recollection" glass shown in these photographs! Atlanta stores had it before Lexington's did!

Reproductions (Con't.)

NEW "MAYFAIR"

Colors: Pink, green, blue, cobalt (shot glasses), 1977 onward. Pink, green (cookie jars), 1982.

Only the pink shot glass need cause any concern to collectors because the glass wasn't made in those other colors originally. At first glance, the color of the newer shots is often too light pink or too orange. Dead give away are the stems of the flower design, however. In the old that stem branched to form an "A" shape; in the new, you have a single stem. Further, in the new design, the leaf is hollow with the veins molded in. In the old, the leaf is molded in and the veining is left hollow. In the center of the flower on the old, dots (another) cluster entirely to one side and are rather distinct. Nothing like that occurs in the new design.

As for the cookie jars, at cursory glance, the base of the cookie has a very indistinct design. It will fell smooth to the touch its so faint. In the old cookie jars, there's a distinct pattern which feels like raised embossing to the touch. Next, turn the bottom upside down. The new bottom is perfectly smooth. The old bottom contains a 1¾" mold circle rim that is raised enough to catch your fingernail in it. There are other distinctions as well; but that is the quickest way to tell old from new.

In the Mayfair cookie lid, the new design (parallel to the straight side of the lid) at the edge curves gracefully toward the center "V" shape (rather like bird wings in flight); in the old, that edge is flat, straight line going into the "V" (like airplane wings sticking straight out from the side of the plane as you face it head on).

The green color of the cookie, as you can see from the picture, is not the pretty, yellow/green color of true green Mayfair. It also doesn't "glow" under black light as the old green does.

So, you see, none of these reproductions give us any trouble; they're all easily spotted by those of us now "in the know"!

NEW "MISS AMERICA"

Colors: Crystal, green, pink, ice blue, red amberina, cobalt blue.

The new butter dish in "Miss America" design is probably the best of the newer products; yet there are three distinct differences to be found between the original butter top and the newly made one. Since the value of the butter dish lies in the top, it seems more profitable to examine it.

In the new butter dishes pictured, notice that the panels reaching the edge of the butter bottom tend to have a pronounced curving, skirt-like edge. In the original dish, there is much less curving at the edge of these panels.

Second, pick up the top of the new dish and feel up inside it. If the butter top knob is filled with glass so that it is convex (curved outward), the dish is new; the old inside knob area is concave (curved inward).

Finally, from the underside, look through the top toward the knob. In the original butter dish you would see a perfectly formed multi-sided star; in the newer version, you see distorted rays with no visible points.

Shakers have been made in green, pink and crystal. The shakers will have new tops; but since some old shakers have been given new tops, that isn't conclusive at all. Unscrew the lid. Old shakers have a very neatly formed ridge of glass on which to screw the lid. It overlaps a little and has neatly rounded off ends. Old shakers stand 3⅜ tall without the lid. New ones stand 3¼" tall. Old shakers have almost a forefinger's depth inside (female finger) or a fraction shy of 2½ inches. New shakers have an inside depth of 2", about the second digit bend of a female's finger. (I'm doing finger depths since most of you will have those with you at the flea market, rather than a tape measure). In men, the old shaker's depth covers my knuckle; the new shaker leaves my knuckle exposed. New shakers simply have more glass on the inside the of shaker-- something you can spot from twelve feet away! The hobs are more rounded on the newer shaker, particularly near the stem and seams; in the old shaker these areas remained pointedly sharp!

New Miss America tumblers have ½" of glass in the bottom, has a smooth edge on the bottom of the glass with no mold rim and show only two distinct mold marks on the sides of the glass. Old tumblers have only ¼" of glass in the bottom, have a distinct mold line rimming the bottom of the tumbler and have four distinct mold marks up the sides of the tumbler. The new green tumbler doesn't "glow" under black light as did the old.

New Miss America pitchers are all perfectly smooth rimmed at the top edge above the handle. All old pitchers that I have seen have a "hump" in the top rim of the glass above the handle area, rather like a camel's hump. The very bottom diamonds next to the foot in the new pitchers "squash" into elongated diamonds. In the old pitchers, these get noticeably smaller, but they retain their diamond shape.

Reproductions (Con't.)

NEW SANDWICH (Indiana)   INDIANA GLASS COMPANY

Tiara Exclusive Line, 1969 . . .

Colors: Amber, blue, red, crystal.

The smoky blue and amber shown here are representative of Tiara's line of Sandwich which is presently available. (See Sandwich pattern for older amber color).

The bad news is that the crystal has been made now and there are only minute differences in this new and the old. I will list the pieces made in crystal and you can make yourself aware of these re-issues if you collect the crystal Sandwich.

Ash Tray Set
Basket, Handles, 10½"
Bowl, 4" Berry
Bowl, 8"
Butter Dish & Cover
Candlesticks, 8½"
Cup, 9 oz.
Cup (Fits Indent in 6 oz. Oval Sandwich Plate)
Decanter & Stopper, 10"
Goblet, 5¼", 8 oz.
Pitcher, 8" Tall, 68 oz. Fluted Rim
Plate, 10" Dinner

Plate, 8" Salad
Plate, 8½" x 6¾" Oval Sandwich
Sandwich Tray, Handled
Saucer, 6"
Sherbets
Tray, 10" (Underliner for Wine
   Decanter & Goblets)
Tumbler, 6½" High, 12 oz.

NEW "SHARON"   Privately Produced 1976 . . .

Colors: Blue, dark green, light green, pink, burnt umber

A blue Sharon butter turned up in 1976 and turned my phone line to a liquid fire! The color is Mayfair blue--a fluke and dead giveaway as far as real Sharon is concerned.

When found in similar colors to the old, pink and green, you can immediately tell that the new version has more glass in the top where it changes from pattern to clear glass, a thick, defined ring of glass as opposed to a thin, barely defined ring of glass in the old. The knob of the new dish tends to stick up more. In the old butter dish there's barely room to fit your finger to grasp the knob. The new butter dish has a sharply defined ridge of glass in the bottom around which the top sits. The old butter has such a slight rim that the top easily scoots off the bottom.

In 1977 a "cheese dish" appeared having the same top as the butter and having all the flaws inherent in that top which were discussed in detail above. However, the bottom of this dish was all wrong. It's about half way between a flat plate and a butter dish bottom, bowl shaped; and it is over thick, giving it an awkward appearance. The real cheese bottom was a salad plate with a rim for holding the top. These "round bottom cheese dishes" are but a parody of the old and are easily spotted. We removed the top from one in the picture so you could see its heaviness and its bowl shape.

The butter/cheese dishes wholesale to dealers for around $6.00.

Reproductions (Con't.)

NEW "SHARON" (Con't.)

The newest reproduction in Sharon is a too light pink creamer and sugar with lid. They are pictured with the "Made in Taiwan" label. These sell for around $15.00 for the pair and are also easy to spot as reproductions. I'll just mention the most obvious differences. Turn the creamer so you are looking directly at the spout. In the old creamer the mold line runs dead center of that spout; in the new, the mold line runs decidedly to the left of center spout.

On the sugar, the leaves and roses are "off" but not enough to DESCRIBE it to new collectors. Therefore, look at the center design, both sides, at the stars located at the very bottom of the motif. A thin leaf stem should run directly from that center star upward on BOTH sides. In this new sugar, the stem only runs from one; it stops way short of the star on one side. OR look inside the sugar bowl at where the handle attaches to the bottom of the bowl. In the new bowl, this attachment looks like a perfect circle; in the old, its an upside down "v" shaped tear drop.

As for the sugar lid, the knob of the new lid is perfectly smooth as you grasp its edges. The old knob has a mold seam running mid circimference. You could tell these two lids apart blind folded!

While there is a hair's difference between the height, mouth opening diameter, and inside depth of the old Sharon shakers and those newly produced, I won't attempt to upset you with those sixteenth and thirty seconds of a degree of difference. Suffice it to say that in physical shape, they are very close. However, as concerns design, they're miles apart. The old shakers have true appearing roses. The flowers really LOOK like roses. On the new shakers, they look like poorly drawn circles with wobbly concentric rings. The leaves are not as clearly defined on the new shakers as the old. However, forgetting all that, in the old shakers, the first design you see below the lid is a ROSE BUD. It's angled like a rocket shooting off into outer space with three leaves at the base of the bud (where the rocket fuel would burn out). In the new shakers, this "bud" has become four paddles of a windmill. It's the difference between this 🌿 and this 🌀

The shakers wholesale for around $6.50 a pair.

221

Publications I recommend

DEPRESSION GLASS **DAZE**

THE ORIGINAL NATIONAL DEPRESSION GLASS NEWSPAPER

Depression Glass Daze, the Original, National monthly newspaper dedicated to the buying, selling and collecting of colored glassware of the 20's and 30's. We average 60 pages each month, filled with feature articles by top notch columnists, readers "finds", club happenings, show news, a china corner, a current listing of new glass issues to beware of and a multitude of ads! You can find it in the DAZE! Keep up with what's happening in the dee gee world with a subscription to the DAZE. Buy sell or trade from the convenience of your easy chair.

Name_____ Street_____

City_____ State_____ Zip_____

☐ 1 Year - $15.00   ☐ Check enclosed   ☐ Please bill me

☐ MasterCard   ☐ VISA   (Foreign subscribers - please add $1.00 per year)

Exp. date_____Card No._____

Signature_____

Order to D.G.D., Box 57GF, Otisville, MI 48463- 008 - Please allow 30 days

A colorful magazine devoted to keeping glass collectors informed about all kinds of glass - antique to contemporary collectibles. Filled with articles, pictures, price reports, ads, research information and more! 12 "BIG" issues yearly.

Name_____ Street_____

City_____ State_____ Zip_____

☐ New   ☐ 1 year - $14.50   ☐ Single Copy $2.00

☐ Renewal   ☐ 1 year Canada or Foreign $16.00 (U.S. Funds please)

Orders to P. O. Box 542, Marietta, OH 45750

Heisey Club Membership To:

Heisey Collectors of America

Box 27GF

Newark, OH 43055

Dues: $12.00 Yearly

THE END

This potty chair in its original condition was found in western Pennsylvania. Several were found in storage at an old hardware store. The "potty" is a Fire-King 6⅞" utility bowl.

Isn't this the absolute end!